THE ENVIRONMENTAL CONSEQUENCES OF GROWTH

The Environmental Consequences of Growth presents a new perspective on the link between economic growth and environmental change. New industries are necessary for economic growth but, far from offering a solution to our current environmental and ecological problems, they foster new problems. Even if some environmental problems can be resolved, others remain irreversible. Douglas E. Booth argues that a new ethical approach to evaluating environmental questions is urgently needed: we should give serious attention to the idea of steady-state economics.

The growth process envisioned in the book draws on the Schumpeterian concept of "creative destruction." However, unlike some other authors, Douglas E. Booth has brought together historical data and case material from the United States and the United Kingdom which provide evidence that the economic growth process is indeed causing a cumulative expansion of environmental problems. The second half of the book provides an ethical framework based on the newly emergent field of environmental evaluation. The author demonstrates that policies based on steady-state economics can simultaneously satisfy human requirements for a decent life, and the moral commitment to preserve the global environment with its diverse life forms.

Written without technical language, this book is suitable for all readers; it assumes no previous understanding of economics. It will be invaluable to students of economics and ecological/environmental studies as well as to environmental policy makers.

Douglas E. Booth is Associate Professor of Economics at Marquette University in Milwaukee, Wisconsin. He is the author of *Valuing Nature: The Decline and Preservation of Old-Growth Forests* and *Regional Long Waves, Uneven Growth, and the Cooperative Alternatives*, as well as numerous articles.

ADVANCES IN SOCIAL ECONOMICS

Edited by John B. Davis
Marquette University

This series presents new advances and developments in social economics thinking on a variety of subjects that concern the link between social values and economics. Need, justice and equity, gender, cooperation, work, poverty, the environment, class, institutions, public policy, and methodology are some of its most important themes. Among the orientations of the authors are social economist, institutionalist, humanist, solidarist, cooperativist, radical and Marxist, feminist, post-Keynesian, behaviouralist, and environmentalist. The series offers new contributions from today's foremost thinkers on the social character of the economy.

Published in conjunction with the Association of Social Economics.

THE ENVIRONMENTAL CONSEQUENCES OF GROWTH

Steady-state economics as an
alternative to ecological decline

Douglas E. Booth

London and New York

First published 1998
by Routledge
11 New Fetter Lane, London EC4P 4EE

Simultaneously published in the USA and Canada
by Routledge
29 West 35th Street, New York, NY 10001

© 1998 Douglas E. Booth

Typeset in Times by
Ponting–Green Publishing Services
Printed in Great Britain by
Creative Print and Design (Wales), Ebbw Vale

British Library Cataloguing in Publication Data
A catalogue record for this book is available
from the British Library

Library of Congress Cataloging in Publication Data
Booth, Douglas E.
The environmental consequences of growth: steady-state economics
as an alternative to ecological decline / Douglas E. Booth
p.   cm. – (Advances in social economics)
Includes bibliographical references and index.
1. Economic development—Environmental apects.
2. Economic development—Moral and ethical aspects.
3. Environmental degradation—Economic aspects.
I. Title.   II. Series.
HD75.6B66   1998
363.7—dc21   97–13793 CIP

ISBN 0–415–16990–9 (hbk)
ISBN 0–415–16991–7 (pbk)

Dedicated to the memory
of
Ruth and Leonard Booth

CONTENTS

List of figures   viii
List of tables   ix
Preface   x

1 Introduction: economic growth and environmental change   1

2 Economic growth and environmental change: theory   7

3 The link between industry creation and environmental change   20

4 Economic growth and environmental change: natural habitat loss   55

5 Economic growth and environmental change: air, water, and pesticide pollution   81

6 Economic growth and the limits of environmental regulation   101

7 Ethics and the limits of environmental economics   125

8 The steady-state alternative   142

9 The macroeconomics of a steady state   161

10 Economic democracy as an environmental measure   170

11 Growth, environmental change, and steady-state economics: conclusion   188

Notes   191
Bibliography   198
Index   212

FIGURES

2.1 Production over the economic life-cycle   14

2.2 Emissions over the economic life-cycle   14

2.3 Cumulative emissions with constant output over the economic life-cycle   15

2.4 Cumulative emissions over the economic life-cycle   15

2.5 Environmental change over time   16

3.1 Total U.S. fossil fuel, petroleum, gas, and coal energy consumption (tril. Btu)   25

3.2 U.S. air pollution emissions (million metric tons)   27

3.3 U.K. air pollution emissions (million metric tons)   29

3.4 Carbon emissions (million metric tons)   31

3.5 Nonpoint water pollution indicators   33

3.6 Habitat loss indicators   43

10.1 Net average revenue product and net marginal revenue product   173

10.2 Scale-increasing investment: cooperative vs. a corporation   175

10.3 Energy/materials productivity-improving investment vs. scale-increasing investment   176

TABLES

3.1 Persistent critical environmental problems and industries
    that caused them   22
3.2 Sector shares of U.S. emissions (%)   26
3.3 Air pollution emissions for the U.S. and energy
    consumption: annual percentage change relative
    to the prior decade   28
3.4 Trends in concentration of selected U.S. water quality
    indicators, 1978–1987   35
3.5 Railroad miles and farmland acres in key prairie states   41
3.6 Prairie remnants   43
3.7 Birth dates for industries or economic activities causing
    major environmental changes   52
4.1 Habitat loss in the British countryside   74
5.1 Some potential ecological consequences of global
    warming   91
8.1 Global warming: options and costs, 2000–2275   146
10.1 Cooperative input efficiency, size and growth relative
    to conventional firms   178

PREFACE

This book arose from my concerns that environmental problems are more deeply rooted and systematic than implied by the usual economics textbook analysis of market failure. The inference I have always drawn from the market failure approach is that with a patch here and a patch there the problem can be solved; underlying economic institutions are fundamentally sound and all that is needed is reform around the edges. My own thinking is contrary to this view and has been profoundly influenced by Herman Daly's work and, in particular, his notion that the scale of the global economy is growing relative to the scale of the global ecosystem, creating serious natural resource and environmental problems that are not easily resolved. While in the end I agree with Daly's call for a steady-state economy, my own approach is a little different than his. My goal here is to find the economic dynamic that drives environmental change. My own conclusion is that environmental change is the direct result of the processes that drive economic growth in modern capitalist economies. If I am right, then to resolve the problem of environmental decline – some would call it a crisis – requires fundamental changes in modern economic institutions.

My goal in writing this book is to also provide a work that is accessible to undergraduate students and lay readers who have had introductory economics. In my own classes I have used the material presented here to provide a counter-point to conventional environmental texts and to foster healthy and interesting debates on whether the modest reforms suggested in the usual texts are enough to resolve environmental problems or whether something deeper is needed. Through these discussions, my students have helped me immeasurably in honing my own thinking.

Finally, in writing this book I wanted undergraduates to have an opportunity to read a work that not only integrates economic and ecological thought, but also is explicitly value-oriented in its premises. This book is not value-free! It is based on the notion of a human duty to preserve the natural environment. Whether such a duty is appropriate or will ever be widely held, I leave to the reader to judge. My point is that it ought to be given serious consideration.

Not only have my students contributed to this work with their comments and insights, but so have a host of others, including a lengthy list of anonymous referees, Herman Daly, John Tomer, and John Davis. Of course, none of these individuals can be held responsible for any remaining errors in my ways. I am also grateful to Marquette University for the opportunity to work as a teacher-scholar and to undertake this book as a part of my normal duties.

1

INTRODUCTION

Economic growth and environmental change

After a quarter century of environmental regulation in the U.S. under the auspices of the Environmental Protection Agency and other governmental bodies, substantial environmental threats remain. Ambient standards for ozone and other air pollutants are frequently violated in urban areas; lakes and rivers continue to be heavily polluted; ambient levels of toxic chemicals in the biotic food chain are at high levels; little has been done about the potentially serious problem of greenhouse warming; and biodiversity is threatened as a consequence of reduced and fragmented natural habitats. A similar story can be told for other prosperous countries of the world such as Great Britain and its fellow members of the European Community. Why has the regulatory system in the U.S. and elsewhere failed to fully address environmental problems?

The goal of this book is to suggest that the roots of environmental change are deeply embedded in the processes that generate economic growth. The central proposition put forth and evaluated in the pages to follow is that forces leading to economic growth in market capitalist economies also lead to environmental change. Technological change, innovation, and the drive for wealth result in the creation of new high-growth industries required for macroeconomic expansion; these same high-growth industries foster environmental change and resist regulatory efforts to limit such change; consequently, economic forces essential to economic growth are responsible for environmental problems.

Because growth itself is the essence of the environmental problem, a new economic vision is needed, one that is rooted in a wider view of human values and ethics. The alternative vision offered here is a steady-state economy, one with the capacity not only to satisfy real human needs, but to preserve the global environment and its full diversity of forms of life. After an exploration of the causes of environmental change in the first six chapters of the book, the alternative vision and its ethical foundations are then addressed in the next five chapters.

Comparison to the conventional view of environmental issues

Because economic growth and growing environmental problems in the absence of effective regulation go hand-in-hand, the environmental problem in this book is seen as fundamentally macroeconomic in character. The conventional view of environmental problems is, to the contrary, fundamentally microeconomic. Environmental problems in the eyes of conventional economists exist because of a failure of the pricing system (Tietenberg 1994). Market-determined prices fail to fully reflect the social costs of environmental damage caused by economic activity, and the solution to the environmental problem is to "get the prices right." This is to be done by internalizing the social costs of environmental damage. Instead of allowing an electric power plant or a chemical plant to externalize environmental costs by emitting pollutants and imposing damage from environmental degradation on the larger society, they should be required to bear the costs of pollution control and environmental damage internally. As a result, prices of products would fully reflect the social costs of using environmental resources and such use would be efficient. While this approach is appealing, in a profit- and growth-oriented economy it is fundamentally problematic, as we will now see.

Economic growth as a cause of environmental decline

The microeconomic insight – that profit-oriented economic agents will have a strong propensity to externalize environmental costs – is indeed compelling. That the internalization of environmental costs would reduce environmental problems is undeniable. However, environmental costs in a profit-driven capitalist economy are typically not fully internalized. Why is this?

Conventional microeconomic thinking does not get at the essence of the cost internalization failure problem, an issue better addressed by considering the nature of the capitalist macroeconomic development process as described by Joseph Schumpeter (1939, 1950) and others. According to a Schumpeterian view, the creation of new industries based on new technologies is fundamental to macroeconomic growth. Growth is driven by qualitative change in the structure of the economy, qualitative changes that inevitably seem to lead to changes in the natural environment. New industries invariably seem to create new environmental problems by virtue of their inherent propensity to externalize environmental costs. Once such industries are created, they often form powerful vested interests that oppose environmental regulations and insure that environmental costs remain externalized to the greatest extent possible. Profit-maximizing electric utilities and chemical companies, for example, typically oppose pollution control regulations that increase their costs and reduce their profits. The consumers of the products of these industries also constitute potentially powerful vested interests not wanting to see their costs of consumption rise as a consequence of environmental regulations. The process of economic growth thus creates vested interests opposed to the internalization of environmental costs. The growth process has the potential to defeat the goal of cost internalization. Consequently, growth is in practice the fundamental issue, not prices. As long as growth in its existing form persists, powerful interest groups will work hard at avoiding environmental cost internalization. Simply put, the forces of economic growth oppose cost internalization.

Ethics and the evaluation of environmental change

Even if all environmental costs were successfully internalized, economic growth could still lead to environmental deterioration. This would occur if the added benefits of growth exceeded the added social costs of environmental damage resulting from growth. The added benefits of continuing to use fossil fuels may well exceed the added social costs of future global warming resulting from carbon dioxide emissions associated with fossil fuel use (Nordhaus 1991).[1] Nonetheless, global warming is likely to cause significant economic harm to future generations and result in the destruction of ecosystems and species (Cline 1992; Abrahamson 1989). Net economic welfare (taking full account of environmental costs to current and future generations) may well be maximized by continuing to use fossil fuels even though the consequences may be catastrophic for individual members of future generations and for species and ecosystems.

This conclusion results from an implicit acceptance of a utilitarian ethical framework underlying cost-benefit analysis, a framework that neglects the moral worth of human individuals in present and future generations, plant and animal species, and ecosystems. If our ethical framework is broadened to include the well being of human individuals, species, and ecosystems, then cost-benefit analysis and social cost internalization are inadequate criteria for determining acceptable levels of environmental damage. If human individuals, species, and ecosystems are viewed as having moral worth, then a dollar value cannot be meaningfully assigned to them in order to assess the extent of external social costs. For any given act of environmental destruction, there will be social costs that *can* be calculated, such as the damage to buildings or loss of crops from air pollution. However, there also may be moral costs that *cannot* be calculated. Most find the idea of assigning a dollar value to human life repugnant. Human individuals may be so poor that they have very little willingness to pay for a clean environment necessary for a full and healthy life. In such circumstances, many would find it morally reprehensible to advocate the continuation of health-damaging pollution even though added social benefits exceed added costs. This suggests that individual human lives are valuable in their own right, not just for the incomes they earn or the utility they deliver to others in society. The same can be said for species and ecosystems, beings that also may have value in their own right apart from any utility they deliver. If so, then assigning a dollar value to them would be repugnant as well.

The point is simple. Social costs are calculable in dollar terms; moral costs are not. Even if social costs are fully internalized, economic growth and environmental deterioration could result in "moral costs" avoidable only through the maintenance of a specified level of environmental quality that may limit economic growth. The moral costs associated with global warming, for example, may be avoidable only by halting or even reversing the global warming trend. This may be the case even though the added social costs of doing so exceed the added social benefits. A central thesis to be explored in the chapters to follow is

3

that the internalization of both the social and moral costs of environmental change will be resisted by those whose interests are tied to unfettered growth, interests that are created by the economic growth process itself.

Sustainability and the steady state

Some argue that economic growth is necessary to provide resources to pay for environmental protection and reverse environmental deterioration (Grossman and Krueger 1993). Herman Daly (1991a) vigorously opposes this view, invoking the entropy principle. For Daly, production is inherently entropic, converting high-quality low-entropy matter and energy into high-entropy environmentally disruptive waste. If Daly is right, then as historically experienced, economic growth is contrary to any notion of sustainability. In its broadest conception, sustainability refers to preserving the ability to produce at existing levels. If our concerns extend beyond production to the protection of human individuals, species, and ecosystems for their own sake, then a more precise definition is needed.

The most concrete concept of sustainability is a steady-state economy. In a steady-state economy, natural resources are consumed at a fixed, sustainable rate and the quality of the environment is maintained at a level that protects the health of human individuals, species, and ecosystems (Daly 1991a). The global ecosystem's ability to provide material inputs to the global economy and to absorb its waste byproducts is inherently limited, and under a steady-state economy the demands placed upon the global ecosystem by the global economy are appropriately restrained. Daly's steady-state economics is really the precursor to modern conceptions of sustainable development calling for the passing on of a stock of natural capital to future generations at least equal to that enjoyed by the current generation (Pearce 1993: 15–19). Some advocates of sustainable development call for a nondeclining total capital stock, mixing capital goods produced by humans and the natural capital stock. This approach is sometimes referred to as weak sustainability and assumes produced and natural capital are substitutes for one another. Daly's version of sustainability denies substitutability and argues for a strong version that passes on a nondeclining natural capital stock to future generations.

Nothing in conventional neoclassical environmental microeconomics suggests the concept of sustainability. If benefit-cost analysis argues for the destruction of a natural area, the extinction of a species, or the using up of a natural resource, so be it. An ethical approach, presuming that the well being of future generations is a matter of present concern, and that human individuals, species, and ecosystems have value in their own right, leads more directly to the concept of sustainability. A properly defined steady-state economy assures the provision of adequate natural resources for future generations and the protection of the health and well being of human individuals, species, and ecosystems.

A steady state does *not* necessarily imply zero economic growth. Economic growth can take place so long as the productivity of natural and environmental resources is increased through technological advance. Rather than labor productivity (output per unit labor) being the focus of attention, environmental resource productivity (output per unit resource) would take center stage in order for there to be significant economic growth. Economic growth would most likely be reduced relative to the historical experience in a steady state since in the past, environmental resource use faced few constraints.

The plan of the book

Each of these claims requires elaboration and justification. Chapters 2 to 5 address the central thesis of the book – new industries are required for long-term economic growth and cause environmental change. The justification for this thesis is necessarily empirical and historical. After the basic theory of the link between economic growth and environmental change has been set out in Chapter 2, historical evidence for the relationship is presented in Chapters 3, 4, and 5. The basic theoretical idea presented in Chapter 2 is the Schumpeterian notion that long-run economic growth proceeds through the addition of new forms of economic activity. If these new forms of economic activity bring forth new kinds of environmental problems, then the forces that lead to economic growth also lead to environmental change. The job of Chapter 3 is to present historical evidence that our existing array of environmental problems can be traced to the industry creation process underpinning economic growth. Chapters 4 and 5 demonstrate the significance of our environmental problems. The serious problem of natural habitat decline is addressed in Chapter 4 and the problems of air, water, and toxic pollution are considered in Chapter 5. To understand and evaluate the full consequences of economic growth for environmental change, we need to know the characteristics of key ecosystems and something about their functioning. Only in this way can we understand what is lost when ecosystems are destroyed or altered by economic growth. This knowledge is especially needed if an ethical framework is adopted where the moral considerability of ecosystems and species must be assessed. Knowledge of something necessarily precedes moral attachment to it, or even the recognition of the possibility of moral attachment. The goal of Chapters 4 and 5 is to give us a better understanding of what is lost exactly as a consequence of environmental change.

In Chapter 6 historical efforts at environmental regulation will be described and assessed. The basic conclusions are that vested economic interests have indeed limited the extent of regulation and that regulation has thus far failed to resolve key environmental problems.

Having established the link between economic growth and environmental change, in Chapter 7 the normative framework for evaluating the problem of environmental decline is presented. The utilitarian benefit-cost framework of conventional neoclassical derivation is rejected in favor of an approach founded on the principles of environmental ethics that sees human individuals, species, and ecosystems as valuable in their own right and thus priceless in the sense that their value is not representable in monetary terms.

Chapter 8 offers the steady-state approach as an alternative to conventional regulation and suggests how a steady state can be implemented. The steady state is justified not in terms of utilitarian benefit-cost analysis, but on the basis of the broader ethical framework suggested in Chapter 7. A steady-state approach is considered for air and water pollution problems, toxins, and natural habitat preservation.

A steady-state economy is a radical departure from a modern high-growth capitalist economy and will require rather different policies for macroeconomic management. This question is addressed in Chapter 9, along with the issue of whether capitalism is even compatible with a steady state. In Chapter 10, the democratically run producer cooperative is evaluated and found to be a more environmentally friendly form of business organization better suited to a steady-state economy than the capitalist corporation.

In the final chapter, the key themes of the book will be brought to bear on the difficult issue of moving from a high-growth to a steady-state economy. Highly developed western economies seem to be hooked on environmentally destructive growth, growth that is largely futile as a means to increase human happiness and expand the opportunity to live decent human lives. The foundation of growth seems to be a zero-sum game in which the participants seek higher incomes as a means to higher relative social status. The problem is, growth can increase average incomes, but it is incapable of bringing forth increases in relative status. The question is, how do we in the prosperous countries of the world become unhooked from socially fruitless, environmentally destructive growth?

2

ECONOMIC GROWTH AND ENVIRONMENTAL CHANGE

Theory

The key points of this and the following three chapters of this book are simple. Technological change, innovation, and the drive for wealth accumulation lead to the creation of new high-growth industries required for macroeconomic growth; these high-growth industries foster environmental change; thus, the same forces that lead to economic growth are responsible for a changing natural environmental. The task here is to explore fully the logic of the economic growth/environment link and to provide historical evidence for it. The starting point is an investigation of the ties between the macroeconomy and the environment. For Herman Daly (1991a), as already noted in Chapter 1, production is inherently entropic, converting high-quality low-entropy matter and energy into high-entropy, environmentally disruptive waste. While Daly's position is compelling on theoretical grounds, to fully justify it requires a more specific conception of the relationship between economic growth and environmental change and more concrete historical and empirical support.

Economic circular flow and the environment

Anyone who has taken macroeconomics is familiar with circular flow analysis. Households purchase commodities produced by businesses, the expenditures of households become the revenues of businesses, and businesses use those revenues to purchase productive services (labor, capital, and natural resources) from households. The incomes of households in turn sustain expenditures on purchases from businesses. In the opposite direction, commodities and services flow from businesses to households and the factors of production flow from households to businesses. Commodities and money flow in an unending circle that never runs down, and, with continuous investment in additional productive capacity, the flow can be ever expanding.

This perception of the macroeconomy is misleading because it ignores scientific laws that place constraints on the flow of inputs into the economic system from the natural environment (Daly 1991a: 195–210). The flow of energy and matter through the economic system is in reality linear and unidirectional, not circular. Energy and matter flow from the environment to the economic system and waste matter and heat flow from the economic system to the environment. The flow begins with the depletion of energy and material resources and ends with the pollution of the environment with waste matter and heat.

As Nicholas Georgescu-Roegen and Herman Daly have gone to great lengths to demonstrate (Georgescu-Roegen 1971, 1973; Daly 1991a), economists have failed in the construction of their macroeconomic models to recognize that the laws of thermodynamics dictate an absolute scarcity of energy and matter. It is this absolute scarcity that in turn negates the macroeconomic concept of circular flow.

The essence of the first law of thermodynamics is that energy and matter can be neither created nor destroyed. In other words, the stock of matter is fixed in availability, as is the maximum flow rate of energy. Thus there is an absolute scarcity of both. If energy and matter could be infinitely rearranged without loss, then this law would matter little for economic activity. The disordering of matter created by consumption could simply be compensated by the re-ordering of matter through production. Perpetual circular flow at a constant or even growing rate would indeed be possible. The problem is, whenever energy is used to re-order matter, something is permanently lost. This is explained by the second law of thermodynamics.

The second law of thermodynamics basically says that when used to perform work, energy is converted to a more dispersed, less useful form. To put it another way, whenever energy is used, some of it is given off in the form of waste heat. The entropy of energy increases. No energy-using process is 100 percent efficient. Entropy is the amount of energy in a system that is not available to do work in that system. An automobile burning petrol converts energy in a concentrated form into motion and waste heat. The automobile moves, but some of the energy is converted into waste heat unavailable for work.

The flow of matter in production and consumption is also an entropic process. Highly concentrated forms of matter are converted into useful artifacts in production, and in consumption those artifacts are converted into dispersed waste material. The energy of nature – sun, wind, rain, oxidation – causes materials to break down and become more dispersed. A house, for example, slowly deteriorates over time. The paint chips off, wood rots, and the roof deteriorates. An increase in entropy is a decrease in order. As the house deteriorates, its material contents become less ordered. To reconcentrate all dispersed matter from a consumption process would require an impossibly large amount of energy, rendering 100 percent recycling an impossibility. Matter, like energy, is subject to entropy.

The extent to which the entropy of energy and matter impinges on the circular flow of commodities in the macroeconomy or harms the human individuals and natural environments that frame the macroeconomy is a fundamental issue that must be addressed by an environmental approach to macroeconomics. The entropic linear flow of energy and matter results in changes to both biotic and abiotic components of what can be called the global ecosystem. Abiotic components include the earth's atmosphere and climatic patterns, the input of solar energy, and the reserves of energy and materials in the earth's crust. The biotic components include a vast array of species and biological communities created and shaped by the interaction of natural evolutionary forces and ecological processes, some of which have been further altered and reshaped by the human hand.

In short, the fundamental problem facing an environmental approach to macroeconomics as an area of intellectual inquiry is this: the global economy is growing while the global ecosystem is stable in terms of its capacity to supply energy and materials, absorb wastes, and provide a host of ecosystem services (Daly 1991a: 180–194). As a result, stocks of nonrenewable resources in the earth's crust are being depleted, waste sinks are filling up, and human-created ecosystems (i.e. agriculture) are taking over a larger and larger percentage of global biotic productivity. Further consequences of these events include a plunge in global biotic diversity, the disappearance of natural habitats (such as tropical rain forests) and numerous environmental problems including global warming, air and water pollution, toxic wastes, and destruction of the protective ozone layer. To fully understand the impact of economic activity on ecosystems we need to know something of the services they provide. Then we will be able to move forward and consider the economy–environment relationship in detail.

Ecosystem services to human beings

Human beings are members of the biotic community and are thus dependent on the materials and services provided by ecosystems. We as biotic consumers need access to the primary productivity of plants, directly or indirectly. In the modern world this has been accomplished primarily through the creation of anthropogenic agricultural ecosystems that favor monocultures composed of species with high net primary productivity. Nonetheless, we do still rely on natural ecosystems for some food resources, such as fish and other marine organisms. Moreover, successful agriculture does rely indirectly on natural ecosystems. The most productive agricultural regions in the world are located on old grasslands with their legacies of extraordinarily rich soils, and the soils themselves constitute an essentially natural ecosystem, albeit one that is in danger of destruction from agricultural practices that cause erosion or the destruction of soil microorganisms. Moreover, the genetic stock of favored agricultural species has ancestral origins in natural ecosystems. This stock has been much modified through plant breeding, and the original ecosystems from which some of these plants were originally taken may no longer exist or may be threatened with extinction (Ehrlich et al. 1977).

In addition to foodstuffs, we extract a variety of fibers and chemicals from natural and anthropogenic ecosystems. For much of the last century, old-growth forests supplied most of the timber used in construction and served as the U.S.'s primary energy resource. Now that old-growth supplies are depleted, timber harvesting has shifted to second-growth plantation forests. Although many modern drugs have their origins in the flora and fauna of the tropical rain forests (Wilson 1988), other ecosystems are potential sources as well, as demonstrated by the recent discovery of taxol, a cancer-fighting chemical, in the Pacific yew, an understory species in Pacific Northwest old-growth forests (Booth 1994). In sum, ecosystems, both natural and anthropogenic, are essential sources of food, fiber, and chemicals for human use, actual as well as potential.

Ecosystems perform a variety of additional functions beneficial to human beings. Wetlands, for example, not only serve as nurseries and habitat for a variety of species, but also purify water and reduce the intensity of floods. Forests, like wetlands, are beneficial because they limit the rapidity of storm water runoff and the erosion that goes with it by storing moisture in their canopies and soils. Old-growth forests often contain the type of streams that are ideal habitat for certain fishes of great benefit to those who fish recreationally and commercially, such as salmon and trout. Forests also store up carbon and reduce the potential for global warming as a consequence of the buildup of carbon dioxide and other greenhouse gases in the earth's atmosphere. Together anthropogenic and natural ecosystems are responsible for the maintenance of the balance of gases in the earth's atmosphere necessary to sustain life (Ehrlich *et al.* 1977; Abrahamson 1989).

These are tangible services that ecosystems provide us. Human beings also enjoy a variety of intangible benefits, especially from natural ecosystems. They are frequently the setting for outdoor recreation, including camping, hiking, mountain climbing, photography, birdwatching, nature study, fishing, and hunting (Rolston 1981). Such intangible uses of the natural world are increasingly important in affluent urban societies where individuals hunger for contact with nature and can afford to devote time and money to its pursuit. Natural ecosystems are also important as the setting for the scientific study of organisms and biotic processes. Finally, natural areas and certain species have cultural significance. In the last century, some of the early national parks were preserved in the U.S. because of their monumental qualities. Wilderness remnants with their dramatic natural and geologic features remind U.S. citizens of their pioneer heritage, as do certain species that are national symbols, such as the bison and the bald eagle (Booth 1994: 173–195). In the U.K., the "countryside" is a prominent cultural icon comparable to wilderness in the U.S. (McCormick 1991: 69). The point is a simple one. Ecosystems provide us with numerous tangible and intangible services, some of which are indispensable.

With its continuous creation of new industries that cause new kinds of environmental disturbances, the economic growth process can easily disrupt ecosystem services. Global warming induced by excessive CO_2 emissions can cause damage and destruction to both natural and anthropogenic ecosystems (Abrahamson 1989). Excessive liquid waste emissions can overload the nutrient recycling capacity of aquatic ecosystems, inhibiting their ability to function and support a diversity of life (Welch 1992). Acid rain and other forms of air pollution can harm the health of both terrestrial and aquatic ecosystems (Gould 1985). Deforestation and poor agricultural practices can cause soil erosion in amounts that exceed the capacity of ecosystems to produce new soils. The conversion of natural to anthropogenic ecosystems can reduce biodiversity and, as a consequence, the range of chemicals and drugs that can be potentially extracted from nature. Destruction of wetlands can reduce the supply of clean water, diminish biodiversity, and increase flooding (Erlich *et al.* 1977). The reduction of natural habitat as a consequence of logging or land development can reduce wildlife populations and cause species extinctions. All such events together reduce tangible and intangible human benefits that derive from ecosystems.

The central argument of this book is that forces leading to economic growth cause the kinds of environmental disturbances just described. The global economy is prone to growth while the global ecosystem is stable in terms of gross productivity and its capacity to provide ecosystem services. While ecosystems individually are subject to disturbance and change, at a global level there is no known natural growth trend in global ecosystem productivity or capacity for service provision. Thus, as the global economy expands, it places increasing demands and stresses on the global ecosystem, reducing its ultimate capacity to serve the human species.

Ecosystems and species, as already noted, can be viewed as having value in their own right independent of any utility they provide to human beings (Callicott 1989; Rolston 1988). This is an approach advocated by many environmental philosophers and one that is finding increasing public favor. Given acceptance of this view, ecosystems and species would have moral standing and the destructive consequences of economic expansion would not be just an economic issue but a moral issue as well. This approach will be given a detailed treatment in Chapter 7. Suffice it to say for now that environmental destruction may be an issue of moral significance involving more than just the welfare of human beings. With a basic understanding of ecosystem functions and their importance, we are now ready to consider the link between economic growth and the environment.

The economic growth process

Our ultimate goal is to understand the relationship between economic growth and environmental change. To accomplish this, theoretical understanding of the economy/environment link is not only needed, but insight into the logic of the economic growth process is required as well. The central issue to be addressed in gaining this insight can be stated simply: why does growth take place?

Because capitalism is rapidly becoming the dominant form of economic organization globally, and is the basis for the world's most prosperous economies, we will focus on the capitalist growth process. Capitalism is by its nature a form or method of economic change, according to the highly respected economist Joseph Schumpeter (1939, 1950). In his view, a capitalist economy never is, and never can be, stationary. The pursuit of profit and capital accumulation brings forth growth and change. The fundamental impulse that sets off the economic growth process comes from new consumer goods, new methods of production or transportation, new markets, and new forms of industrial organization. The process of change is qualitative as well as quantitative. Old industries are constantly being reduced in scope or even destroyed and new ones created. The result is not only a quantitative expansion of the economy, but a qualitative change in its structure as well. New forms of economy activity are created and the old decline and sometimes even disappear (Schumpeter 1939, 1950). To describe this process, Schumpeter coined the term "creative destruction." The analogy in evolutionary biology is the creation of new species through genetic mutation and evolution and the destruction (extinction) of species unable to adapt to changing conditions. New firms and industries are constantly appearing while old ones are declining and disappearing.

Because new industries bring forth new forms of environmental damage, the creative destruction process is of great significance for environmental change. Even though old firms and industries decline or even disappear, their environmental legacies often do not. When this happens the environmental impact of the creative destruction process is cumulative over time. New industries add environmental problems to those of the old.

The idea of creative destruction calls forth a form of competition substantially different from that encountered in neoclassical microeconomic theory. The economic process envisioned by Schumpeter relegates the purely competitive equilibrium driven by price competition to a relatively minor role. The real threat to an existing enterprise is the introduction of a new product or new technology by a competitor. New businesses with new products will take away markets from the old. New firms with new products or technologies will attain quasi-monopoly positions, only to see their market eroded away by still newer firms with newer products and technologies (Schumpeter 1950).

According to Schumpeter, innovations in products, production technologies, markets, and methods of organization come in waves or clusters. Entrepreneurs are attracted to the latest new products or technologies. These become the engines of economic growth driving the economy forward through market expansion. During the high-growth phase, capital and entrepreneurs are attracted to the growth engines and ignore other possibilities. Often a pioneer enterprise initiates a new technology and fosters a number of spinoff enterprises that fill related product niches or emulate the pioneer.

While new industries indeed experience more rapid expansion than old, Schumpeter probably overemphasized the destructive side of the growth process. Old industries, such as printing, paper manufacture, food processing, lumber, and steel, seldom disappear entirely, because they serve key economic functions in society. They get transformed from time to time by new technologies, but they remain an essential part of the economy. Creative destruction no doubt operates with full force at the level of the firm, but to a lesser extent at the level of the industry. As Nell (1988) has emphasized in his work, economic growth is built on pulling into the market arena social and economic functions that were previously served through nonmarket arrangements (i.e. in household production).

Schumpeter's theory of creative destruction suggests that industries have life-cycle patterns of development characterized by initial rapid growth, a subsequent slowing of growth, and in some instances decline. An industry grows rapidly until it reaches market saturation where all those who desire a product at a given income are consuming it. This part of the growth process involves diffusion of information about the new industry's product or technology, including advertising to convince the public of the product's importance. Once this period has ended, growth in demand for the product is related to income and population growth and the rate at which competing new products and technologies enter the market and attract consumer attention. As already suggested, older industries don't necessarily disappear, because they often continue to serve essential economic functions. They may disappear, however, from a particular country as their production facilities are located offshore to take advantage of lower production costs elsewhere (van Duijn 1983: 20–32).

The Schumpeterian growth process has found empirical support in the work of Arthur Burns (1934), who established in his path-breaking work 60 years ago that retardation of growth in specific industries is a universal phenomenon.[1] Burns also established that the economy as a whole does not experience growth retardation, even though individual industries inevitably do. The inference of this conclusion is that new industries step into the breach and take on the job of growth engines and, in the process, prevent a retardation of growth in the aggregate economy. Without the addition of new sectors to the economy, the economic growth rate would decline. A central feature of the long-run economic growth process is, thus, the creation of new industries. Economic growth proceeds by adding new forms of activity to the economy.

The life-cycle pattern for an individual industry is illustrated by the graph in Figure 2.1. Rapid initial output growth is followed by a retardation of growth, and output eventually declines in absolute terms. This life-cycle pattern could be modified and disrupted if political or social barriers to growth must be first overcome, or if historical events intervene to alter it. The disruption of the automobile industry growth pattern by the Great Depression and World War II is an example.

The industry life-cycle and environmental change

The environmental impact of an industry will be related to industry output and the extent of environmental regulation. In the absence of regulation, emissions of pollutants and other environmental effects will vary from being proportional to output, at one extreme, to being irreversible and cumulative at another. The volume of particulates in the air at a given location will be approximately proportionate to the amount of local particulate emissions for given weather conditions. If emissions are brought to a halt, particulates in the air will fall to zero as they settle out or are blown away. At the other extreme, the volume of PCBs in the Lake Michigan ecosystem will accumulate as production takes place. Even if emissions are brought to a halt, the accumulated amount will remain constant because PCBs do not readily degrade by biotic or chemical action.

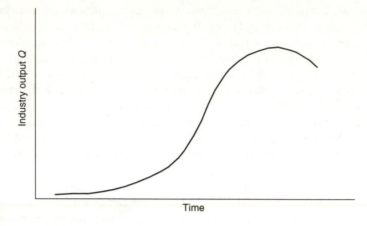

Figure 2.1 Production over the economic life-cycle

If the emission of a pollutant or other environmental impact is proportionate to output, then $E = bQ$, where Q is output, b is a constant, and E is the emission, and the emission will mirror the industry life-cycle over time as indicated in Figure 2.2.

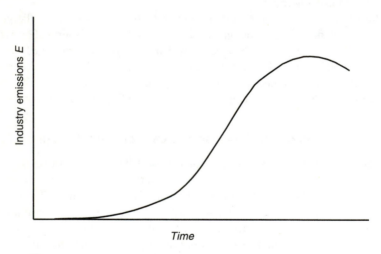

Figure 2.2 Emissions over the economic life-cycle

The actual damage to the environment from pollution emissions could be less than proportionate or more than proportionate to output. In many cases, damage increases at an increasing rate as emissions increase. Moreover, damage may depend on interaction between pollutants and environmental conditions. For example, ozone, a form of smog, results from the interaction of volatile organic compounds, nitrous oxides, and sunshine. Below a certain threshold, the harmful effects of smog will be small, but beyond a certain threshold they can increase rapidly (Ehrlich *et al.* 1977; Stern *et al.* 1984).

If the impact or emission is cumulative or irreversible, then the impact will be proportionate to the sum of production over time. $E_t = b\Sigma Q_t$, where b is a constant and Q_t is output in time t. The graph in Figure 2.3 illustrates the growth of the emission over time for a constant level of output, while the graph in Figure 2.4 indicates the behavior of emissions over the typical industrial cycle. As long as production is increasing, cumulative emissions will increase at an increasing rate. In the case of an emission or impact that is cumulative, the only way to stop its growth is to bring production to a halt in the absence of emission controls.

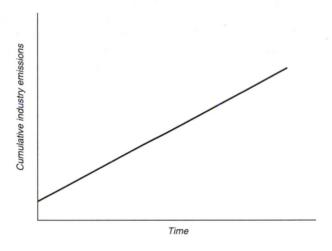

Figure 2.3 Cumulative emissions with constant output over the economic life-cycle

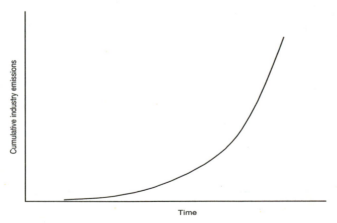

Figure 2.4 Cumulative emissions over the economic life-cycle

15

The growth of a particular industry not only may result in health-threatening wastes being emitted into the environment, but also may alter or even eliminate natural ecosystems. Waste emissions from industries can damage natural ecosystems in addition to causing harm to human health. Moreover, the growth of industries, such as agriculture, mining, timber production, and housing construction, can be at the expense of natural ecosystems and the organisms they contain. To summarize, waste emissions and land development associated with the growth of particular industries can cause environmental damage that is in some cases reversible and disappears when industry output disappears, and in some cases cumulative and irreversible.

Because new industries are being created over time, and because some are disappearing, the environmental consequences of economic growth in terms of specific environmental problems will have a pattern like that illustrated in Figure 2.5. Over time, new environmental problems will emerge as new industries are created. Some problems will disappear as old industries decline or as effective regulations are instituted. Problem 1, for example, might be urban smoke pollution, which has largely disappeared as a consequence of reduced use of coal for home heating and improved pollution regulations. Problem 2 could be the decline in U.S. natural prairie habitat associated with agricultural land use, Problem 3 could be increased nonpoint water pollution associated with fertilizer and pesticide use in agriculture, and Problem 4 could be the buildup of carbon in the earth's

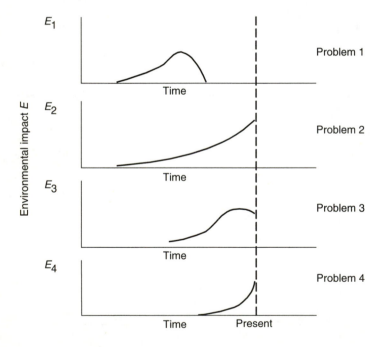

Figure 2.5 Environmental change over time

atmosphere leading to global warming. To reiterate the central premise underlying this analysis, new industries create new environmental problems. Some problems disappear over time, but some don't. As a result, environmental problems accumulate over time. Historical evidence for this process will be presented in Chapters 3, 4, and 5. Before moving on to the question of evidence, however, we need to understand more fully why it is that businesses and consumers impose the social and moral costs of environmental problems on society at large, rather than taking them on individually themselves.

Economic growth and the problem of cost externalization

Individual businesses and consumers are the agents whose activities not only foster economic growth but bring forth environmental change as well, much of which is detrimental to human beings, ecological systems, species, and populations of plants and animals. If such activities are indeed damaging, why don't economic agents exercise restraint in order to minimize the resulting costs of such damage?

The reason they don't is fairly simple. In the framework of a capitalist economy, where the seeking of material gain by economic agents is the central principle, individual businesses and consumers will attempt to avoid the costs of their actions by externalizing them. Profits for individual businesses and utility for individual consumers can be maximized by emitting pollutants into the air or water, rather than bearing the cost of emissions control equipment that would limit the discharge of pollutants. By doing so the costs of the emissions are externalized and borne by the society as a whole. Gain-seeking promotes cost externalization (Kapp 1970).

This is even the case when the cost to society (assuming that it is measurable) greatly exceeds the internal costs of avoiding the environmental damage through some form of emissions control. We all, for example, contribute to the problem of air pollution when we drive our automobiles, but the reduction in air quality we experience as a result of our own individual actions is imperceptible, while emissions control devices are quite expensive for each of us individually. Consequently, few of us are willing to voluntarily install control devices on our own, even though the collective costs of damage from air pollution we bear as a society much exceed the total cost of control devices. This line of reasoning applies to businesses as well that emit pollutants or cause other forms of environmental damage. The tendency is to push the burdens of limiting environmental damage off on others in a gain-seeking society, and the net result is that everyone suffers.

Some argue that if property rights to pollution are assigned to someone, then the problem will be self-correcting (Coase 1960). Those who experience damage from pollution need only bargain with those emitting the pollutants to reach an agreement where the damaged parties compensate the polluter for the cost of reducing emissions. This assumes the polluter has the right to pollute. If the property right is reversed, then in order to undertake emissions, the polluter would have to compensate damaged parties for costs incurred in order to reach a successful agreement. The problem with this approach is that links between emissions and damage are often difficult to establish, and the parties involved in a given negotiation could easily number in the millions, resulting in astronomical transactions costs.[2] Consequently, if the polluter has the right to pollute, emissions will not be limited because transactions costs will exceed the benefits to be achieved from negotiations. If individuals have a right to a pollution-free environment, then no emissions at all will be undertaken, again, because the transactions costs will exceed any benefits from negotiations. This set of circumstances could be socially undesirable if, for example, the cost of avoiding some amount of pollution control by emitting some pollutants into the environment is greater than the social costs of the environmental damage that would result. These conclusions are supported by the absence of any observed voluntary negotiations over pollution control. Pollution control in practice is the consequence of regulations imposed by government.

Even if property rights in the environment could be specified in some workable fashion, the problem of environmental damage harmful to human beings, ecosystems, species, or plant or animal populations will still not be necessarily resolved. If any such entities are of moral concern, then to cause them harm through some form of economic activity would be precluded on ethical grounds, unless doing so served some higher moral purpose. In other words, cost externalization as a consequence of economic activity may result not only in social costs for which compensation is at least theoretically possible, but in moral harm for which compensation is impossible. If impairing the health or causing the death or destruction of a human being, species, ecosystem, or population of plants or animals is an immoral act, then any economic activity causing such an event is ethically precluded. In short, where human or ecosystem health is involved, environmental damage is not ethically permitted unless it serves some higher end. This means that environmental damage that is legitimate in a property rights context may well be illegitimate in an ethical context.

To put this in the framework of industry life-cycles, as new industries emerge and experience growth, they externalize the costs of environmental damage rather than bear them internally. These externalized costs take form as social costs of environmental damage borne by members of the larger society, or as moral costs borne by ethically significant human beings, ecosystems, species, or plant or animal populations. In the absence of environmental regulation, as economic growth proceeds, such social and moral costs grow in extent.

Summary

The creative destruction process described by Schumpeter leads to the creation of new industries that become engines of macroeconomic growth. A given set of industries based on a particular technology eventually saturates its market, and the mantle of growth is picked up by still newer industries based on still newer technologies. Each new industry not only fosters economic growth, but generates new environmental problems as well. As economic growth proceeds, environmental changes result and new environmental problems are added. Over time some environmental problems are resolved as the consequence of the decline of aging industries and regulatory efforts, but some are not, and new problems appear. Environmental problems today are thus the consequence of a cumulative process of adding new forms of economic activity to the economy.

3

THE LINK BETWEEN INDUSTRY CREATION AND ENVIRONMENTAL CHANGE

The previous chapter suggests that environmental problems expand in number and seriousness as a consequence of economic growth. Certain environmental conditions, such as urban smoke pollution, may worsen for a time and then disappear, but many environmental problems don't, and new ones emerge along with new forms of economic activity. How can the proposition be substantiated that environmental problems are cumulative because of the cumulative addition of new kinds of economic activity? To answer this question is the central goal of this chapter.

The dynamics of environmental change

Consider Figure 2.5 again. If environmental problems 2 and 3 were resolved soon after they arose, their environmental effects would fall to zero before the present and only environmental problem 4 would appear on a list of contemporary environmental issues. Environmental problems would not be cumulative. If, however, problems 2 and 3 remain unresolved, as they are in Figure 2.5, then they appear on the list of contemporary environmental problems and such problems accumulate in number over time. Moreover, if contemporary environmental problems are cumulative, their birth dates will be spread out over time. Were the process of environmental change not cumulative, birth dates of current environmental problems would all be close to the present because all environmental problems would be resolved soon after their appearance. Spread out birth dates for contemporary environmental problems thus indicate that the process of environmental change is cumulative in the sense that the number of environmental problems is expanding as time passes.

   The proposition that environmental problems are cumulative over time can be historically verified by listing current critical environmental problems, determining the industries whose formation and growth are largely responsible for those problems, and then identifying the birth dates of those industries and their associated trends in environmental deterioration. If birth dates are spread out in time, then current environmental problems are the consequence of the cumulative creation of industries.

Some environmental problems disappear over time and they may disappear first in wealthy countries that spend more per person on regulation. This phenomenon is consistent with the so-called "Kuznets curve hypothesis" suggesting that in developing countries environmental conditions first worsen as per capita income growth occurs and then improve (Grossman and Krueger 1993). Evidence supports this hypothesis for some environmental problems such as SO_2 and particulate air pollution emissions. Amelioration of the most visible environmental problems such as these does not necessarily mean, however, that environmental quality in all its many dimensions improves as economic growth proceeds. Some growth-induced environmental changes are simply irreversible, and new environmental problems may be added by the economic growth process at a more rapid rate than old ones are resolved. Constructing a meaningful aggregate index of environmental quality is impossible, given the difficulties in comparing the importance of different problems. Is urban smoke pollution, which has largely disappeared in prosperous countries, more or less important than global warming or species extinctions, problems that have loomed larger in more recent years? In order for environmental quality to be unambiguously improving, *no* new environmental problems can be added over time and some indices of environmental deterioration would have to be trending downward while none were trending upward. Even then we could be stuck with a permanent legacy of growth-induced environmental problems that are simply irreversible. If all environmental problems were reversible, if none were added over time, and if the Kuznets hypothesis were universally true, then economic growth would indeed solve our environmental problems. Unfortunately, if a Schumpeterian growth dynamic is at work adding new kinds of environmental problems, some of which may be irreversible, then economic growth may well worsen environmental conditions.

Critical contemporary environmental problems

A partial list of critical contemporary environmental problems is provided in Table 3.1 along with the industries and types of economic activities fostering those problems. While the list is not intended to be comprehensive, it does cover a broad range of environmental problems considered by many to be serious. In particular, the list includes environmental problems, such as habitat destruction, loss of biodiversity, and global climate change, that the U.S. Environmental Protection Agency judges to be in a high risk category, and problems, such as pesticide contamination, toxins and nutrients in surface waters, and acid deposition, that it judges to be in a medium risk category (Goodstein 1995: 93).

The status and consequences of each environmental problem listed in Table 3.1 are treated in detail in Chapters 4 and 5 where evidence is presented to justify the view that these problems constitute major environmental threats. The central purpose of the present chapter is to establish the relationship between environmental problems and the industry creation process, taking as given the seriousness of the problems in Table 3.1. The first step is to establish the link

Table 3.1 Persistent critical environmental problems and industries that caused them

Environmental problem	Responsible industries, activity
Air pollution: urban ozone, acid rain, global warming; ozone layer destruction.	Coal, steam technology, petroleum, motor vehicles, electrical goods, electricity, organic chemicals.
Nonpoint water pollution: urban, rural.	Motor vehicles, petroleum, highway construction, suburban development, agriculture, fertilizer, pesticides.
Organic toxic chemicals pollution: agricultural pesticides.	Organic chemicals, agriculture.
Destruction and fragmentation of natural areas: disappearance of the tall grass prairie; decline of old-growth forests in northern Great Lakes; decline of semi-natural areas in the U.K.; fragmentation and destruction of riparian habitat from dam construction; decline of Pacific Northwest old-growth forests; habitat fragmentation, riparian area damage in the Yellowstone area.	Agriculture, railroads, lumber, pulp and paper, electricity, irrigation, suburban development, microelectronics and advanced telecommunications.

between specific environmental problems and the complex of industries that created them. Then industry and environmental trend birth dates can be determined to see whether they are spread out in time. If they are, the creation of environmental problems is historically a cumulative process dependent on the cumulative creation and growth of new forms of economic activity.

Before moving on to a historical investigation of environmental problems, let's summarize the central proposition to be investigated. If contemporary environmental concerns all have recent birth dates, then the life span of such problems must be short. Past environmental concerns would have been resolved expeditiously. If, however, the list of contemporary environmental concerns is full of problems with early birth dates and long life spans, and if unresolved environmental problems are periodically added to the list, then the Schumpeterian-style industry creation process that drives economic growth is progressively creating enduring new environmental problems, and the evolutionary path of economic activity is mirrored in the current content of environmental concerns. Case materials used to illustrate the historical path of economic development and environmental change will be predominantly drawn from the U.S. experience, but supplementary materials for the U.K. will also be presented to demonstrate that a Schumpeterian environmental dynamic can be widely applied.

New forms of economic activity and environmental change

Each of the environmental problems listed in Table 3.1 can be traced historically to the emergence of new forms of economic activity. Environmental changes related to fossil fuel use, nonpoint water pollution, and pesticides are considered first and landscape-modifying environmental changes second.

Environmental change and fossil fuels

Fossil fuel use, the source of most air pollution problems (Stern *et al.* 1984), originated in the nineteenth century in the U.S. with the development of steam technology and its need for an efficient and abundant energy source (Tylecote 1992). The shift from wood to fossil fuels as the primary energy source in the U.S. was also aided by innovations in the iron and steel industry that led to increased use of coal as an industrial fuel, by local shortages of timber and increased demand for wood as a building material, and by the development of rail transportation to bring coal from mines to cities (Melosi 1985). U.S coal consumption grew rapidly from the 1850s through the 1920s, after which coal began to be supplanted by petroleum and natural gas. In 1850, coal provided only 9.3 percent of U.S. energy consumption, and by 1900 it provided 71.3 percent (U.S. Department of Commerce 1975).

With abundant forests as a source of fuelwood for both domestic and commercial uses, the rise of coal as a major fuel in the U.S. awaited the industrial revolution. In Great Britain, on the other hand, deforestation to make way for cropland and pasture occurred very early in the country's history, reducing the availability of fuelwood, and, as a consequence, coal became an essential domestic fuel in cities like London as early as the sixteenth century (Green 1985: 121; Brimblecombe 1987: 29–36). Nonetheless, explosive growth of annual coal consumption in the U.K., as in the U.S., coincided with the industrial revolution. The U.K. ushered in the modern industrial economy and experienced rapid growth in coal consumption much earlier than the U.S., with an expansion of use from around 13 million tons in 1801 to 225 million tons in 1900 (Mitchell 1984: 3, 12). This growth was driven by the rapid expansion of the iron and steel industry, the use of the steam engine in manufacturing and transportation, and the expansion of coal exports.

The growing use of electricity from the end of the nineteenth century on in both the U.S. and U.K. further stimulated the demand for fossil fuel energy. In the 1870s and 1880s a number of inventions materialized in rapid succession, including the ring dynamo, electric motor, telephone, incandescent lamp, and electric railway (Byatt 1979; Passer 1953; Tylecote 1992: 50–51). The telephone revolutionized communication, and the electric tram took intra-urban transportation out of the personal realm and placed it in the market, at least for the middle class. The tram also began the process of suburbanization in the U.S. that eventually revolutionized land use patterns in urban areas (Warner 1974). Electric lighting initiated a vast new consumer market in electrical goods, and the use of electricity as a power source diffused rapidly in manufacturing. By 1929 75 percent of primary horsepower in U.S. manufacturing was provided by electricity, whereas at the turn of the century the figure was only 4 percent (Woolf 1984). In British industry around 50 percent of total power used was from electricity by 1924 (Byatt 1979: 73).

Technological changes are often interlinked not only in space, but over time as well. Certain technological changes and industry births necessarily precede other technological changes. The steel and electricity industries, for example, together made possible the production of mechanized goods on a large-scale basis and thus set the stage for another new technological system, the Fordist assembly line method of mass production. The idea of the assembly line goes back to Adam Smith's pin factory and the Chicago slaughterhouses, but it could not be readily implemented in nineteenth-century manufacturing because of two fundamental problems. First, parts had to be genuinely interchangeable, and they had to be made of a strong, durable yet shapable material like steel to be effectively produced on a mass basis. Cutting tools that could shape such steel parts had to await the development of high-quality steel alloys, unneeded in the nineteenth century when metal cutting requirements were less exacting. Second, a centralized steam power source would not do for a spread out assembly line style production process. The system of belts needed to supply power to all the different machines would be too complex. This problem was solved with the electric motor, a highly decentralized and flexible source of power (Tylecote 1992: 51–52; Woolf 1984; Schurr et al. 1990: 21–42; Rae 1984: 31–39; Church 1994: 1–11). Steel and electricity thus set the stage for the Fordist technological system and its assembly line process.[1]

Although the concept of the assembly line can be applied to virtually any mass-produced mechanical or electrical good, it was applied first to the one product that has perhaps more than any other transformed the way we live, the automobile.[2] The automobile was made possible by the discovery of liquid petroleum in the nineteenth century and the advancement of refining processes to cheapen automobile fuels.[3] The impact of the automobile on industrial development in the U.S., the U.K., and elsewhere cannot be easily overstated. The automobile provided a large new market for the steel and machinery industries and created a whole array of part suppliers; it is largely responsible for the growth of the petroleum industry and thus indirectly fostered the eventual development of the petrochemical industry in the 1940s; it created a large service industry to keep the auto and truck fleet running; and it stimulated road construction and accelerated the suburbanization process and attendant housing construction by reducing commuting times and costs (Tylecote 1992: 53; Hogan 1971b: 661–686; Melosi 1985: 105–112; Williamson et al. 1963; Richardson 1977; Church 1994). The automobile completed the process of transferring individual transportation from the personal to the market realm begun by the railroad and tram (Ling 1990: 64–94). The emergence of the automobile industry caused a revolution in processing technology in the petroleum industry and led to petroleum becoming the U.S. economy's predominant energy source with the motor vehicle as the leading consumer (Williamson *et al.* 1963). While European per capita motor vehicle ownership is significantly less and vehicle fuel efficiency somewhat greater in comparison to the U.S., even so European motor vehicle ownership and fuel consumption is substantial and growing rapidly (OECD 1995: 207–230).

The pattern of growth in U.S. energy consumption for the period 1948–1990 as shown in Figure 3.1 is driven by fossil fuel use. The dominance of oil, coal, and gas in energy consumption extends to European countries and Japan, although the share of nuclear power is somewhat greater outside the U.S. (OECD 1991: 223). The link between fossil fuel use and modern air pollution problems is discussed in detail in Stern *et al.* (1984) and MacDonald (1982) and will be only briefly summarized here. The three predominant sources of air pollution emissions for the U.S. are the transportation, fuel combustion, and industrial sectors. Stationary-source fuel combustion emissions are primarily from electric utilities (70–80 percent), most of which are coal-fired (U.S. Department of Commerce 1993). Particulate emissions are shared by all three sectors, with the most coming from the industrial sector (Table 3.2). The major source of sulfur oxide

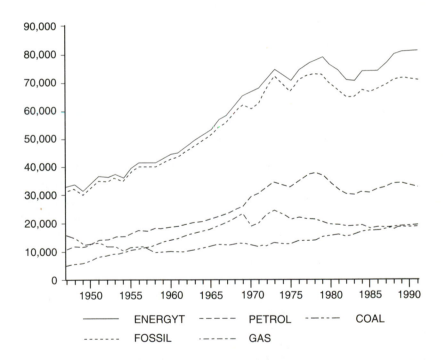

Figure 3.1 Total U.S. (ENERGYT) fossil fuel (FOSSIL), petroleum (PETROL), gas (GAS), and coal (COAL) energy consumption (tril. Btu)
Sources: U.S. Department of Commerce (1975, 1976–1993).

Table 3.2 Sector shares of U.S. emissions (%)

Year	1970	1980	1990
Particulates			
Transportation	6.3	14.3	21.2
Fuel combustion	26.8	33.0	25.6
Industrial	55.3	36.3	34.4
Sulfur oxides			
Transportation	2.2	4.0	4.8
Fuel combustion	75.0	79.3	79.8
Industrial	22.5	16.3	15.2
Nitrous oxides			
Transportation	44.7	53.0	38.7
Fuel combustion	47.9	42.8	56.4
Industrial	3.7	3.0	3.2
Volatile organic compounds			
Transportation fuel	46.7	37.2	30.1
Combustion	2.2	4.6	4.0
Industrial	32.5	41.7	46.6
Carbon monoxide			
Transportation	78.4	77.4	70.0
Fuel combustion	3.4	6.6	7.5
Industrial	7.3	6.3	7.6

Source: U.S. Department of Commerce (1993).

emissions is fuel combustion, while the transportation sector and fuel combustion share emissions of nitrous oxides (Table 3.2). Volatile organic emissions come primarily from the transportation and industrial sectors, while carbon monoxide emissions are mostly from the transportation sector (Table 3.2).[4]

Emissions of air pollutants in the U.S. have been mediated by regulatory efforts. Prior to the 1970 Clean Air Act Amendments, regulation of U.S. air quality was essentially left to states and municipalities, and the impact of these regulations was comparatively modest. Particulate emissions declined in the 1950s and 1960s before significant national regulation, probably as a result of reduced coal use for home heating and tighter local regulations. National regulations after 1970 resulted in particulate emissions dropping fairly rapidly (Figure 3.2; Table 3.3). Sulfur oxide emission trends are tied historically to coal consumption patterns as well as efforts to regulate emissions (Stern *et al.* 1984: 363–373). In the 1950s, sulfur oxide emissions grew very slowly at a time when coal use was declining. However, sulfur emissions surged in the 1960s in response to growth in coal use by electric utilities (Figure 3.2; Table 3.3). Even though coal consumption continued to grow after 1970, sulfur emissions fell in response to tighter regulation. Under the 1970 Clean Air Act, new source performance standards were established for newly constructed stationary emission sources that limited

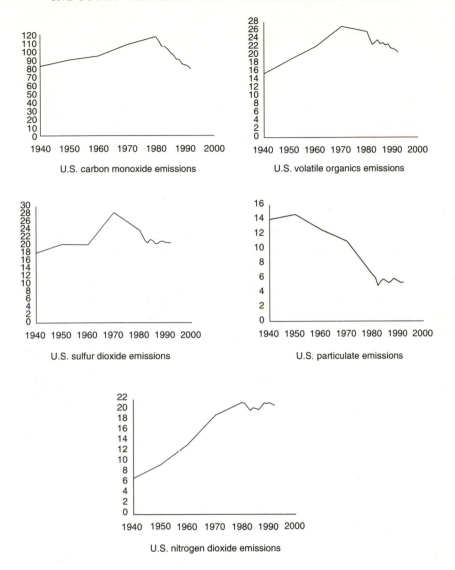

Figure 3.2 U.S. air pollution emissions (million metric tons)
Sources: U.S. Department of Commerce (1993); U.S. EPA (1991).

sulfur oxide as well as particulate and nitrous oxide emissions. States also had the option of regulating existing sources in order to meet ambient air quality standards required by the Clean Air Act (Stern *et al.* 1984: 446, 356–358).

Of all U.S. air pollutants, nitrous oxides have been the most difficult to control. Nitrous oxide emissions are the result of fossil fuel combustion at high emperatures, and their dominant sources are the internal combustion engine and

27

Table 3.3 Air pollution emissions for the U.S. and energy consumption: annual percentage change relative to the prior decade

Year	1950	1960	1970	1980	1990
Emission					
Particulates	0.84	−1.29	−1.37	−7.36	−2.06
Sulfur oxides	1.15	0.64	3.41	−1.77	−1.20
Nitrous oxides	3.24	3.40	3.64	1.24	−1.96
Volatile organics	1.98	1.74	1.97	−2.29	−2.14
Carbon monoxide	0.73	1.82	1.77	−2.12	−3.90
Energy use					
Motor vehicle fuel	4.83	4.85	4.67	2.19	1.28
Coal	0.30	−2.20	1.92	1.92	2.14
Coal-util.	5.86	6.78	6.11	5.74	5.74
Industrial		1.71	3.15	0.49	−0.69

Sources: U.S. Department of Commerce (1975, 1993)

the electric utility. The rapid increase of nitrous oxide emissions up to 1970 is the result of increased motor vehicle use and the expansion of coal-fired electrical generating capacity (Table 3.3). Some of the increase in nitrous oxides emissions can be traced to higher electric utility boiler operating temperatures, undertaken to improve fuel consumption efficiency (Gould 1985: 28). Nitrous oxide emissions continued to grow in the 1970s, although at a slower rate because of increased regulations. Beginning in the mid-1970s, emissions control devices were required on U.S. automobiles to reduce nitrous oxide emissions (Stern *et al.* 1984: 483), and in the 1980s, nitrous oxide emissions began to decline.

Two other major pollutants, volatile organics and carbon monoxide, have trajectories of growth and decline similar to one another in the U.S. (Figure 3.2; Table 3.3). Transportation is the predominant source of carbon monoxide, while transportation and industry share responsibility for emissions of volatile organics. Carbon monoxide emissions grew up to 1970 in response to growth in motor vehicle use, while volatile organics increased as a result of both industrial expansion and growing motor vehicle use (Table 3.3). Growth in hydrocarbon emissions from motor vehicles was restrained somewhat after 1963 with the installation of crankcase ventilation systems that recycle crankcase gases (Stern *et al.* 1984: 481–482). In the 1970s catalytic converters and other control devices were required on most new cars, resulting in reduced emissions of carbon monoxide and hydrocarbons as well as nitrous oxides (Stern *et al.* 1984, 882–884).

In sum, air pollution emissions in the U.S. were significantly reduced after 1970 as a consequence of reduced growth in energy consumption and increased regulation. The decline in emissions has been relatively more substantial for sulfur, particulates, and CO than it has for nitrous oxides and volatile organics. Progress on emissions reductions slowed significantly for all pollutants in the early 1990s and a significant emissions problem remains (Figure 3.2).

The history of air pollution emissions provides a rather different story in the U.K. than the U.S., even though the primary source in both instances is fossil fuel use. Air pollution problems in the U.K. are symbolized by the deadly London smog of 1952, caused by smoke pollution from coal used mostly for domestic heating, while air pollution in the U.S. brings to mind the photochemical smog that appears frequently in the Los Angeles basin. Pollution control regulation in the U.K. has focused mostly on smoke and SO_2 emissions rather than on pollutants that cause photochemical smog, although now that the number of sunny days is on the rise in cities like London because of smoke control, photochemical smog is increasing (Brimblecombe 1987: 161–177). As a consequence of the smoke control emphasis in the U.K., sulfur emissions have declined fairly significantly, but the emission of carbon monoxide, volatile organics, and nitrous oxides continued to increase up to 1990 (Figure 3.3). Despite reductions in SO_2 emissions, the U.K. remains the second largest source in Europe (World Resources Institute 1996: 331). More recently, motor vehicles have come under stricter regulation as the result of European Community directives requiring the installation of catalytic converters since 1992 (Button 1995: 182). The growth of U.K. motor vehicle emissions in recent years can be traced to a substantial growth in road traffic (*ibid*.: 178–180). The cycle of rise and decline of auto emissions in the U.K. appears to be occurring somewhat later than in the U.S. (Figures 3.2 and 3.3).

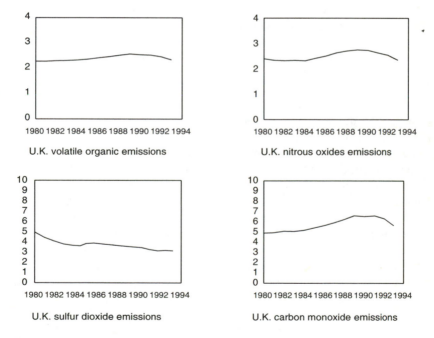

Figure 3.3 U.K. air pollution emissions (million metric tons)
Source: OECD (1995).

The one air pollutant that has not been significantly regulated in the U.S., the U.K., or elsewhere is carbon dioxide, the primary cause of the global warming problem.[5] Global carbon dioxide concentrations have risen from a relatively stable level of about 270 parts per million (ppm) in 1850, prior to massive use of fossil fuels, to a current level of about 350 ppm (Abrahamson 1989). Atmospheric carbon acts like a window to incoming high-energy solar radiation, but absorbs low-frequency energy re-radiated from the earth's surface, increasing atmospheric temperatures above levels that would otherwise prevail (MacDonald 1989). Other heat-trapping gases include methane, nitrous oxides, chlorine-containing chemicals, carbon monoxide, and ground-level (tropospheric) ozone.

The most important of the greenhouse gases, carbon dioxide, is increasing in atmospheric concentration because of a substantial modification of the carbon cycle. Carbon is taken up through photosynthesis by the earth's biota and is released back into the atmosphere through respiration by plants, animals, and microorganisms. The global carbon sinks are the biota and soils, the oceans (which chemically absorb carbon), the atmosphere, and fossil fuel deposits in the earth's crust. With the extraction and use of fossil fuels, and with increase global deforestation, the balance between sinks has been upset. Combustion of fossil fuels currently is increasing the release of carbon to the atmosphere by 5–6 billion metric tons per year, while deforestation is increasing carbon releases by 1–3 billion metric tons per year. The oceans and other carbon sinks are unable to absorb the full amount of the extra carbon being released, resulting in a net annual accumulation in the atmosphere of around 3 billion tons (Woodwell 1989).

The contribution to global carbon emissions from fossil fuel use by the U.S. is by no means trivial (Figure 3.4), running at 1.3–1.5 billion metric tons per year in the 1970s and 1980s, or approximately 24 percent of the global total in 1990. The contribution of the U.K. is rather smaller (2.5 percent) by virtue of its greater energy efficiency and smaller population, and U.K. emissions have declined slightly in the last two decades while U.S. emissions have continued to rise. The decline in U.K. carbon emissions can be attributed in part to a shift toward (lower carbon content) oil and gas and away from (higher carbon content) coal undertaken for the purpose of reducing sulfur emissions (Maddison and Pearce 1995: 129). The European Community as a whole contributes a relatively significant 14 percent to global carbon emissions from fossil fuel use (Cline 1992: 330–331). Carbon emissions in the U.S. are directly tied to fossil fuel energy consumption patterns, and emissions grew rapidly in the U.S. up to the 1970s along with rapid growth in fossil fuel consumption (Figure 3.1). Coal consumption is weighted somewhat more heavily in the calculation of carbon dioxide emissions because it emits 25 kg of carbon per million Btu of thermal energy, as opposed to 20.5 kg for petroleum and 16.3 kg for natural gas (MacDonald 1982: 18). Since approximately 50 percent of carbon emissions remain in the atmosphere, emissions accumulate (Cline 1992: 16). Even though emissions in the U.S. are growing slowly, the U.S. contribution to cumulative emissions continues to grow relatively rapidly (Figure 3.4), and it is cumulative emissions that count in the global warming problem.

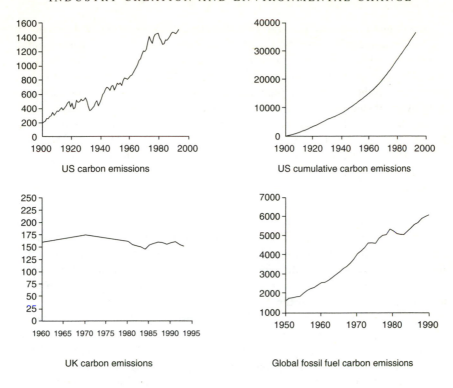

Figure 3.4 Carbon emissions (million metric tons)
Sources: U.S. Department of Commerce (1975, 1976–1993); MacDonald (1992: 18); World Resources Institute (1995).

To summarize, continuing fossil fuel use is the root cause of continuing relatively high levels of air pollution emissions. Fossil fuel use is in turn the historical consequence of the creation of a complex of industries including steam power, coal, motor vehicles, petroleum, chemicals, and electricity and electrical goods.

Nonpoint water pollution: suburbanization and urban sources in the U.S.

A trend of great environmental significance in the U.S. has been the rapid growth of suburbs since World War II. Suburbanization and the consequent need for greater motor vehicle use has not only caused air pollution problems, but has aggravated nonpoint water pollution problems as well. Prior to the turn of the century, cities simply moved their boundaries outward to accommodate increasing populations. Since then, older central cities in the East and Midwest have become surrounded by suburban municipalities, inhibiting the outward expansion of central city boundaries. Until recently, some cities in the South and Southwest have avoided this problem by virtue of favorable annexation laws. The ring of suburban municipalities around central cities permits a simple measure of the extent of suburbanization. For 135 metropolitan statistical areas in the United States, in 1950 57 percent of the metropolitan population lived in central cities and 43 percent in the suburbs. By 1980, 40 percent lived in the central cities and 60 percent in the suburbs. In many metropolitan areas, this shift was accompanied by an absolute drop in central city population. Private sector employment also underwent a dramatic shift over this period of time, with 70 percent concentrated in the central cities in 1950, and 50 percent in 1980 (Mills and Hamilton 1994: 81–85). Clearly, population and employment growth have concentrated predominantly in the suburbs since 1950.

The auto, truck, and freeway accelerated the pace and increased the extent of suburbanization. Before the truck, transporting goods within cities was relatively costly, and, as a consequence, manufacturers concentrated their facilities near ports and rail lines. Before the auto, retailing concentrated heavily in the central business district, and to a lesser extent along mass transit lines. Cities were much more densely packed, and the amount of housing space consumed per person was less (Muth 1969). The truck and freeway untied manufacturing from ports and rail lines, the auto and the freeway along with the outward movement of employment stimulated suburban population growth, and retailing followed population to the suburbs (Mills and Hamilton 1994). In essence, the auto, truck, and freeway significantly reduced the cost of moving goods and people in urban areas, permitting an outward spread of both population and employment.

The vast spreading out of cities after World War II made possible by highway construction and increased motor vehicle use contributed significantly to the U.S. urban nonpoint pollution problem. Storm water that formerly was absorbed by soils or flowed into natural drainage channels now runs off acres of concrete highway and parking lot surfaces into streams, rivers, and lakes, carrying with it metals that come from the wear and corrosion of vehicles, lubricating oils that leak from vehicles, waste oils purposely dumped into street drains, and road salts used to melt ice and snow in the winter (Welch 1992). Acres of suburban lawns contribute fertilizers, pesticides, yard wastes, and pet feces to the chemical mix of nonpoint runoff, along with the suspended solids that wash off urban construction sites. The symbol and the measure of suburbanization and its associated nonpoint water pollution problem is the mileage of urban highways. As can be seen in Figure 3.5, urban highways grew rapidly after World War II and continue to grow.[6]

This relatively new and largely unregulated source of water pollutants is one of the reasons for limited progress in improving U.S. water quality. Prior to 1972, point sources of pollution went largely untreated, and water quality in major rivers and lakes was in a highly deteriorated state. Under the 1972 Clean Water Act, all point sources of water pollution emissions were required to have a permit, and to get one certain discharge limits had to be met. While the process of determining permit standards has been slow and enforcement of standards has sometimes been weak, progress has been made in reducing discharges. All

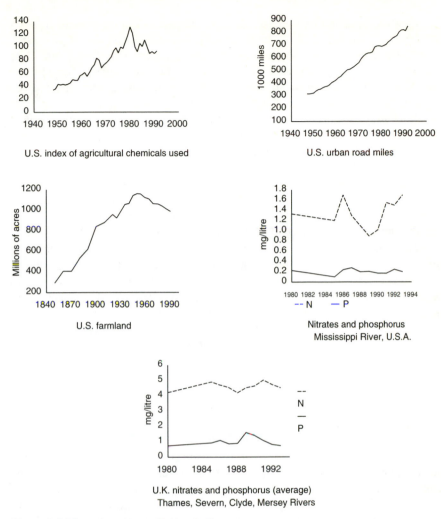

Figure 3.5 Nonpoint water pollution indicators
Sources: U.S. Department of Commerce (1975, 1976–1993); U.S. Federal Highway Commission (1947–1965); U.S. Council of Economic Advisors (1995); OECD (1995).

municipal sewer plants are required to undertake secondary treatment, and all industrial sources are required to install treatment facilities. As a consequence, by the mid-1980s, industry was spending $6 billion a year on water pollution control. Because of improved treatment, the EPA claims that the release of organic wastes has been reduced by 46 percent and the emission of selected toxic pollutants has declined substantially (Adler *et al.* 1993).

The extent to which water quality in lakes, rivers, and estuaries has actually improved as a consequence of pollution control efforts is difficult to ascertain because of the inadequacy of water quality monitoring. The limited evidence that is available suggests that water quality has improved near many point sources. However, serious problems remain, and some streams and lakes have experienced deterioration in quality. The percentage of waters of sufficient quality to support their designated uses under the Clean Water Act actually decreased in the 1980s, although some of the decrease may be the consequence of increased monitoring efforts (Adler *et al*. 1993).

The continuation of serious water pollution problems in the face of point source control suggests that nonpoint sources may be the root cause. Urban runoff contains many of the same pollutants as uncontrolled municipal sewage discharges, but in somewhat different concentrations. While one may think that urban runoff is likely to be cleaner than raw sewage, in fact urban areas yield approximately equal annual volumes of total suspended solids (TSS) in sewage and runoff. Urban runoff contains less total biochemical oxygen-demanding organic matter (BOD), nitrogen, and phosphorus than untreated sewage, but relatively more heavy metals (zinc, copper, and lead). Because storm water episodes tend to be infrequent and sometimes yield large volumes of runoff, the concentration of pollutants can rise to much higher levels for a period of time in local water bodies than occurs from continuously flowing sewage. While the high concentrations may be short in duration, they can do significant damage to aquatic flora and fauna. Consequently, urban runoff constitutes a pollution problem as serious as that caused by untreated sewage (Welch 1992).

Nonpoint water pollution: U.S. rural sources

An even more serious nonpoint pollution problem originates in the countryside. Runoff from farm fields and barnyards has caused a deterioration in local stream and lake quality since the beginning of intense cultivation in the U.S. Turbidity in local waters increases as the result of erosion, and, where manure is spread on fields, runoff results in nutrient enrichment of local streams and lakes. Since World War II, however, the nutrient enrichment problem has increased in severity as a consequence of an eightfold increase in the use of fertilizers between 1940 and 1970 (U.S. Department of Commerce 1975). Phosphorus at high levels in local waters is toxic to fish, and at low levels it stimulates algae production that can use up local dissolved oxygen supplies during decomposition and cause fish kills. Applications of nitrogen fertilizers can cause buildups of nitrate to toxic levels in streams and groundwater (Adler *et al*. 1993; Patrick 1992). Increased pesticide use since World War II also constitutes another major source of nonpoint pollution. Surges of pesticide contamination in streams that correspond with planting cycles are now a relatively common phenomenon (Welch 1992; Adler *et al*. 1993). Much expanded U.S. agricultural land use beginning in the nineteenth century and the more intensive use of agricultural chemicals beginning in the 1940s have together caused increased emissions of pollutants into streams, rivers, and lakes and have reduced water quality.

Although direct measures are unavailable, the amount of rural nonpoint pollution is probably related historically to the amount of grazed and cultivated land (acres of farmland) and the use of agricultural chemicals. As shown in Figure 3.5, the growth of both in the U.S. leveled off in the 1980s, a trend that is apparently mirrored in water quality measures. The only continuous national system of water quality monitoring is the U.S. Geological Survey's National Stream Quality Accounting Network (NASQAN), initiated in the 1970s. The monitoring stations used for NASQAN are generally located relatively far downstream and thus measure water quality conditions associated with land use patterns in the watershed as a whole, rather than local water quality conditions associated with local point sources of pollution. Some of the results of a time trend analysis of these data for the period 1978–1987 are presented in Table 3.4 (Lettenmaier *et al.* 1991). The most obvious and important conclusion of this study is that for all water quality indicators most monitoring stations show no trend, implying that water quality is neither improving nor declining at these stations. This finding is broadly consistent with slight declines in farmland and agricultural chemical use and a slight increase in urban development as measured by urban road miles (Figure 3.5). The lack of a clear trend in water quality is confirmed for nitrate and phosphorus concentrations in the Mississippi between 1980 and 1993, a river that drains a very large area of the continental U.S. (Figure 3.5). In short, over the period 1978–1987 large-scale U.S. land use patterns, and their contribution to nonpoint pollution, have not changed substantially.

Table 3.4 Trends in concentration of selected U.S. water quality indicators, 1978–1987

Pollutant	Number of stations	Stations with plus trend	Stations with minus trend	Stations with no trend
Sulfate	393	64	36	293
Chloride	392	65	32	295
Dissolved solids	388	84	22	282
Nitrogen	390	82	24	284
Phosphorus	389	12	69	308
Suspended solids	153	13	19	121
Oxygen deficit	316	12	39	265
Fecal coliform	390	24	51	315
Copper	371	17	27	327
Zinc	381	3	20	358
Lead	374	4	45	325

Source: Lettenmaier *et al.* (1991).

Water pollution in the U.K.

Because of more concentrated urban development and relatively less road mileage, urban nonpoint water pollution is less of an issue in the U.K. than the U.S.

This is not to say that the U.K. is free of surburban development. The road network in the U.K. expanded 9 percent between 1970 and 1988, a rate that is only slightly below the 11 percent figure for the U.S. (OECD 1991: 212). While the land use planning process in the U.K. is not lacking for criticism (Norton-Taylor 1982: 199–234), it has probably constrained the spatial extent of suburban sprawl, a result that is immediately apparent to visitors from the U.S. (Vogel 1986:161). While the road network in the U.K. has indeed expanded, the number of kilometers of roads per capita is only one-fourth the U.S. figure (OECD 1991: 212, 241). The compactness of urban land use in the U.K. is also partly attributable to a relatively extensive system of intra- and inter-urban rail transportation, a phenomenon that goes a long way in explaining a U.K. rate of motor vehicle ownership per capita that is about half that of the U.S. (*ibid.*: 215).

The reduced potential for urban nonpoint pollution by no means leaves the U.K. free of water quality problems. Early water pollution problems on the Thames and other rivers were notorious; the stink from the Thames was so great during a heat wave in 1858 that Parliament was forced to adjourn (Clapp 1994: 71–76). The most serious problems in U.K. rivers and estuaries up to World War II were the consequence of untreated sewage and industrial discharges. The first water quality legislation, the River Pollution Prevention Act of 1876, called for the control of discharges by the "best practicable means" and left enforcement to local sanitary authorities who were in charge of sewerage facilities. Sewage farms and treatment facilities began to appear by the early twentieth century, and industries began to treat some of their waste discharges. However, in both world wars, water quality deteriorated, with low priority given to investment in sewage treatment (*ibid.*: 82–88). Unlike in the U.S., a river basin approach has been taken to water quality with River Boards (later renamed River Authorities) given authority in 1951 to negotiate emissions limits, or consents, for new sources that consider the condition of the receiving waters in non-tidal rivers (Kinnersley 1994: 43–44). This authority was extended by 1961 to estuaries and coastal waters and to sources of pollution existing prior to 1951. On the grounds of preventing trade secret disclosure, the process of negotiating and enforcing consents was kept confidential and out of public view until the 1974 Control of Pollution Act, and even then exemptions were kept in place for another 10 years. Because members of local government councils who were responsible for sewage treatment also sat on the River Boards, enforcement of consents for sewage treatment plants was often lax (Kinnersley 1988: 76–78).

The net result of pollution control efforts has been mixed. Between 1958 and 1990, the percentage of river length in England and Wales that was "grossly polluted" declined for non-tidal rivers from 6 percent to 2 percent and for tidal rivers from 13 percent to 3 percent. For non-tidal rivers, however, the percentage of river length that was "poor" increased from 7 percent to 9 percent, and the percentage that was of "doubtful" water quality increased from 15 percent to 25 percent. Water quality in tidal rivers, on the other hand, improved, with river length in the "poor" category declining from 14 to 7 percent and in the "doubtful" category declining from 32 to 24 percent (Clapp 1994: 92). While progress has occurred in the tidal stretches of rivers like the Thames, quality has apparently deteriorated on the non-tidal stretches of some rivers. The deterioration has been concentrated on the non-tidal Thames and in the southwest of England. The apparent deterioration on the Thames, which runs through an intensively developed urban landscape, may be partly the result of improved water quality monitoring rather than a real decline in water quality. The deterioration in the southwest of England, however, has occurred in an area that is predominantly rural and agricultural, suggesting that nonpoint sources are playing an increasing role in the determination of water quality (Kinnersley 1994: 124–127).

Prior to World War II, the U.K. agricultural sector had not yet felt the hand of modern industrial methods. Mechanization was relatively low and mixed farming was the rule. Maintenance of cropland fertility was accomplished through crop rotation and application of manure. Abundant imports and relatively low agricultural commodity prices kept the agricultural sector in a state of depression from about 1870 to 1939 (Green 1985: 79–81; Holderness 1985: 1–6). Hedgerows and small fields must have kept erosion and polluted runoff to a minimum.

For British agriculture, World War II proved to be a watershed. The threat of German U-boats to imports made it abundantly clear that as a matter of necessity the U.K. had to rely much more on its own farmlands for food. From this moment forward government policy called for self-sufficiency in food, and this policy was more or less continued after the war. With abundant governmental subsidies, U.K. agriculture modernized. Grassland was plowed up for arable crops; mechanization increased; hedgerows were torn up to make bigger fields suited to large tractors and farm implements; the population of beef cattle and pigs increased significantly; and the use of fertilizers and pesticides rose dramatically (Holderness 1985: 6–27, 42–74; Green 1985: 81–92). These changing farming methods have contributed significantly to increased nonpoint water pollution problems in the English countryside, although attempts to modify farming practices in order to reduce nonpoint runoff have begun (Green 1985: 90–92; Kinnersley 1994: 134–137). Nitrate concentration in three U.K. rivers more than doubled between 1960 and 1980, paralleling a more than twofold increase in fertilizer use over the same period (Meybeck *et al.* 1989: 126–127). The application of nitrogen fertilizer per hectare in the U.K. is more than twice the amount typically applied in the U.S. (Conway and Pretty 1991: 159). In the 1980s, growth in fertilizer consumption leveled off, and nitrate and phosphorus concentrations in U.K. rivers have remained relatively constant since (OECD 1995; Figure 3.5). In brief, the growth of industrial agriculture in the UK from 1940 on has resulted in substantial new water pollution problems that have yet to be significantly resolved.

Pesticides

Increased use of pesticides has aggravated nonpoint water pollution problems, but has created other, larger environmental problems as well and thus deserves separate treatment. Prior to World War II, the use of pesticides was limited in scope. Pest problems were often addressed by such techniques as crop rotation, early planting and crop maturation, and the breeding of pest-resistant plant varieties. Arsenical compounds and hydrogen cyanide were used as pesticides to a limited extent beginning in the late nineteenth century. In 1917 and again in the early 1920s calcium arsenate was used to fight off a boll weevil attack on the U.S. cotton crop (Davis 1984: 148–150; Brown 1978: 2).

These pesticides were inorganic chemicals, and they were generally used for specific pest attacks. Consequently, demand for them was highly variable and so was their price. The market for calcium arsenate boomed in years when the boll weevil was a problem, but collapsed in other years. In order for the chemical industry to make significant and continuous profits from pesticides, broad-spectrum chemicals were needed that could be effective against a variety of pests. This problem was solved in 1939 with the discovery by a Swiss chemical firm that DDT was a powerful and persistent insecticide, effective against a wide variety of pests. The chemical was extremely useful to the Allies in World War II because of its effectiveness in suppressing insect-borne diseases such as malaria and typhus (Davis 1984: 150–151).

Following the war, the chemical industry set out to develop a variety of broad-spectrum synthetic organic pesticides. Two major categories of insecticides have emerged: the chlorinated hydrocarbons, including DDT, chlordane, heptachlor, dieldrin, aldrin, and endrin, and the organic phosphates, such as parathion, malathion, and diazinon. The latter group was developed by the German chemical industry as modifications of chemical warfare agents. In addition, carbamate insecticides, such as Sevin, and synthetic organic herbicides, such as 2,4-D, 2,4,5-T, silvex, and atrazine were developed in the 1940s and 1950s (Davis 1984: 153; Brown 1978: 2–9).

From 1951 to 1959, the growth of pesticide production in the U.S. was explosive, increasing from a total of 464,000 pounds to 468,833,000 pounds (Davis 1984: 145; U.S. Tariff Commission 1959). From 1959 to 1974, growth continued to be relatively rapid in the U.S., and by 1988 on a global scale Western Europe was a close second to the U.S. in pesticide use (Pimentel *et al.* 1991; Conway and Pretty 1991: 20). Since 1974, the volume of total pesticide use has declined in the U.S., primarily because of reduced use of insecticides. One major reason for the volume decline has been a ten- to one-hundredfold increase in the toxicity of new pesticides (Pimentel *et al.* 1991). The use of herbicides in the U.S. has remained fairly stable since 1974, and relative use patterns of insecticides and herbicides are similar in the U.S. and Western Europe (U.S. International Trade Commission, 1974–1988; Conway and Pretty 1991: 20). The application of pesticides fits hand-in-glove with the increasing capital intensity of agriculture. Herbicides could be substituted for costly hand-weeding. Pesticide use permitted cotton growers to introduce longer-season varieties that benefited from heavy irrigation and fertilization. Pesticide use also allowed corn farmers to eliminate crop rotation for the purpose of controlling rootworm and thus resulted in a greater degree of crop specialization and larger, more capital-intensive farms. The heaviest users of insecticides and herbicides in the U.S. respectively have been cotton growers and corn farmers (Davis 1984: 151–152; Brown 1978: 10–15). Pesticide and herbicide use has also been adopted as a key component of modern agricultural methods in the U.K. (Green 1985: 87–90).

Environmental problems associated with the chemical industry, such as growing concentrations of pesticides in wildlife food chains, were brought to public attention by Rachel Carson's path-breaking book, *Silent Spring* (1962). Although DDT and other pesticides that are not easily broken down by biological processes have been banned from general use in the U.S. and from the most damaging uses in the U.K., they continue to be employed elsewhere, persist in the environment for long periods of time, and pose a health threat to biotic life in general (Vogel 1986: 184; Pimentel *et al.* 1991). In the meantime, many potentially dangerous pesticides continue to be used in U.S. and U.K. agriculture whose health and environmental threats have yet to be fully addressed (Bosso 1987; Davis 1984; Brown 1978; Pimentel *et al.* 1992).[7] The emergence and growth of the organic chemicals industry thus led to the chemically based agricultural system that predominates today and the associated problem of environmental toxins causing economic damage and harm to human health and wildlife populations.

Natural habitat destruction and fragmentation: tallgrass prairie

While most think of various forms of pollution in reference to environmental problems, the destruction and fragmentation of natural habitats in the U.S. and elsewhere is a longstanding environmental problem that is closely associated with agricultural settlement and production and the extraction of wood fiber and other natural resources. The loss of the U.S. tallgrass prairie can be traced directly to the settlement of the Midwest on the foundation of commercial agriculture (Madson 1982).

Agriculture was the dominant sector in the U.S. economy in the last half of the nineteenth century, and a significant portion of its growth in this period of time can be attributed to settlement of the Midwest. The fourfold rise in U.S. agricultural production from 1850 to 1900 resulted primarily from a threefold rise in the amount of land in farms, much of which occurred in the prairie states (Gallman 1960). By 1859, Illinois, Indiana, and Wisconsin had taken the three leading positions in wheat production for states previously held by Ohio, Pennsylvania, and New York (North 1974: 141). From 1850 to 1880, the Midwestern prairie state share of total U.S. farmland increased from 21 percent to 39 percent (U.S. Department of Commerce 1975: 460). Prairie settlement was driven in turn by the single most influential change in transportation in the nineteenth century, construction of the steam railroad.

Transportation improvements, especially the expansion of the railroad, were necessary for the commercialization and growth of prairie state agriculture. Since overland transportation costs quickly absorbed the market value of such commodities as wheat and corn as distance to urban markets increased, the transporting of agricultural commodities by wagon was too costly for long-distance shipment. Consequently, Midwestern commercial agriculture was water-oriented to take advantage of market access by way of waterborne transportation prior to 1850. Population density tended to be heaviest along navigable waterways, and the flow of commodities was predominantly to the south following the flow of Mississippi watershed rivers (Cronon 1991: 97–109; North 1974: 141–142).

After 1840 commodity flows began to be redirected to the east through the Erie Canal as a consequence of waterborne transportation improvements in the Great Lakes region (North 1974: 142). This processes was accelerated in the 1850s with the development of an extensive rail network emanating from Chicago (Cronon 1991: 55–93). Chicago thus became the lynchpin of the Midwestern economy, funneling commodity flows from west to east, manufactured goods from east to west, and lumber, essential for farm building, from the north woods to the prairie.

Notwithstanding the extensive debate in the historical literature over the role of the railroad in the aggregate development of the U.S. economy,[8] the railroad significantly accelerated agricultural settlement in the prairie states.[9] In the 1850s, interior counties in Illinois lacking access to navigable waterways experienced much more rapid population growth as a consequence of gaining railroad service than peripheral counties (North 1974: 146–152). These same counties experienced increases in wheat production at a much more rapid rate than the state as a whole, as well. With the coming of the railroad, settlers who had previously been attracted to the river valleys were now moving into the rich upland prairies (Cronon 1991: 109). Grain shipments increased not only from newly settled areas, but from previously settled localities as well because of declining transportation costs (Fishlow 1965: 205–215). The proportion of wheat output growth coming from counties served by railroads was 75 percent for Indiana, Illinois, Wisconsin, and Iowa between 1850 and 1860, and 63 percent of this was from counties lacking water access (Fishlow 1965: 211).

The data in Table 3.5 provide evidence that railroads stimulated agricultural settlement where no other transportation options were available. Both Illinois and Iowa had water access on their periphery and thus agricultural settlement prior to significant railroad development. The Dakotas and Kansas, however, lacked significant water transportation routes and did not experience substantial farmland settlement until after major railroad development. The process and pattern of settlement in Iowa and South Dakota have been respectively investigated at a more detailed level by Clare C. Cooper (1958) and James F. Hamburg (1981), and they confirm the importance of railroads in stimulating settlement in the open prairie. The eastern and south-central sections of Iowa were already heavily settled prior to railroad construction. The wooded valleys of these areas provided pioneers with the necessities of life, and water transportation along the Mississippi was relatively close at hand. Settlement of most of the rest of the state, however, either coincided with railroad development or

Table 3.5 Railroad miles and farmland acres in key prairie states

	Year	Railroad miles	Acres of farmland (000)	Acres of improved farmland (000)
Illinois	1850	111	12,037	2,040
	1860	2,790	20,912	13,096
	1870	4,823	25,883	19,330
	1880	7,851	31,674	20,115
	1890	10,116	30,498	25,669
	1900	11,058	32,795	27,699
Iowa	1850	0	2,736	825
	1860	65	1,007	3,793
	1870	2,683	15,542	9,396
	1880	5,400	24,753	19,867
	1890	8,416	30,492	25,429
	1900	9,392	34,574	29,898
N. and S. Dakota	1850	0	0	
	1860	0	26	
	1870	65	302	
	1880	1,225	3,801	1,150
	1890	4,726	19,056	11,617
	1900	5,773	34,614	20,931
Kansas	1850	0	0	0
	1860	0	1,778	405
	1870	1,501	5,657	1,971
	1880	3,400	21,417	10,740
	1890	8,892	30,214	22,303
	1900	8,714	41,663	25,041

Sources: Poor and Poor (1868–1900); U.S. Census Office (1854–1902).

else followed it. In the western part of the state, railroads were generally built in advance of settlement. In some areas, settlement lagged substantially behind railroad development because of the absence of the means for draining wet prairies. The strongest correlation between population growth and railroad development occurred in counties lacking in woodlands, supporting the view that railroads were needed to bring in the necessary materials for farm building (Cooper 1958: 136–141).

Prior to railroad construction in South Dakota, settlement proceeded slowly, and most towns were located along waterways (Hamburg 1981: 2, 41). The settlement of the state accelerated only after railroad construction commenced (Hamburg 1981: 4). The central conclusion of Hamburg's work is that anticipated and actual railroad construction was the primary factor in determining the timing and location of towns. He arrives at these conclusions through a historical analysis of the relationship between railroad construction and the plating or incorporation of towns.

Although the prairie soils were richer than those found in the more wooded river valleys and floodplains, early settlers stuck to the river bottoms, seldom venturing out onto the open prairie for farm building. The settlers' initial reluctance to farm the prairie was partly the consequence of their eastern woodland origins and lack of experience with prairie cultivation, but there were other good reasons as well. Before the railroad, crops could only be shipped to market by water transportation on navigable rivers. To engage at all in commercial agriculture, a farmer could not be too far from a navigable waterway, given the high cost and difficulty of transporting crops by horse and wagon. While sod houses afforded temporary shelter, the availability of timber for farm building and fuel was an important if not essential determinant of farm location. Before development of the farm windmill and deep well drilling, being close to a stream or river was important for an assured water supply. Finally, the prairie sod itself was a barrier to cultivation. The plows the early settlers brought with them were simply not up to the task of breaking the thick sod so a crop could be planted. The services of a heavy breaking plow drawn by oxen could be hired, but for many farmers the cost was prohibitive. Not until the 1840s was the problem solved with the development of light steel plows by John Deere and others (Gates 1960: 80–83; Bogue 1963: 1–85; Cronon 1991: 97–104; Cooper 1958: 33–38).

The coming of the railroad solved the problem of transporting commercial crops to market at bearable costs and the problem of obtaining reasonably priced lumber for farm building. The development of the railroad thus significantly accelerated the settlement of the prairie (Cronon 1991: 109–110; Hamburg 1981; Cooper 1958). Railroad construction did not mean immediate cultivation of all of the prairie, however. Prairie lands within the boundaries of the Wisconsin glaciation were very fertile but often too wet for cultivation, because of poorly developed natural drainage systems. Except for relatively dry uplands, the cultivation of these areas had to await the development of artificial drainage technologies in the 1880s (Bogue 1963: 85; Cooper 1958: 79).

The settlement and cultivation of the prairie proceeded rapidly from 1850 to 1900 (Figure 3.6). The increase in farmland in the 1860s and 1870s can be traced in large measure to railroad development and the resulting increased prospects for commercial agriculture, while a combination of railroad construction and improved drainage technologies permitted more land to be brought under cultivation in the 1880s and 1890s (Figure 3.6). After the turn of the century, additions to farmland occurred primarily in the mixed-grass prairies of western North and South Dakota.

How much of the original prairie remains today and how much is protected from exploitation? A recent survey suggests that only 4 percent of the original tallgrass prairie remains. Large tracts of tallgrass prairie can be found only in the Flint Hills of eastern Kansas and northeast Oklahoma and on the glacial moraines of northeastern South Dakota, and much of these areas lack any form of protection from exploitation. Otherwise, most prairie remnants are quite small (Steinauer and Collins 1996). In his survey of protected prairie preserves, Madson (1982) lists 149 in the tallgrass prairie

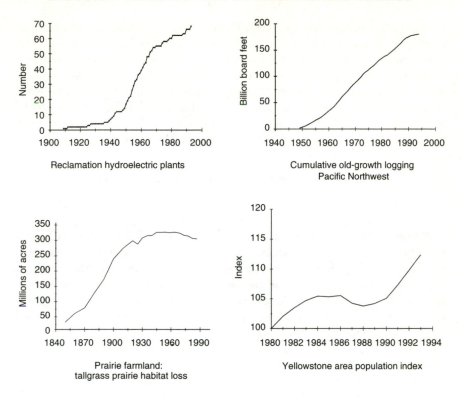

Figure 3.6 Habitat loss indicators
Sources: U.S. Department of Commerce (1975, 1976–1993); Wall (1972); U.S. Department of Commerce, Bureau of Economic Analysis (1995); U.S. Department of the Interior (1991).

Table 3.6 Prairie remnants

State	Prairie preserve acres	Number of preserves	Average acres per preserve
Illinois	6,551	29	226
Iowa	2,649	32	83
Kansas	10,896	3	3,632
Minnesota	4,940	25	198
Missouri	5,813	20	291
Nebraska	1,711	3	570
North Dakota	46,449	15	3,097
South Dakota	8,071	6	1,345
Wisconsin	867	16	54
Total	87,947	149	590

Source: Madson (1982).

states, containing approximately 88,000 acres with an average size of 590 acres (Table 3.6). This is an infinitesimal proportion of the original tallgrass prairie, covering some 228 million acres (Risser *et al.* 1981: 13). While the size of these protected prairie patches ranges from 1 to 8,600 acres, most are very small. Certainly all prairie patches are not included in current surveys. Unrecorded prairie relicts could no doubt be found in old cemeteries and alongside railroad rights-of-way and country roads (Madson 1982: 261), but even if these were taken into account, the proportion of the original prairie remaining would still probably be very small.

Habitat transformation: northern Great Lakes forests

The decline of the tallgrass prairie and the alteration of forest habitats in the Great Lakes area are inextricably linked. Beginning with the New England states in the late eighteenth and early nineteenth centuries, regional dominance in timber cutting and lumber production shifted westward and southward over time. By 1860, the Great Lakes states were producing more lumber than any other region, a position they held until the turn of the century when they were overtaken by the South and the West Coast. When one region of the country was logged out, the industry would pull up stakes and move on to new unexploited forest lands in other regions (Williams 1989: 193–197).

While the Great Lakes region would have eventually taken its turn in the timber production cycle as eastern forests were depleted, the process of exploitation was accelerated by the settlement of the prairie. For purposes of economic development, the prairie and the northern Great Lakes constituted an integrated whole, each supplying something needed by the other. Lumber was needed to build prairie farms, and the Great Lakes forests were a rich source of timber in relatively close proximity to the prairie. While the plow followed the ax in the woodlands to the east and south, the Great Lakes forests lay too far north for an adequate growing season and contained soils of insufficient fertility for successful agriculture. The prairie thus supplied the food crops that could not be successfully grown on cleared Great Lakes timberlands (Cronon 1991: 151–159; Williams 1989: 197).

Several forest types were found in the northern Great Lakes, including upland mixed stands of white pine, hemlock, and hardwoods; mixed stands of pine (white, red, and jack) and oak; pure stands of jack pine on relatively infertile outwash plains; and wet forests of spruce and tamarack (Whitney 1987). The most highly prized by lumbermen of all the trees was the towering white pine. Large white pine reach as much as six feet in diameter and several hundred feet in height. The wood is light, strong, and straight-grained, and white pine logs float readily, permitting their transportation down streams and rivers (Cronon 1991: 152; Williams 1989: 198). Hemlock was also harvested for its bark, which was used in the tanning industry.

Logging the northern Great Lakes was significantly eased by the natural geography of the landscape. The comparatively flat terrain simplified the task of logging, the forests were dissected with relatively high-velocity streams that could be used for log-drives, and streams and rivers ran into either the Great Lakes or the Mississippi River, facilitating the transportation of logs or lumber to market (Williams 1989: 198). The lumber mills on Lake Michigan fed the Chicago wholesale lumber market, which in the 1870s was the largest of its kind. While lumber moved from mill to market by ship on the Great Lakes, it found its way from wholesaler to the prairie retailer by way of the rail lines that fanned out into the prairie from Chicago (Cronon 1991: 159–183). Close to half the lumber arriving in Chicago served the home market (*ibid.*: 204). The balloon frame architectural system invented by a Chicago builder revolutionized urban construction and opened a vast new market for light milled softwood (*ibid.*: 179).

The growth of Chicago and the settlement of the prairie were part of the same developmental process. Chicago, with its network of rail lines and access to Great Lakes shipping, was the funnel through which commodities and industrial goods flowed to and from the prairie. It also became a manufacturing center for new labor-saving farm machinery that revolutionized the planting, tilling, and harvesting of prairie crops (*ibid.*: 313–318). Without an urban center to feed it with necessary industrial goods, the creation of a commercial agricultural system on the prairie would have been much slower. The urban economy of Chicago, the timber economy of the north woods, and the agricultural economy of the prairie were thus a part of a single regional economic system (*ibid.*: 97–309). They grew and prospered together.

While Chicago was an important link in the Midwestern lumber distribution system of the 1870s, it did not monopolize it. An alternative path from woods to market was available for the timber of Wisconsin and Minnesota. Much of the forest land of both states was drained by tributaries of the Mississippi. The Mississippi River Logging Company, under the direction of Frederick Weyerhaeuser, established a large reservoir for logs in a slough on the Mississippi just below the mouth of the Chippewa River, a stream that gave access to some of the richest pinelands in Wisconsin. The purpose of this reservoir was to feed downstream lumber mills in Iowa and Illinois that served the rapidly growing prairie market (Williams 1989: 203–206).

The exploitation of the Great Lakes forests was facilitated by a variety of technological innovations in the last half of the nineteenth century. Improvements in the quality of steel led to the development of more efficient saws; the application of steam technology to lumber mills along with other innovations increased the scale of milling operation; and steam technology was applied to the hauling of logs in the woods. Logging initially was confined to the winter months when logs could be hauled by horse-drawn sleds along iced roads. Steam traction engines were developed to replace horses, and eventually narrow-gauge logging railroads spread through the woods to collect logs and haul them to transshipment points or milling centers. The railroads made year-around logging possible. The development of main-line railroads to milling centers in the north woods eventually aided in the decline of the Chicago market by permitting the direct shipment of lumber from mill to retailer (Williams 1989: 201–216; Cronon 1991: 183–199).

The harvesting of Great Lakes timber was a boom–bust phenomenon. Lakes states timber production peaked in the 1890s at approximately 9 billion board feet per year, and declined precipitously thereafter. As exploitation proceeded, harvesting moved farther north to remoter stands. With the exhaustion of the white pine, loggers turned to hemlock and the hardwoods, but they could not replace the timber volume generated by white pine harvests (Williams 1989: 222–230).

Unlike in the cutover forests of the east, the plow did not follow the ax, as already noted. The soil was too poor, and what humus it contained was often burned off in the forest fires that raged over the northern Great Lakes in the wake of timber cutting. The loggers sought only the best-grade pine, leaving behind great piles of slash and brush. In the infernos that followed, vast areas of forest and cutover were burned clean. The growing season was not long enough for corn and just barely long enough for hay. While property developers attracted many to stumpland farming, most who tried it failed. With the decline of logging came a significant depopulation of the north woods. Only when a pulping industry took hold in the 1920s on the basis of aspen and jack pine did an alternative to the lumber industry of any significance appear (Williams 1989: 228–237; Whitney 1987).

As the result of this whole process, the Great Lakes forests were transformed from forests containing a mix of species and substantial stands of old growth to forests where fast-growing early successional trees, such as the aspen, dominate and serve as a prime source for pulpwood for paper industry (Cronon 1991; Whitney 1987). From the end of the nineteenth century on, pulp mills tended to follow in the wake of lumber mills as the center of logging activity shifted from one area to another (Guthrie 1972: 4–5). With the best timber stands cut over, states that at one time were leading lumber producers became major pulpwood producers. The net effect of this transition was to assure that forest stands would no longer be allowed to grow old.

The agricultural revolution, forestry, and habitat modification in the U.K. countryside

The U.K. countryside lacks what in the U.S. would be called wilderness – areas relatively free of human impact. Nonetheless, the U.K. is blessed with an abundance of what can be called semi-natural habitat, or at least has been until recently (Pye-Smith and Rose 1984: 1). At the beginning of settlement by Neolithic agriculturalists around 3000 BC, the English countryside was predominantly forested, although open areas were maintained above the tree line or where waterlogging, coastal land accretion and erosion, avalanches, lightning fires, windthrows, and herbivore grazing occurred (Green 1985: 28–30). With the slow advance of agriculture over the centuries, forests receded to the point where they cover less than 8 percent of the English landscape today (NCC 1984: 32). The loss of forestland combined with exploitation and persecution led to the extinction of such large mammals as the beaver, brown bear, wolf, and wild boar. Nonetheless, many woodland species continued to survive in remaining forest fragments, and landscape diversity increased, at least up to World War II, with species occupying open habitats prospering. The grazing of domestic livestock on unsown lands maintained conditions similar to those created by wild grazing animals (Green 1985: 33–41). Eighteenth- and nineteenth-century enclosures and increased cultivation dealt a blow to some of these habitats, but the expansion of arable land came to a halt with increased competition from imported agricultural commodities beginning in the later part of the nineteenth century (*ibid* .; Holderness 1985: 1). In short, traditional agriculture replaced relatively uniform forest habitats with a mixture of meadow, heath, and woodlands, increasing the habitat diversity of the landscape. While some large mammals were rendered extinct as a result of settlement, much of the openlands was devoted to a pastoral husbandry that provided habitat to a diverse array of native species. A relatively uniform natural forested landscape was converted over centuries into a semi-natural landscape of mixed habitats.

World War II brought forth a revolution in U.K. agricultural production, as already noted in the discussion of nonpoint water pollution. This revolution has dramatically altered the landscape. To increase arable land, uncultivated grasslands and heaths have been plowed and wetlands drained. The amount of rough grazing land declined from 42 percent of the English and Welsh landscape in 1939 to 26 percent in 1971. Over the same period the amount of arable land increased from 26 percent to 38 percent of the landscape (Green 1985: 81). The reclamation of heathland has been aided by the application of fertilizers to increase fertility, a process that has been accelerated by government subsidies. Hedgerows that serve as a refuge for woodland species have been ripped up at a rate of about 8,000 kilometers per year to make room for the use of large unwieldy farm equipment in cultivation (*ibid.*: 82). These and other practices have reduced the amount and diversity of habitat in the rural landscape (Pye-Smith and Rose 1984: 23–28; Green 1985: 78–99). The physically heterogeneous agricultural landscape of the 1930s, with its relatively large array of semi-natural characteristics and diverse flora and fauna, has been progressively replaced by biologically sterile fields of monocultural crops.

British forestlands face similar pressures. Although the remaining woodlands of the British countryside have been cut and exploited for centuries, they retain many species and ecological characteristics of the original primeval forests (Pye-Smith and Rose 1984: 78). Wildwood patches have been extensively utilized for grazing, the production of wood products, and game, but they still contain many of their original species and continue to be biologically diverse in structure as well as composition (*ibid.*: 78–90; Green 1985: 121–130). Primary woods that have been continuously forested with a predominance of native species constitute important semi-natural habitat in the U.K. countryside.

Not surprisingly, with so little forestland the U.K. is heavily dependent today on imports for its wood products needs, meeting only 9 percent of them from domestic sources (*ibid.*: 121). With imports cut off in World War I and the resulting massive felling of domestic woodlands, political leaders created the Forestry Commission in 1919 and charged it with the task of reforestation and the creation of strategic timber reserves. The Commission manages 1.2 million ha of its own lands and oversees the activities of 3,700 private foresters, inducing reforestation through tax incentives that are of primary benefit to large landowners (Pye-Smith and Rose 1984: 39–44). The Commission has created a modern forest industry wherein traditional woodsmanship is replaced by plantation monocultures utilizing exotic tree species. This replacement process along with conversion to farmland caused a 46 percent loss of semi-natural woodland in 23 counties of England and Wales between 1933 and 1983 (NCC 1984: 56). Both industrial agriculture and forestry are making inroads into traditional woodlands habitat. Although species diversity is relatively high in young plantation forests, as the canopy closes with tree growth, species diversity declines to low levels. These forests are not allowed to grow sufficiently old before they are harvested and therefore fail to gain the habitat diversity that goes with tree death and its resulting creation of snags, downed logs, and openings attractive to a variety of species. Even if they are allowed to age, conifer forests would not regain the same complement of species found in the predominantly deciduous wildwoods they replace (Pye-Smith and Rose 1984: 45–46, 78–90; Green 1985: 121–142). In sum, the emergence of both industrial agriculture and industrial forestry is threatening remaining semi-natural wildwood habitat in the U.K. countryside.

U.S. suburbanization and the decline of old-growth forests

Like the Great Lakes forests and the forests of the U.K., the forests of the Pacific Northwest have been substantially altered by modern timber harvesting practices. Instead of being linked to agricultural settlement, as it was in the nineteenth century, the decline of U.S. old-growth forests in the decades since World War II has been predominantly driven by the growth of suburbs around major cities. The post-war suburbanization process not only added to air and water pollution problems, but also played a role in the acceleration of timber harvesting in virgin stands of old-growth forests. The spreading out of population through suburbanization increased the supply of urban land and reduced its average price. As a result, the amount of land consumed per dwelling increased, and, with lower land prices, a shift from multi-family to single-family dwellings occurred. For an equal amount of floor space single-family units consume more lumber than multi-family, and with lower land and transportation costs more funds could be devoted to increasing floor space, further stimulating the consumption of lumber.[10] The point is simple. Lower transportation and land costs resulted in population spreading out in more spacious detached dwellings that required more lumber.

48

At the same time as the beginning of the suburban housing boom in the 1950s, the lumber industry was turning increasingly to relatively untouched forests on public lands for its timber supply. In 1929, approximately 1.6 billion board feet of timber was cut from the national forest system, or about 4 percent of the U.S. timber supply. By 1952, national forest timber production was up to 4.5 billion board feet and 13 percent of the U.S. timber supply, and by 1962 it was up to 9.2 billion board feet and 22 percent of the total (U.S. Department of Commerce 1975; Nelson 1985). The suburban housing boom thus coincided with increased cutting of virgin timber from the national forests.

One region in particular, the Pacific Northwest, was significantly affected by expanded demand for lumber. Log production in western Oregon and Washington increased from an annual average of 9.6 billion board feet in the 1920s, the historical peak production period prior to World War II, to an annual average of 14.4 billion board feet in the 1960s (Booth 1994: 89). From 1949 to 1970, log production from the national forests in this region increased from 10 percent of the total harvest to 24.6 percent, and log production from all public lands increased from 22 percent to 40 percent of the harvest (Wall 1972). By the 1950s, low-elevation privately owned old-growth forests (two hundred years and older) had been largely cut, leaving higher-elevation old growth as the primary source of large, old trees.

The U.S. Forest Service, charged with the management of the national forests, had operated primarily in a custodial capacity prior to World War II. Because ample timber supplies were available before the war on private lands at low elevations in the Pacific Northwest, little interest was shown by the lumber industry in the higher-elevation public lands where timber harvesting was relatively more costly. With surging timber demand after the war, the Forest Service expanded its scope of activity, and thus the size of its bureaucracy and its budget, through dramatic increases in timber sales. This meant that previously untouched old growth fell to the ax, even in localities that had been previously set aside as primitive or wilderness areas. This brought the Forest Service into sharp conflict with a burgeoning wilderness and forest preservation movement. A lengthy series of struggles followed over preservation of upland forests involving wilderness advocates, the Forest Service, and the forest products industry. These struggles culminated in law suits in the 1990s over the preservation of an old-growth dependent endangered species, the spotted owl, that virtually halted logging on the national forests in western Oregon and Washington. By then, however, probably less than 10 percent of the original old growth remained (Booth 1994). The decline in old-growth forest habitat on public lands can be approximated by the cumulative volume of logs harvested in western Washington and Oregon (Figure 3.6), and the cumulative volume logged increased in the 1960s and 1970s along a relatively stable linear trend line. The cumulative harvest represents a permanent loss of old growth, given that the areas logged are converted into short-rotation stands for harvest every 40–100 years.

Dam construction and riparian habitat fragmentation

Along with timber harvesting, dam construction ranks very high as a phenomenon bringing forth significant environmental change. Almost 70 percent of freshwater mussel and crayfish and close to 40 percent of freshwater fish species are at risk of extinction according to a recent Nature Conservancy report (1996). Some of these species are at risk because of water pollution problems, but many are threatened by riparian habitat modification, of which dam construction is among the most serious (Petts 1984).

Dams have been constructed for centuries for flood control and, more importantly, for irrigation. Civilization itself marks its birthplace in irrigation agriculture, and the control of irrigation, some argue, has been the foundation stone for the building of highly centralized despotic societies whose centrality of control was directly related to the scale of their irrigation systems (Wittfogel 1957; Worster 1985). Irrigation and aridity go together, and irrigation was integral to the development of the arid regions of the western U.S. Even in a laissez faire capitalist economy, irrigation requires centrality of power, and the dominant institution in the irrigating of the West was a government agency, the U.S. Bureau of Reclamation. The beneficiaries of irrigation, subsidized by interest-free government loans for project capital costs, were more often than not land speculators and relatively large-scale farmers, rather than the smallholders originally intended by the legislation that established the Bureau (Worster 1985; Reisner 1987). The Bureau was not the only government dam builder on the scene, however. In the name of flood control and navigation, the Army Corps of Engineers competed with the Bureau to control and reshape the rivers of the West.

Dam construction accelerated around the turn of the century because of improvements in cement technology and, more notably, because of the growing demand for electricity, one that could be supplied in part by hydroelectric projects (Petts 1984). Because they were relatively lucrative, hydroelectric projects were incorported into most large-scale Bureau of Reclamation projects. Many reclamation projects were economically feasible only because of the revenues generated from electricity sales (Worster 1985: 241; Reisner 1987: 283–284). As can be seen in Figure 3.6, the number of hydroelectric projects operated by the Bureau has grown continuously and the rate of growth has diminished only recently.

High technology and natural habitat deterioration: the Yellowstone area

In recent years, economic growth has come to depend less on industries causing air and water pollution problems and resource-based industries, such as lumber and hydroelectric power, that lead directly to natural habitat loss, and more on the so-called "clean" high-technology industries. On the face of it, environmental problems associated with a booming high-technology sector based on microelectronics appear to be relatively innocuous. However, further investigation reveals that high-technology advances may be playing a role in fostering development in sensitive natural habitats previously protected by their isolation. With sophisticated personal computers, modems, faxes, and the Internet and its global communication connections, many can now locate their businesses in remote areas featuring dramatic scenic beauty and immediate access to abundant outdoor recreation opportunities. New kinds of "knowledge-based" businesses in the area surrounding Yellowstone National Park, for example, include pharmaceutical testing, computer software design, environmental engineering and management consulting, publishing, architecture, and financial consulting (Rasker 1993; Rasker and Glick 1994). Between 1969 and 1989, 79 percent of new jobs and 65 percent of the increase in total personal income in the Yellowstone area local economy occurred in the services sector (Rasker *et al.* 1991). Between 1980 and 1989, more than half of the 15,000 jobs created in the area were nonfarm, self-employed. While the services sector was advancing, employment in mining, manufacturing, and agriculture were declining in the Yellowstone region.

Although the shift away from economic dependence on natural resource extraction may bring pressure to reduce extractive activities that degrade the natural environment, the new forms of economic activity have their own environmental consequences. While private lands make up only 20 percent of the Greater Yellowstone ecosystem, these lands include critical winter range for elk and mule deer, lower-elevation river corridors, and wetlands (Glick *et al.*, 1991). Such areas provide critical habitat for 62 sensitive species as identified by the Nature Conservancy (Rasker *et al.* 1991), and these are precisely the lands that are under heavy development pressure. Population growth in the Yellowstone area (Figure 3.6) is probably a reasonable proxy for the amount of critical habitat loss.

Conclusions: industry birth dates and environmental trends

The analysis of the relationship between continuing environmental problems and the industries that have either directly or indirectly caused them is necessarily descriptive. There is no simple quantitative relationship between production and consumption levels and the extent of environmental problems. The relationships are complex and the current understanding of these relationships can only be summarized in a descriptive fashion. The summary provided here suggests that environmental problems originate as the consequence of the creation and development of complexes of industries. Some would argue that in the end it is really the consumer that is at fault because, after all, industry is merely the handmaiden of the consumer. While there is an element of truth to this view, invention and product creation come prior to consumption.

In Table 3.7, rough estimates of birth dates for industries causing contemporary environmental problems are established on the basis of historical accounts. The point of doing so is to demonstrate that continuing environmental problems

51

Table 3.7 Birth dates for industries or economic activities causing major environmental changes

Industry or activity	Approximate U.S. birth date
Midwestern railroads[a]	1850
Midwestern agriculture[b]	1840
Midwestern lumber industry[c]	1850
Western lumber industry[d]	1850
Coal U.K.[e]	1800
Coal U.S.[f]	1870
Electricity; electrical goods[g]	1880
Pulp and paper[h]	1900
Motor vehicles (mass production)[i]	1915
Petroleum (modern)[j]	1920
Highway construction (modern)[k]	1920
Chemicals (organic)[l]	1930
Modern U.K. agriculture[m]	1940
Suburban development (large-scale)[n]	1950
Microelectronics[o]	1970

Notes [a] In the 1850s, an extensive rail network was developed in the Midwest emanating from Chicago, and by 1852 the city was linked to the east coast by rail (Cronon 1991; Fishlow 1965). In 1850 Illinois had only 111 miles of railroad; in 1860 it had 2,790 miles (Poor and Poor 1868).
[b] The first wave of western expansion into the prairie states occurred in the period 1816–1818 and initiated a modest commercial agriculture provisioning the southern cotton states. The first really substantial wave of prairie state expansion occurred in the 1830s and was accompanied by an unprecedented boom in land sales. This and subsequent waves of expansion in the next two decades set the stage for large-scale prairie state commercial agriculture (North 1974).
[c] Williams (1989); Whitney (1987).
[d] The Pacific Northwest lumber industry began with the California gold rush and the shipment of lumber from Puget Sound waterside mills to San Francisco (Booth 1994).
[e] Mitchell (1984).
[f] In 1850 coal provided only 9 percent of U.S. energy consumption, but by 1900 this figure had risen to 71 percent (U.S. Department of Commerce, 1975). The growth of coal consumption from 1850 on was rapid, taking over much of the home heating market and fueling rapid industrial expansion (Melosi 1985; Schurr and Netschert 1960).
[g] The ring dynamo came into general use in the 1870s, rendering arc lighting economically feasible. The first electric motor of commercial significance was exhibited in 1873, the telephone was patented in 1876, and incandescent filament lamps were invented by 1880 (Tylecote 1992; Passer 1953; Byatt 1979).
[h] Prior to 1900, materials other than wood pulp, such as rags and straw, were mostly used to produce paper. By 1900 wood was increasingly used as the raw material for paper, and from this point on the pulpwood industry grew rapidly (Guthrie 1972: 1–15).
[i] Henry Ford opened his first assembly line plant in 1915 (Rae 1984; Tylecote 1992). For the history of the U.K. auto industry, see Church (1994).
[j] The modern petroleum industry dates from the development of the cracking process, allowing a much higher yield of gasoline from a barrel of oil (Williamson *et al*. 1963).
[k] The modern highway construction industry can be dated roughly to the passage of the Federal Aid Act of 1921 creating the Federal Aid Highway System. The 1920s were the first boom years for highway construction (Melosi 1985: 109).
[l] The post-war growth of organic chemicals is at least partly rooted in the rapid pace of scientific advance and innovation in the industry in the 1920s and 1930s (Davis 1984; Kleinknecht 1984). The shift to petroleum from coal as the main feedstock for organic chemicals also facilitated rapid growth of the industry from the 1940s on (Freeman *et al*. 1982: 95–96).
[m] Green (1985).
[n] Suburbanization based on the electric tram dates from the late nineteenth century (Warner 1974). However, suburbanization on a large scale did not begin until after World War II and the shift to the automobile as the primary mode of urban transportation (Jackson 1985; Mills and Hamilton 1994).
[o] The microprocessor was invented in 1971 (Tylecote 1992: 56).

are the result of the historical process of industry creation. Even if the dates are off by one or two decades, the conclusion that industry birth dates are spread out in time will not be altered. The problem of atmospheric carbon accumulation is a product of the entire history of fossil fuel use, just as the problem of the accumulation and continued use of highly toxic chemicals in agriculture is a product of the entire history of the organic chemical industry. The modern problem of inadequate habitat areas to maintain biodiversity is the product of the whole history of habitat change caused by agricultural and industrial forestry practices. Contemporary environmental problems are thus rooted in the historical process of new industry formation. As economic growth proceeds by adding new industries, new environmental problems are added to the list. Some problems may fall off the list along the way, but many remain. In other words, the problems created by older industries are not always solved by regulatory processes, and new industries are bringing forth new environmental problems. Some problems are probably irreversible. Pulling carbon back out of the atmosphere and DDT back out of the environment on a large scale and significant restoration of the tallgrass prairie, northern pinery, riparian habitats, or Pacific Northwest old-growth forests are probably impossible tasks. Even where mitigation of environmental problems is feasible, such as in the case of air and water pollution emissions, environmental problems persist. As the economy grows, environmental changes and problems accumulate.

The continued accumulation of environmental problems is perfectly compatible with significant and successful efforts to address certain environmental problems. Life-threatening pollution of urban water supplies in the nineteenth century, dangerous and harmful smoke pollution prevalent in urban areas as late as the 1950s, indiscriminate dumping of solid wastes in cities common in the nineteenth century, highly toxic incidents of urban smog, rampant use of DDT, and perhaps even damage to the stratospheric ozone layer are all environmental problems that have been substantially mitigated. While these problems may have indeed dropped off the list of environmental concerns in the U.S., the U.K., and elsewhere, many problems have not, and new problems continue to be added as economic growth proceeds.

The continued accumulation of environmental problems over time at a global level is also perfectly compatible with cross-sectional studies (Grossman and Krueger 1993) that have found higher levels of air and water quality in wealthier nations. Wealthy nations with more active environmental movements may indeed successfully tackle the most immediately dangerous and visible environmental problems while still experiencing additions to the list of environmental threats emanating from new forms of economic activity essential to long-run economic growth processes.

The environmental trend data presented in Figures 3.2–3.6 present a picture comparable to the theoretical description in Figure 2.5. Measures of environmental decline and their proxies for specific environmental problems individually follow a trend of rapid growth early in their history and then experience a slowing of growth and in some cases decline. This pattern reflects underlying industry growth trends as well as regulatory actions. Over time, new environmental problems and their trends are added to the old. With the exception of air pollution, U.S. agricultural land, and the volume of agricultural chemicals consumed, all trends of environmental decline in Figures 3.2–3.6 are positive at the end of the period of available data, suggesting that a claim of an improvement in aggregate environmental quality cannot yet be made. The decline in the volume of agricultural chemicals applied, as already noted, has been partially offset by an increase in the toxicity of pesticides. As noted in the beginning of this chapter, absent a mechanism for comparing environmental problems, a claim of aggregate improvement in the environment is possible only if there are no positive trends in environmental deterioration for specific problems and if some trends are negative.

The key points of the analysis can be summarized rather simply. New forms of economic activity are periodically added to the economy, providing the underpinning for continued economic expansion. These new forms of economic activity in turn create new kinds of environmental problems. Some problems may disappear over time, but many remain, as the historical material in this chapter has shown. The birth dates of contemporary environmental problems will as a result be spread out in historical time. The history of the economic development process will thus be reflected in a modern listing of environmental concerns. The next task taken up in Chapters 4 and 5 is to provide evidence that the environmental concerns examined in this chapter are indeed serious and worthy of our attention.

4

ECONOMIC GROWTH AND ENVIRONMENTAL CHANGE

Natural habitat loss

Economic growth is fostered by the development of new forms of economic activity, and new forms of economic activity bring forth new kinds of environmental change. For this view to be worth anything, the resulting environmental change must be of some significance. To judge whether environmental decline resulting from economic growth is a serious problem, we need a detailed understanding of its effects. Consequently, the goal of this and the following chapter is to document the significance and importance of the environmental changes and problems discussed in Chapter 3 and listed in Table 3.1. In this chapter, the problem of natural habitat loss will be addressed for the U.S. tallgrass prairie, the forests of the northern Great Lakes, Pacific Northwest old-growth forests, the U.K. countryside, riparian areas fragmented and altered through the construction of dams, and the Yellowstone area. In the next chapter, air and water pollution problems will be addressed as well as the problem of toxic agricultural chemicals.

The loss of the tallgrass prairie

To understand exactly what was lost as a consequence of agricultural settlement in the tallgrass prairie region requires knowledge of the pre-settlement landscape. Consequently, the tallgrass prairie ecosystem will be described briefly before we consider how the settlement process altered it.

The prairie ecosystem

On reaching the open lands of Illinois, the settlers, who were accustomed to the eastern woodlands from which many of them had migrated, marveled at the lushness and openness of the tallgrass prairie (Madson, 1982: 8–19). The tallgrass prairie covered much of Illinois, all of Iowa, the northwestern half of Missouri, the western edge of Minnesota, and the eastern edges of the tier of states beginning with North Dakota and extending south to Oklahoma. The western portion of this tier of states was covered mostly by medium-height mixed-grass prairie, and the land further west up to the front ranges of the Rocky Mountains was covered by shortgrass prairie (L. Brown 1985: 21). The tallgrass prairie covered some 351,000 square miles, the mixed-grass prairie 356,000 square miles, and the shortgrass prairie 645,000 square miles (Risser *et al.* 1981: 13). While all three areas have been profoundly altered by settlement, the focus of attention here will be on the tallgrass prairie.

The grassland biome on the North American continent contains relatively young plant community types. The tallgrass prairie and the treeless Great Plains the settlers saw have come into existence only since the last glacial retreat some 10,000 years ago, when the Midwest was largely covered by spruce and fir forests (Madson 1982: 35; Wright 1970). Open grassland extended well into the eastern forests of Indiana and Ohio during a very dry period 4,000 years ago. Since that time, the tallgrass prairie has been in retreat, with woodlands slowly advancing westward (Madson 1982: 36–37).

While the debate continues over whether climate or fire is the dominant element in determining the extent of the prairie, both play their part. The defining characteristic of the prairie, aridity, is determined by the rain shadow created by mountains to the west. Since westerly Pacific air currents are forced to rise over three separate mountain ranges and lose moisture to rain and snowfall as the air is chilled with increasing elevation, the moisture content of these air masses has been significantly reduced by the time they reach the Great Plains. From west to east on the prairies, however, rainfall increases, from 16 inches in eastern Colorado to 24 inches in western Kansas. This rainfall pattern controls the type of prairie: short grasses in the dry West, mixed grasses in the eastern Great Plains, and tall grasses in the more humid Midwest. A botanist, Edgar Transeau, found in the 1930s that it was not rainfall that determined the boundaries of the prairies, but the ratio of potential evaporation to rainfall. The prairie coincides with an area where the ratio of rainfall to potential evaporation is 60 to 80 percent (Transeau 1935; Madson 1982: 40).

Prior to settlement, fire was a frequent event on the prairie landscape. In periods of drought or the dry season, fire moved rapidly across the flat prairie landscape driven by the ever-present winds. The grasses of the prairies were adapted to fire and recovered quickly after burning, while shrubs and trees were usually destroyed. Fires were not only caused by lightning, but were often set by Indians for the purpose of driving game or improving the quality of the grasses for game animals. Fires set by Indians may have delayed the natural conversion of prairie in Illinois into woodlands (Madson 1982: 45–49). Some argue that without fire, the prairie would have been converted to woodland or a savannah with scattered trees and grasses (Axelrod 1985; Wells 1970), noting that trees readily invade wherever fire is controlled in the prairie, and that forests are commonly found on the east side of streams and rivers large enough to break fires driven by westerly winds. These phenomena suggest that fire, not a lack of moisture, preserved the open prairie.

The dominant feature of the prairie landscape is its grasses. These are the most important primary producers and largely determine the structure of the prairie ecosystem (Weaver 1954: 14). The grasses of the prairie evolved in a dry period some six million years ago after the formation of the Rocky Mountains and the creation of its rain shadow to the east (Risser *et al.* 1981: 26–28; Axelrod 1985: 172–173). Axelrod argues that the evolution of prairie grasses occurred not in treeless plains, but in savannahs where grasses and woodlands intermixed. If he is right, then the treeless grassland biome is indeed very young, taking form sometime in the last 4,000 to 8,000 years.

Grasses are admirably adapted to drought, wind, and fire. Prairie grasses are generally deep-rooted perennials able to seek moisture sources well below ground. Biotic production is manifested not only in the growth of stems and leaves, but in the creation of a deep, heavily organic sod. In periods of drought, grass leaves for some species roll up to conserve moisture. Grass stems are strengthened with silicon and are flexible enough to bend to the force of the wind without damage. Because more than half of the plant is typically below ground, out of reach of intense flames, grasses readily withstand fire. Unlike trees, grasses keep their winter buds below ground, from which new shoots can develop after a fire (Weaver 1954: 3–32; Madson 1982: 48–59).

While the prairie is generally thought of as being uniformly flat, there is enough variation in topography to create different soil moisture levels and thus different habitats for grasses. In the true prairie, slough grass (*Spartina pectinata*) is found in the low, wet areas, while somewhat farther up the moisture gradient, but still in well-watered soils, the "mesic" grasses occur, such as switch grass (*Panicum virgatum*), Canada wild rye (*Elymus canadensis*), and the tallgrass prairie dominant, big bluestem (*Andropogon gerardi*). Finally, in the driest upland areas, the "xeric" grasses are found, such as little bluestem (*Andropogon scoparius*), sideoats grama (*Bouteloua curtipendula*), and Junegrass (*Koeleria cristata*). The characteristic grass of the relatively humid true prairie is big bluestem, reaching as much as 12 feet in height. The drier mixed-grass prairie of the Great Plains is dominated by the shorter grasses, such as little bluestem. The composition of the grasses also varies from north to south, with cool season grasses, which are dormant in the summer, more prevalent in the north, and warm season grasses, whose growth continues in the summer, more prevalent in the south (Madson 1982: 49–79; Weaver 1954: 23–67). While as many as 150 species of grasses can be found in the tallgrass prairie, only 10 of these achieve a significant presence in those parts of the prairie to which they are adapted.

Perhaps the prairie is most noted for its pageant of color that begins in early spring and continues into late fall. While prairie forbs constitute a small proportion of primary producer biomass in comparison to the grasses, when in bloom they are one of the prairie's most attractive features. The pageant begins with the ground-hugging flowers of the prevernal aspect in late winter. These plants, including the pasqueflower (*Anemone patens*) and prairie cat's-foot (*Antennaria neglecta*), must bloom and fruit before the tallgrass canopy overtakes them. The somewhat taller spring flowers (vernal aspect) then begin to emerge and flower, including the shooting star (*Dodecatheon meadia*) and prairie violet (*Viola pedatifida*). These in their turn are overtaken by the grasses, and the prairie moves on into the summer (esteval) and autumn aspect, with blackeyed Susan (*Rudbeckia hirta*), leadplant (*Amorpha canescens*), asters (*Aster spp.*), goldenrods (*Solidago spp.*), and sunflowers (*Helianthus spp.*) reaching above the grasses (Madson 1982: 81–98; Weaver 1954: 123–133; Risser *et al.* 1981: 51–54).

Like the grasses, the prairie forbs are well adapted to fire, drought, and insects. Prairie forbs are generally perennials whose roots penetrate deep into the soil in search of moisture. Plant leaves are often resistant to damage from both insects and drought. An extensive underground presence assures that forbs have the ability to recover from wildfire. Wildfire may actually be advantageous to forbs and grasses by killing off invading weeds, which are mostly annuals, and by releasing nutrients and clearing out dead plant matter that chokes off growth (Madson 1982: 100–103).

As the dominant primary producer in the prairie, the grasses provide an abundance of nutritious plant material that is potentially available to primary consumers. Grasslands worldwide are noted for their vast herds of grazing mammals. The tallgrass prairie once contained bison and pronghorn, but it was apparently marginal habitat for both. It was in the mixed- and shortgrass prairies to the west that both thrived. The tallgrass prairie, however, did contain a variety of less noticeable herbivorous invertebrate and vertebrate primary consumers. A variety of invertebrate primary consumers such as grasshoppers occupy above- and below-ground habitat in the prairie. Because of the openness of the prairie habitat, most herbivorous small mammals are found below ground. Small mammals apparently consume a very small proportion of the herbage available in any given area. Both small mammals and the few seed-eating birds found in the prairie can, however, place significant pressure on seed supplies in a given area (Madson 1982: 125–165; Risser *et al.* 1981: 185–283). In the absence of large grazing herbivores, primary consumers in the prairie have a very limited impact on the standing stock biomass. Annual above-ground production is thus recycled primarily through the decomposer pathway of the food chain.

Of the 100-plus mammals that originally took up residence in the true prairie, most originated in adjacent woodlands. Few were truly grassland species. Of the 24 secondary consuming carnivores in the prairie, only two, the swift fox (*Vulpes velox*) and the black-footed ferret (*Mustela nigripes*), are true grassland species. In comparison to the woodlands, the prairie contained a meager collection of avian species. The lack of a vertical physical structure to the prairie reduced the number of possible habitat niches available to birds. While as many as 300 different species were found in the geographic confines of the tallgrass prairie, few of these were restricted to a prairie habitat (i.e., few were endemics). Birds utilizing the prairie are either seed-eating primary consumers, omnivores feeding on both seeds and insects, insectivores, or carnivores (Risser *et al.* 1981: 74–107, 213–283).

The true prairie is most remembered for its waving sea of tall grasses punctuated by the color of its wild flowers. The other defining feature of the tallgrass prairie, one that proved so attractive to settlers, was its deep, rich soils. The raw material for most of the prairie soils was either a fine-grain rock flour called loess, produced in the ice mills of the glacial rivers, or else glacial till (Madson 1982: 108–110). While the underlying mineral soils were rich in basic nutrients in the true prairie, it was the soil-building activities of the grasses and forbs that were largely responsible for the deep loams found by the settlers. The deep-rooted grasses drew minerals up from the underlying soil layer, using them in the production of a massive underground root system as well as above-ground shoots. Because above-ground productivity was so massive – too massive to be completely cropped by grazers or destroyed by fire – substantial amounts of dead plant matter were contributed to the soil each year, to be broken down by earthworms, millipedes, fungi, and bacteria. The normal life and death of the below-ground root system also made abundant contributions to soil formation. The net result was a thick upper soil layer of highly organic humus. Eventually, as the prairie soils formed, a rough balance was achieved between humus production and its breakdown into mineral nutrients. The result was a soil rich in accumulated basic plant nutrients (Madson 1982: 110–115). With cultivation, however, the balance was broken between humus production and its conversion to mineral nutrients, forever altering the character of the soil (*ibid*. 122–123).

The consequences of settlement for the prairie ecosystem

There was much to be gained by settlement of the prairie. Settlement and expansion of the agricultural sector was a driving force in nineteenth-century U.S. economic growth. The tall- and mixed-grass prairies continue today to be the nation's breadbasket, supplying U.S. consumers with most of the grains and much of the meats that they consume. But what was lost?

While much reduced in scale, the prairie was not totally destroyed by settlement, because of the inadvertent preservation of remnants. Is the essence of the prairie ecosystem retained in these remnant patches? If it is, then the extent of the loss is diminished. To answer this question requires application of certain principles from the discipline of conservation biology.

The breaking up of a single continuous habitat into relatively isolated fragments is akin to creating small habitat islands. The theory of island biogeography suggests that habitat islands will have fewer species than continents, and that the number of species present will bear a positive relationship to the area of a habitat island (MacArthur and Wilson 1967). Because smaller islands have smaller and less diverse habitats than larger islands, they support fewer species. To put it somewhat differently, smaller islands will have a greater species extinction rate for a given number of species than larger islands. A herd of bison, for example, would be more likely to eventually die out on a small prairie remnant of a few hundred acres than in a large area, such as the Flint Hills of Kansas. Also, a small prairie remnant will have less variation in habitat features and thus support fewer species than a large area. A large area may contain both uplands and wet areas, supporting both upland bird species and waterfowl, while a small area may contain only one of the two habitat types. Moreover, a small isolated island is likely to have a smaller species immigration rate for a given number of species than a larger, less isolated island. Small islands are harder to find than large and are less likely to receive wind-transported migrants from other areas. Small isolated prairie remnants, for example, will receive a less diverse influx of prairie flower seeds than larger areas. As a consequence of the interplay of two forces, species immigrations and extinctions, the equilibrium number of species on a small habitat island will tend to be smaller than on a larger habitat island.

The theory of island biogeography thus suggests that bringing the prairie under cultivation and leaving behind a few isolated prairie fragments would result in a reduction of the number of species within any given preserved area once fragmentation is complete. Before fragmentation, a given area would contain more species because of a higher species immigration rate from the surrounding area and a lower species extinction rate. Afterwards, the number of species would eventually decline because of a drop in the immigration rate and a rise in the extinction rate on remaining habitat islands.

While the relationship between the number of species and area apparently has not been investigated for prairie remnants, it is known that any given remnant contains a very small proportion of the total prairie flora in a given area (Weaver 1954: 184). This may be the consequence of any given prairie relict being so small as to have a highly homogeneous habitat. A prairie remnant may encompass only a wet or a dry habitat, in contrast to a larger prairie area that may have covered the full moisture gradient. Studies of prairie remnants have generally found that a few grass and forb species are very common in a given habitat type, such as a dry prairie, while many species that could occur are quite rare (Curtis 1959: 269, 274). Thus, even for a given habitat type, any remnant is unlikely to contain the full complement of species that could occur there (*ibid.*: 306). Moreover, some habitat types are less likely to be preserved because of their exceptional value in agricultural production, such as highly fertile and easily cultivated middle-level mesic prairies, and species confined to such habitats may be eventually lost. Once fragmentation has occurred, remaining rare habitat fragments themselves may disappear because of catastrophic random events (most likely human actions), taking rare species with them.

Because no remnant is equivalent to the prairie as a whole, observing and experiencing a remnant can never be equivalent to doing the same for a large contiguous prairie. The opportunity to experience the true prairie landscape with its full complement of species has been lost. Similarly, the true prairie ecosystem with its full complement of species and all their interactions has been lost. An ecosystem fragment is not the same as the ecosystem as a whole.

This is especially apparent when considering species that require relatively large habitat areas. For these species conservation biologists suggest that ecosystem fragmentation creates special dangers (Soule 1985; Saunders *et al.* 1991). The dividing of populations of species into small subgroups and the shrinkage of habitats to suboptimal levels creates risks for the survival of wide-ranging species. Small populations are subject to demographic accidents. In a small population, a sudden shift in sex ratios could mean extinction, as could inbreeding and the resulting loss of genetic variation. Top predators and large grazers may not be able to survive on the resources of isolated habitat fragments. While the bison was reduced to small remnant herds by hunting prior to significant settlement in the Midwest, it obviously could not survive today on the small pieces of remaining tallgrass prairie habitat.

Because the pre-Columbian open prairie probably did not come into existence until after the last glaciation some 10,000 years ago, the grassland biome and prairie ecosystems are of relatively recent origin on a geologic time scale. Although the prairie habitat offers significant potential for evolution because of its unique habitat niches, species unique to the prairie apparently have not yet evolved because of its relative youth as an ecosystem type (Wells 1970; Axelrod 1985). The prairie flora and fauna are both lacking in very many endemic species (those not found in the adjacent forest and desert biomes) (Ross 1970; Mengel 1970). The flora and fauna in the tallgrass prairie are also generally found in open woodland meadows in the eastern U.S.

Given the absence of a large number of prairie endemics, the decline of the prairie would be unlikely to result in the endangerment or extinction of very many species, unless similar habitats elsewhere were also in decline. Curtis suggests that the full complement of prairie grasses and forbs is preserved in remnants, although it is at least a possibility that some species were lost prior to detailed botanical surveys of prairie plants (Curtis 1959: 306). Nonetheless, many prairie species are locally threatened, and at least a few are threatened globally. In Minnesota, for example, 105 vascular native plant and animal species associated with the prairie biome are either locally threatened or endangered (Coffin and Pfannmuller 1988: 12). Two species that find their greatest abundance in Minnesota prairie fragments, the prairie fringed orchid (*Platanthera leucophaea*) and the prairie bush clover (*Lespedeza leptostachya*), are threatened at the national level. Other tallgrass species that are imperiled globally, according to the Nature Conservancy, include Mead's milkweed (*Asclepias meadii*), western prairie white-fringed orchid (*Platantherea praeclara*), and prairie moonwort (*Botrychium capestre*).[1]

Even though avian prairie endemics are few in number (Risser *et al*. 1981: 74–88), two prairie species, the prairie chicken (*Tympanuchus cupido americanus* Reich) and the sandhill crane (*Grus canadensis tabida* Peters), are apparently endangered. The sandhill crane ranged over the prairie for food and nested in marshy areas, and the prairie chicken also found its optimum habitat in the prairie (Schorger 1942; Madson 1982: 137–138). According to the Nature Conservancy (personal communication), two other prairie species, Baird's sparrow (*Ammodramus bairdii*) and Henslow's sparrow (*Ammodramus henslowii*), are respectively vulnerable and uncommon. Of the nine endemic prairie bird species, six are faced with serious population declines (Knopf 1996: 142).

While the replacement of the prairie with farmland may not have caused many avian species extinctions, it has dramatically altered the composition of the avian communities. Native prairie species have declined in number while introduced species adapted to a farmland habitat have flourished (Wilson and Belcher 1989; Graber and Graber 1963). The filling in of prairie potholes and wet areas has reduced the number of resident and migratory water fowl as well (Madson 1982: 143–146). In Illinois alone, prairie marshland declined from 560,000 acres in 1907 to 60,000 acres in 1958 (Graber and Graber 1963). In general, the prairie landscape has been transformed from a habitat with varied niches to a managed landscape having highly specialized uses. Although they support bird populations in high densities, these highly specialized landscapes support a lesser variety of bird species than natural habitats (*ibid*. 1963). Moreover, managed habitats are often dominated by introduced exotic, not native, species. The decline of grass-land bird populations has accelerated since 1950 with the increased intensity of row cropping and the decline of introduced forage grasses and legumes that offered a pseudo-prairie habitat (Warner 1994). While some prairie birds have suffered significant population declines, most mammals native to the tallgrass prairie have held their own (apart from the bison), perhaps because of the ability of many to live in a woodland habitat or to adapt to an agricultural setting (Madson 1982: 152–158).

The lack of very many endemics in the North American grassland biome suggests an absence of significant evolution and speciation in the past, but, because of the youth of the biome, this does not necessarily mean an absence of evolutionary potential. The breaking up of the prairie into very small remnant fragments, however, has probably precluded extensive future evolutionary development. Although prairie grasses are not endemic to the open grasslands, in the tallgrass prairie they possess extensive in-species ecotypic adaptions to differences in photoperiod, moisture, and nutrients. Genetic variation of this type is essential for evolutionary processes to function, and such variation will not necessarily be preserved adequately in prairie remnants. Remnants of tallgrass prairie in the middle or mesic range of the moisture gradient are exceedingly rare because of the ideal conditions such prairie areas present for agriculture (Curtis 1959: 277). Ecotypic genetic variations unique to the mesic prairie areas thus could be lost. Moreover, in a highly fragmented ecosystem, gene flows between subpopulations needed to maintain genetic variation are much reduced, and in some cases completely truncated. With reduced genetic variation, adaptations to new environmental conditions and specialized niches are less likely to occur. Fragmentation, in sum, curtails the evolutionary potential of an ecosystem.

Apart from the question of evolutionary potential, a serious problem for the local preservation of prairie flora is the danger that prairie fragments will themselves disappear. One of the most significant changes brought on by settlement was the controlling of prairie fires. Without fire, dead plant matter builds up and reduces the vigor of prairie plant growth (Madson 1982: 49). Also, in the absence of fire, prairie areas are often invaded by trees, especially along the eastern border of the tallgrass prairie. Prairie remnants are thus threatened by the absence of fire. Prairie remnants are common along railroad rights-of-way because of the past practice of burning these areas to keep down woody plants and prevent wildfire (Curtis 1959: 306). With the abandonment of such rights-of-way and increased use of herbicides for brush control, prairie remnants will be increasingly threatened, and along with them prairie plant species, some of which are already endangered (Madson 1982: 258).

Prairie species confined to fragments may also be endangered if major changes in climate occur. A warming of the climate, for example, would shift climatic zones northward. However, northward migration may be prevented by habitat fragmentation because species intolerant of warmer temperatures will lack suitable habitat farther north in a fragmented landscape. Fragmentation creates barriers to northward migration, particularly for grasses and forbs that require a relatively continuous habitat for migration (Peters 1989).

Not all of the prairie was put to the plow, particularly the mixed- and shortgrass prairies of the Great Plains. The Flint Hills tallgrass prairie in Kansas was not plowed because of thin soil, and became bluestem pastures (Madson 1982: 281), demonstrating the possibility of maintaining prairie grasses under moderate grazing. Under intense grazing pressure, however, prairie grasses decline, sometimes to be replaced by exotics, such as Kentucky bluegrass capable of withstanding heavy grazing pressure (Weaver 1954: 273–296). Bluegrass recovers quickly from grazing because its growing point is at the soil surface and is not removed, whereas for many of the prairie grasses the growing point is above the soil surface and is often eaten, preventing a new leaf from growing (Madson 1982: 73–75). Bluegrass, however, is poorly adapted to fire and could not survive for long under the natural prairie fire regime.

The point of all this is comparatively simple: natural habitat loss and fragmentation as a consequence of settlement and agricultural cultivation has for all practical purposes caused the disappearance of the pre-Columbian prairie ecosystem. Something of significance has indeed been lost.

The ecological consequences of forest exploitation in the northern Great Lakes

Because prairie farm-building required a source of lumber, the logging of the northern Great Lakes forests occurred simultaneously with prairie settlement. The result was a significant modification of Great Lakes forest habitats. The original forests of northern Michigan, Wisconsin, and Minnesota consisted of several forest types, as already noted. In the wet lowland areas, swamp forests were dominated by black spruce (*Picea mariana*), tamarack (*Larix larician*), and white cedar (*Thuja occidentialis*). Of all the forest types, these were least disturbed by logging. In the more mesic areas (mid-range of the moisture continuum), the forests were dominated by a mixture of hardwoods, with sugar maple (*Acer saccharum*) and hemlock (*Tsuga canadensis*) the most prevalent. These forests were interspersed with white pine (*Pinus strobus*) as well, perhaps two or three large trees per acre. The drier areas were covered with mixed stands of white and red pine (*Pinus resinosa*) that included some oak (*Quercus spp.*). On the very driest sites, pine barrens were often found composed primarily of jack pine (*Pinus banksiana*) with red pine and oak sometimes mixed in. In the most northerly reaches of the Great Lakes area, small areas of boreal forests dominated by balsam fir (*Abies balsamea*) and white spruce (*Picea glauca*) occurred (Curtis 1959: 171–257; Whitney 1987).

The pre-logging northern Great Lakes forests were significantly shaped by two powerful forces: fire and wind. In the absence of disturbance, highly shade-tolerant species, such as sugar maple, beech (*Fagus grandifolia*), and basswood (*Tilia americana*), would dominate the forests, especially sugar maple. The shade-intolerant pines would eventually die out. Disturbance by fire and blowdown, however, created a place for pine in the forests. On the dry, droughty outwash plains, fire returned every 80 to 170 years, maintaining almost pure stands of jack pine. Because the pine cone produced by the jack pine is serotinous, and thus must be exposed to intense heat before it opens and releases its seeds, the tree actually requires fire for successful reproduction. The stands of mixed pine were also dependent on either fire or windthrow to expose the mineral soils needed for successful seedling growth. The large isolated pine trees found in the maple–hemlock forests may have originally sprouted in soils created by the decaying roots of windthrown trees. While less shade-tolerant than maple, white pine seed-lings could survive under shaded conditions in the understory, awaiting a distur-bance-generated canopy opening. Although the mesic maple–hemlock forests experience fire infrequently, they were subject to fairly frequent disturbance by wind (Bourdo 1983; Curtis 1959: 171–257; Canham and Loucks 1984; Whitney 1987; Ahlgren and Ahlgren 1983). Hemlock seedlings apparently reproduce best on decayed pine and hemlock stumps and logs created by windthrow.

The harvest of white pine was massive in scale and exceptional in its thorough-ness. The total harvest in Wisconsin alone was estimated to be 103.4 billion board feet. Every stand of pine was cut and the hemlock hardwood forests were culled for their two or three white pines per acre (Curtis 1959: 218–220). The forests might have been able to eventually recover from logging, but the fires that fol-lowed changed them forever.

While the Great Lakes forests were adapted to fire, the frequency and intensity of fires following logging were unprecedented. Under the belief that the plow would indeed follow the ax, the loggers left behind piles of highly combustible slash. These were ignited by farmers clearing fields, berry pickers, vandals, and sparks from passing trains. Fires raged across the landscape, clearing away any trees that remained and, as in the case in the famous Peshtigo fire, causing loss of life and extensive property damage (Curtis 1959: 219–220; Whitney 1987).

Consequently, mixed pine forests were devastated by fire, and in many areas the white pine was virtually extirpated. These forests were largely replaced by aspen, white birch, oak, and maple. Fire favored the aspen, with its capacity for sprouting from roots protected under the soil cover. Jack pine stands spread because of their adaption to fire into what were formerly mixed pine forests. White and red pine regeneration was inhibited after the fires because of the lack of seed sources. More recently, white pine has suffered from the introduction of a fungus, white pine blister rust. Today stands of white pine cover just 1.6 percent of the total forest area in northern Wisconsin and 1.4 percent in northern Michigan. Most of these stands were planted in reforestation projects, and only about 9 percent of all white pine forests are more than 120 years old (Spencer 1983; Smith 1986; Whitney 1987). Although logging-induced fires were less of a problem in the damper mixed conifer–hardwood forests, the opening up of the canopy by logging and the resulting drying of the soil hinder hemlock reproduction. As a result, old-growth forests of sugar maple, hemlock, and white pine were frequently converted to second-growth maple forests.

Since the 1920s and the instituting of fire protection, the forests of the Great Lakes have recovered, but their composition and age structure have changed dramatically. Aspen, a minor species in the pre-logging forest because of its shade intolerance, is now dominant over much of the old mixed pine forestlands and has replaced some of the old conifer–hardwood forests. In northern Wisconsin aspen now covers 26 percent of the forest area, and in northern Michigan it covers 17 percent of the forest area (Spencer 1983; Smith 1986). This dominance is maintained in part by a pulpwood industry that cuts on a 30- to 60-year cycle. The cutover areas invariably come back to aspen because of the tree's ability to reproduce from suckers. Where pulpwood cutting is undertaken, forests are not allowed to grow old. Where forests are allowed to age, sugar maple is more prevalent and hemlock and beech less so than in the pre-logging days. Swamp conifer forests and jack pine have maintained their pre-logging presence, although there is some concern that jack pine will decline over time because of fire control. While artificial regeneration of red pine is common, white pine is unlikely ever to be able to recover to its pre-logging status (Whitney 1987; Ahlgren and Ahlgren 1983).

Logging and post-settlement uses of the forests thus have significantly altered their compositional structure. The modern northern Great Lakes forest ecosystems differ significantly from those the settlers first saw. Because the key structural element of a forest is its trees, changing the composition of forests as well as their age structure can have consequences for other plants and animals. What species have experienced decline as a consequence of logging and settlement, and what species have benefited? Have any species become endangered or rendered extinct as a result?

A number of mammals have been reduced to very low numbers or have become locally extinct in the Great Lakes forests. Moose was originally found in the northerly areas of the region, but is present now only on Isle Royale in Lake Superior. Apparently deer carry a parasite that is harmless to them but lethal to moose. The explosion of deer populations in the wake of timber harvesting may have helped push moose populations farther north. The caribou (*Rangifer caribou caribou*) was originally abundant in northern Minnesota but has disappeared

65

from the state. Fur-bearing mammals, including the fisher (*Martes pennanti pennanti*), wolverine (*Gulo luscus*), and marten (*Martes americana americana*), have become exceedingly rare in the Great Lakes states. The same is true for two top predators, the cougar (*Felis concolor couguar*) and the timber wolf (*Canis lycaon*), although the timber wolf seems to be making a comeback in some areas. Hunting and trapping were the primary reasons for the disappearance of these species, although habitat loss played a role for some. The marten favored pine, the forests that disappeared as a consequence of logging, and the caribou favored the muskeg country, much of which was susceptible to post-logging fires (Schorger 1942; Gates *et al*. 1983).

On of the most interesting consequences of logging has been the eruption of deer populations in the Great Lakes forests. The mixed hardwood–conifer old-growth forests (200–300 years old) that covered almost half of the region have now been reduced to patches totaling less than 5 percent of the original forest. With their sparse understory, old-growth forests were poor deer habitat. The early successional aspen forests that have replaced the old growth are excellent deer habitat, containing an abundance of browse. The creation of open areas through clearcut timber harvesting has also been beneficial to deer by increasing foraging opportunities. As a consequence of habitat improvement, deer populations increased several-fold relative to their pre-settlement levels (Alverson *et al*. 1988).

Large populations of deer, through selective browsing, can in turn have a dramatic impact on the vegetational structure of a forest. In the winter, deer favor the seedlings and saplings of such species as Canada yew (*Taxus canadensis*), eastern hemlock, and white cedar. The deer thus suppress reproduction of these species and in the long term alter the character and composition of the forest canopy. Deer also favor certain herbaceous species, such as the showy lady's-slipper orchid (*Cypripedium reginae*), purple fringed orchid (*Habenaria psycodes*), tall northern bog orchid (*Habenaria hyperborea*), yellow lady's slipper orchid (*Cypripedium calceolus*), blunt-leaved orchid (*Habenaria obtusata*), Indian cucumber root (*Medeola virginiana*), and large-flowered trillium (*Trillium grandiflorum*). The orchids in particular are subject to extirpation by deer. The loss of mature hemlock and cedar from the canopy and their replacement by maple will eventually alter understory light regimes and change the composition of shrubs and herbs on the forest floor (Alverson *et al*. 1988).

In the aftermath of logging, the northern forests were more fragmented than they had been. While farming is difficult, today forests are interspersed with fields in some areas, and the practice of clearcutting for pulpwood leaves numerous open patches in the forests. This fragmenting has increased the extent of edges between forest and fields and has altered environmental conditions within the forests near edges (Alverson *et al*. 1988; Harris 1988; Yahner 1988; Saunders *et al*. 1991). In particular, species that utilize open habitat or the edge can penetrate into the forest, threatening forest interior species. The decline of songbirds in eastern deciduous forests is partly attributed to nest predation by edge species and nest parasitism by cowbirds (*Molthrus ater*). Nests are subject to predation by raccoons, skunks, foxes, squirrels, blue jays, and crows. Brown-headed cowbirds feed in open areas but parasitically deposit their eggs in songbird nests. Cowbirds have spread north and east from the plains and prairies into the forests as a result of agricultural settlement and logging. In the north woods, cowbird parasitism is threatening the Kirtland's warbler (*Dendroica kirtlandii*), a bird that nests in the jack pine barrens of Michigan (Brittingham and Temple 1983). The barrens themselves are threatened by the controlling of fire, inhibiting jack pine reproduction.

Exploitation of the hardwood–conifer forests occurred in stages. In the last century the white pine were removed. Then the hemlock were harvested for the use of their bark in the tanning industry. And finally many forests were clearcut for their hardwoods in the 1920s (Alverson *et al.*, 1988). The result was the disappearance of habitats within which certain woody and herbaceous species could avoid overbrowsing by deer, and songbirds could avoid nest parasitism and predation. Now most of those habitats are gone. What is needed to preserve these species is to allow large tracts of northern forests to grow old and become marginal deer habitat and safe habitat for songbird reproduction. This would mean reducing the amount of acreage now devoted to fast-rotation pulp production. This is one of the few opportunities we have to undo the damage done to the Great Lakes forests by the economic development process. Again, as in the case of the tallgrass prairie, certain kinds of natural habitats have disappeared. Something of significance has been lost.

The loss of Pacific Northwest old-growth forests

Like the northern Great Lakes forests, the forests of the Pacific Northwest have been substantially altered by logging. As of the early 1990s, 90 percent of the original stands of old growth in the Pacific Northwest were gone and along with them elements of an ecosystem with unique structural and functional characteristics that served as a habitat for certain rare species such as the spotted owl, the marbled murrelet, and the western yew. For many years, old growth was viewed with disdain by foresters as a biotic wasteland containing decaying timber. The conventional thinking was that such forests should be harvested as quickly as possible and converted to rapid-growth young stands of timber (Booth 1994).

The research of Jerry Franklin and many others, however, has substantially altered this view (Franklin *et al.* 1981). After a major disturbance, such as wildfire or clearcut logging, a Pacific Northwest forest will go through several successional stages, including the grass–forb (0–5 years), shrub (5–15 years), open pole–sapling (15–30 years), closed sapling–pole–sawtimber (30–80 years), large sawtimber (80–200 years), and old growth (200+ years). As redevelopment of the forest proceeds through these different seral stages, the physical structure of the forest undergoes significant changes. Young forests contain dense stands dominated by pioneer species, such as Douglas fir, and support limited vegetation on the heavily shaded forest floor. As the forest ages, a natural thinning process occurs, the forest floor becomes more open, a multilayer canopy forms, and stand composition shifts from being almost entirely Douglas fir to a mixture of old-growth Douglas fir, western hemlock, western red cedar, and other species. An old-growth forest is characterized by a patchy herb–shrub layer, large living trees, large dead snags, and an abundance of organic litter on the forest floor, including large logs in various stages of decay. These are the key physical or structural characteristics that distinguish an old-growth forest from other seral stages. Young and mature forests lack large trees, large snags, and large downed logs, except where they have been carried over from the predisturbance forest. Young and mature forests also have a relatively uniform single-layered canopy and limited penetration of sunlight to the forest floor (E. R. Brown 1985; Franklin *et al*. 1981).

The most apparent feature of an old-growth forest is its large coniferous trees. In the Pacific Northwest, conifers are able to dominate over deciduous trees because of their ready ability to adapt to the moderate wet winters and warm, dry summers characteristic of the area. Deciduous trees are at a relative disadvantage because of their high rates of water loss in the droughty summer months and their inability to undertake photosynthesis in the wet, mild winter months. Unlike many ecological systems where the primary production of biomass is quickly cropped by heterotrophic consumers, biomass accumulates to unparalleled magnitudes per unit of land area in Pacific Northwest old-growth forests. Except in a very old forest, Douglas fir is likely to be the dominant species among the large trees. Douglas fir is the typical pioneer species in disturbed areas, but it persists in relatively old stands because it is long-lived. As a result of the periodicity of disturbance, a climax condition in which Douglas fir has completely disappeared is seldom reached in the Pacific Northwest (Waring and Franklin 1979; Franklin *et al*. 1981).

Large trees, a key structural element in old-growth forests, first and foremost have their origins at the functional level as the dominant primary producers, transforming atmospheric carbon into organic material through photosynthesis. While this function does not differ conceptually from that of small trees in earlier successional stages, it differs quantitatively in the sense that production in old-growth forest stands is heavily concentrated in a comparatively few large individual trees per unit area. These stands have high rates of gross productivity, but because of high rates of respiration and tree mortality, there is typically little if any net increment to living tree biomass. By contrast, young stands have high rates of net productivity and biomass accumulation, but relatively small amounts accumulated in individual trees. The large trees in old-growth stands with their massive accumulations of organic material ultimately become the source of energy that drives the entire forest ecosystem, particularly when they are transformed through tree death into standing snags or fallen logs on the forest floor (*ibid*.).

As structures, large living trees have an important role to play in the functioning of the ecological system. The upper branches of large trees are prime habitat for nitrogen-fixing lichens, which draw their nutrients from rainwater and convert atmospheric nitrogen into a form useful to plants. Since nitrogen-fixing lichens, such as *Lobaria spp.*, are uncommon in young forests, apparently because of the absence of adequate thermal buffering in young stands, the amount of nitrogen fixation is greater per unit area in old-growth forests. Because of its large capacity to store water from rainfall and consequently to buffer temperatures, the canopy of old-growth forests provides an ideal microclimate for *Lobaria*. Old-growth forests also make a significant contribution to hydrologic budget relative to young forests, through the interception of fog and mist by the branch and needle system of large trees, particularly in coastal areas where fog and mist is common. The irregularity of the crown of large trees and their relatively distant spacing from one another contribute to the availability of light on the forest floor and the patchiness of the understory. In densely packed young stands, the understory may be entirely absent or composed of a relatively few species adapted to low-light conditions (Spies and Franklin 1988a; Franklin *et al*. 1981).

Large old-growth trees, with their tall, large-diameter trunks, heterogeneous crowns and branch systems, and microclimatic gradients beginning with the cool damp forest floor and ending at the exposed weather conditions at the top of the crown, provide a wide variety of habitat niches for a range of vertebrate and invertebrate animal species as well as a variety of mosses and lichens. The cavities and irregularities of the crown are attractive nesting habitats for the rare spotted owl, and large protruding branches near the treetop serve as perches for the bald eagle along waterways. An abundance of insects is found around, on, and within the bark of large, old-growth trees, and these insects serve as a food source for a variety of birds and mammals, including bats that feed on flying insects above the crown. Birds and mammals also feed on the abundant foliage. As many as 1,500 species of invertebrates can be found in, on, and around a large old-growth Douglas fir (*ibid.*).

The unique role of large trees in old-growth ecological functioning by no means ends with tree death. Dead trees become standing snags, downed logs on land, or downed logs in streams, and in these capacities continue to play a major ecological role for many years. Douglas fir snags last 50 to 75 years, while western red cedar snags can last 75 to 125 years. The life span of downed logs on land is even longer, ranging up to 480–580 years for a 30-inch diameter Douglas fir log. The volume of snags and downed logs in old-growth Douglas fir forests is among the highest reported for temperate forests (Franklin *et al*. 1987; Spies and Franklin 1988b).

Snags are common in forests of all ages, but only old-growth forests and recent burns contain large snags. Large snags, with their large accumulations of biomass, become the feeding ground for a variety of bacteria, fungi, and insects. The unique function of snags, however, is as nesting sites for cavity-excavating birds, such as the pileated woodpecker. Hole-nesting birds are normally confined to snags over 24 inches in diameter at breast height. Cavities in snags are used by mammals as well as birds, and the species use of snags shifts as the state of snag decay changes. Cavities are often created by primary excavators in hard snags and are then used by other hole-nesting birds and mammals (Franklin *et al.* 1981; Mannan *et al.* 1980).

In addition to the creation of snags, tree death can lead to an abundance of downed large logs on land in old-growth forests, logs that perform important nutrient and hydrologic cycling functions. They are principal energy sources for a variety of decomposer organisms that recycle phosphorus and nitrogen for use by primary producers. Downed logs are also an important habitat for nitrogen-fixing bacteria, which convert atmospheric nitrogen into a form usable by primary producing plants. Both nitrogen and phosphorus concentrations in downed logs increase as decay progresses. The volume of water in downed logs also increases with decay, making them more attractive as habitat for both plants and animals (Franklin *et al.* 1981; Solins *et al.* 1980; Maser and Trappe 1984).

Downed logs perform a variety of habitat functions for a wide range of organisms, including mycorrhizal fungi, moisture-loving amphibians and reptiles, mammals, and birds. The logs are used as food sources, rearing and food storage sites, perches and lookouts, and paths for travel. They play an important role in the recolonization of fire-disturbed sites by providing a store of nutrients protected from fire by a high moisture content and by providing a pathway for small mammals from the surrounding forest into the burned-over area. Mycorrhizal fungi form a symbiotic relationship with tree roots absorbing sugars produced by the tree and supplying nutrients to the tree roots from the surrounding soil. In a burned-over area, mycorrhizal fungi disappear completely and must be reintroduced for successful tree growth. Downed logs play a role in reintroduction by providing a pathway into bare areas for small animals that eat mycorrhizal fungi and spread the spores to new areas through defecation. Certain mycorrhizae, such as truffles, fruit in rotten wood close to the tunnels of California red-backed voles found beneath downed Douglas fir logs. The voles in turn disperse the spores of the truffles, assuring the reproduction and genetic diversity of mycorrhizae. Mycorrhizae have been found to play an important role in biomass release as well as nutrient cycling in the Douglas fir ecosystem. In addition to red-backed voles, flying squirrels feed heavily on fruiting fungi, dispersing their spores (Franklin *et al.* 1981; Maser and Trappe 1984; Maser *et al.* 1978, 1986).

Fallen logs are also an important habitat for tree seedlings for such species as western hemlock, Sitka spruce, and Pacific silver fir. Seedlings are generally more numerous on nurse logs than the adjacent forest floor, particularly in the damper coastal forests. Tree seedlings seem to encounter difficulty competing for space with the mosses and herbs of the forest floor and, consequently, are more successful rooting in recently fallen logs where competition is less intense (Harmon and Franklin 1989).

Downed logs also play a major ecological role in forest streams. Large logs in streams not only affect the carbon and nutrients available to aquatic organisms, but also significantly influence the physical profile of small- and medium-sized streams. In small streams, logs act like dams, creating a stepped profile of pools and riffles. In the process, the energy of the flowing water is dissipated and the potential for stream bank erosion is reduced. In intermediate-sized streams where logs can be redistributed by the flowing water, dams are less common, but clumps of logs nonetheless alter flow patterns and create habitat variety. In larger streams, logs become highly dispersed and have a minor impact on stream profile. While large logs may persist in streams through the development of second-growth forests after major disturbances, in managed stands converted to a short rotation, logs will eventually disappear as major structural elements (Franklin *et al.* 1981).

In small streams, downed logs as well as litter fall from the surrounding forest provide a major source of organic carbon and nutrients for aquatic organisms. Because of canopy shading, primary production in streams is limited, and most of the energy used by aquatic organisms is imported from the surrounding forest. The pools and riffles are ideal habitats for a variety of invertebrate and vertebrate organisms, including a number of salmonids. The imported (allochthonous) organic debris is first attacked by bacteria and fungi. These organisms increase the palatability of organic debris for invertebrate shredders, which in turn further reduce it to a form that is usable by collectors. The shredders and collectors are food for invertebrate and vertebrate predators, the latter of which can include salamanders and cutthroat trout (*ibid.*).

The relative impact of the surrounding forest on a stream depends on the size or order of the stream. A small, first-order stream is one that has no other streams flowing into it. A second-order stream results from the confluence of two first order streams. Similarly, a third-order stream results from the confluence of two second-order streams. As the order increases, the width of the stream enlarges and the canopy opens, permitting light energy to radiate directly on the stream's surface, shifting the energy base relatively in the direction of primary production by attached algae (periphyton) and plants (macrophytes). Not only does the forest become less important as a determinant of the physical profile of a stream, but the energy base also shifts from imported organic debris to in-stream primary production. This causes a shift in the food web toward grazer organisms that feed on periphyton and macrophytes and away from shredders. Stream productivity also tends to increase as the canopy opens (Murphy and Hall 1981).

A number of studies have shown that opening the canopy over streams through timber harvesting initially increases the productivity of higher predators, such as juvenile coho salmon and cutthroat trout. Timber harvesting negatively affects the emergence of fry from coho salmon eggs through sedimentation, but the impact of this on salmonid populations is apparently offset by earlier fry emergence due to warmer waters and higher levels of in-stream primary productivity and feeding opportunities for juvenile salmonids in unshaded clearcuts. For a time, the original pool and riffle stream profile may be preserved after timber harvesting, but without further inputs of large woody debris, the stepped profile will be replaced by a channelized profile with its rapid water flow and absence of pools. Consequently, once the postharvest canopy closes, both the habitat favored by salmonids and the higher productivity of the open stream are lost. Thus, for most of the rotation in a managed forest, salmonid productivity will be reduced relative to the initial clearcut as well as the old-growth forest. The old-growth forest will likely be intermediate in total stream productivity because of its partially open canopy in comparison to the closed canopy of the young forest and the completely open canopy of the clearcut. After several rotations, the stepped profile of streams will likely disappear completely, and the increased salmonid productivity associated with subsequent clearcuts would as a result be reduced because of the loss of pool and riffle habitat. Although it has yet to be proven, old-growth forests may be necessary to sustain the productivity of salmonids at historic levels. The input of large organic debris to streams as a stabilizing element may be required to provide salmonids with adequate habitat for rearing and feeding (Holtby 1988; Thedinga *et al*. 1989; Scrivener and Brownlee 1989).

Recent research on old-growth forests thus suggests that they are not biological deserts of overmature timber, as once thought. Rather, old-growth forests are unique biological structures with unusual physical characteristics that carry out key biotic functions in ways that are much different from forests in earlier successional stages. They also support a variety of species that appear to be dependent on old growth, including, as already mentioned, the western yew, marbled murrelet, and spotted owl. Old-growth forest ecosystems have unique structural and functional characteristics, and contain a unique collection of species. As a result of the cutting of these forests, something of significance has indeed disappeared. Although it is not immediately apparent to the casual observer, U.S. suburbanization with its expanded use of lumber in housing has played a significant role in the decline of old-growth forests (Chapter 3), which constitute an increasingly rare and threatened ecosystem type.

Habitat loss in the U.K. countryside

None of the U.K. rural landscape can be said to be "natural" in the sense of being lightly touched by the human hand. Grasslands, heath, and woodlands, however, often contain a sufficient diversity of native species to be called "semi-natural." Remaining patches of primary woodlands never converted to other uses are by virtue of their complement of species and habitat characteristics lineal descendents of their prehistorical counterparts. These woodlands are ecologically identifiable by their understory species, such as dog's mercury (*Mercurialis perennis*) and yellow archangel (*Galeobdolon luteum*). Because such species are slow to disperse to new forest habitats, they are good indicators of primary forest (Pye-Smith and Rose 1984: 78–87). While primary forest patches have been heavily exploited, they are resilient enough to retain a diversity of native plant and animal species. Grasslands and heath created by centuries of deforestation are also composed of complexes of native species expanding out of coastal and upland refuges and forest glades (ibid.: 90–96; Green 1985: 103–104). Over centuries, the British countryside has been converted from a forested landscape with a few openings to an open landscape with a few forests. During this transition some large mammal species and birds of prey have been rendered extinct by habitat loss or persecution, but surprisingly the U.K. retains much of its pre-settlement flora and fauna (Green 1985: 33–41). Nonetheless, the emergence of intensive mechanized agriculture and plantation forestry in recent years is threatening the continued presence of a number of species in woodland, grassland, heath, and wetland habitats.

Woodland habitat loss

Temperate deciduous forest is the climax ecosystem type in most of the British landscape. By virtue of historical land clearance, less than 8 percent of the U.K. land area contains forests, and less than this is primary woodland (NCC 1984: 32). Depending on soil type and moisture, long-lived canopy species include oaks (*Quercus spp.*), elms (*Ulmus spp.*), limes (*Tilia spp.*), alder (*Alnus glutinosa*), beech (*Fagus sylvatica*), and hornbeam (*Carpinus betulus*). The shorter-lived species invading openings created by tree-falls and other disturbances are ash (*Fraxinus excelsior*), aspen (*Populus tremula*), birches (*Betula spp.*), and willows (*Salix spp.*). Because oak has been favored by forest management for centuries, it tends to dominate in areas where beech would otherwise be more common (Green 1985: 124–127). The understory of mature forests often contains small trees and shrubs such as the whitebeam (*Sorbus aria*), yew (*Taxus baccata*), and hazel (*Corylus avellana*). While woods dominated by dense canopies of beech have a limited ground flora, forests with relatively open canopies have a richer ground layer, including dog's mercury, yellow archangel, and a variety of orchids (ibid.: 127). These woodlands support a variety of mammal and bird species as well as a host of invertebrates including rare butterflies (ibid.: 129; NCC 1984: 61).

Traditionally, woodlands have been exploited for wood products, grazing, and wildlife harvesting. Forests with large trees but an impoverished ground layer were often preserved historically as royal hunting grounds, and some forests were grazing grounds for pigs that foraged for acorns (pannage). Wildlife browsing and grazing were not conducive to timber production because animals would browse on the immature shoots of trees. Woodlands used for timber production were consequently enclosed for protection from browsing and grazing. One of the more common methods of wood extraction was coppicing. Understory shrubs such as hazel and many trees will send out masses of shoots when cut at a young age. This permits a continuous cutting of pole-sized timber on a rotation of 10–25 years. Coppicing maintained a relatively open woodland with a rich ground layer and understory. With the cessation of coppicing in the modern era and the emergence of a thick canopy, species diversity has fallen (Green 1985: 131–132, 137–138).

The amount of woodland habitat lost to clearance for agriculture, cessation of coppicing, and conversion to conifer plantations is substantial, and this loss has resulted in the decline of a number of rare and threatened species. In 23 U.K. counties, 46 percent of all natural woodland disappeared because of agricultural clearance and plantation forestry between 1933 and 1983 (Table 4.1).

As a consequence of this and other habitat changes, butterflies have been among the most affected. Of 55 native butterfly species in the U.K., one has become extinct and 23 are either endangered, vulnerable, or declining in population. Of these, 14 have suffered from woodland habitat losses and changes (NCC 1984: 61). Flowering plants and ferns have also suffered from woodland habitat loss. Of the 149 species showing at least 20 percent decline since 1930, 18 are woodland species, and of 117 nationally rare species showing at least 33 percent decline since 1930, eight are found in woodlands (NCC 1984: 64).

Table 4.1 Habitat loss in the British countryside

Habitat type	Pre-modern	Modern
Permanent pasture – north Kent (ha) 1935–1982	14,750	7,675
Chalk grassland – Dorset (ha) 1934–1972	7,700	2,268
Lowland acid heath – 6 districts (ha) 1930–1980	82,000	39,450
Semi-natural woodland – 23 counties (ha) 1933–1983	142,000	76,500
Lowland fens – East Anglia (sq. km.) 1934–1984	100	10
Lowland peatlands – 5 areas (ha) 1948–1978	4,146	1,216

Source: NCC (1984: 50–59).

Grassland and heathland habitat loss

In the primeval British landscape, grassland and heath were comparatively rare. In the traditional mixed farming landscape they became significant semi-natural habitats, but in the modern landscape they are in decline as a consequence of conversion to arable land and conifer afforestation (Table 4.1; Green 1985: 100). Rich lowland meadows for hay and winter grazing and rough upland pasture for summer grazing were essential components of the traditional farm economy. Grasslands in the U.K. are categorized according to their underlying soil type: limestone, neutral, or acidic. The "chalk" (limestone) grasslands are relatively rich in species; the neutral lowland grasslands are the most productive and tend to be most closely managed; and the acidic grasslands are the most infertile and tend to be relatively species-poor. The blue pasque flower, a slow disperser, is an indicator of old limestone grassland (Pye-Smith and Rose 1984: 91). Under intense grazing, acid grasslands often come to be dominated by heather and experience a transformation to healthland and moorland plant communities (Green 1985: 103–110).

In many areas, grasslands and heathlands are in rapid decline (Table 4.1). Relatively infertile lowland heath is being converted to cropland with the help of fertilizers; in lowland meadows the most productive species are being favored through fertilizer and herbicide application, reducing plant diversity; and upland heaths are being lost to conifer plantations (*ibid.*: 100; Pye-Smith and Rose 1984: 90–102). The loss of these habitats has had serious consequences for a variety of plant and animal species, including the extinction of the big blue butterfly and population declines for 10 other species of butterfly, declines of at least 20 percent since 1930 for 59 of 149 species of flowering plants and ferns, and declines of at least 33 percent for 74 of 117 species of flowering plants and ferns that are nationally rare (NCC 1984: 61–64). Of a dozen recent plant extinctions, five were for plants found in grassland, arable, or heathland habitats.

Wetlands

Wetlands are an extremely important natural habitat by virtue of the functions they perform. They mitigate water pollution problems by trapping sediments and filtering out toxins; they reduce the magnitude of floods by serving as sponges that soak up surges in runoff and stream flow; and they serve as habitats for a variety of species. Wetlands are also among the world's most threatened types of ecosystems. The central threat to wetlands is drainage for agriculture, urban development, hydroelectric and irrigation projects, and control of mosquitoes. In Britain, another important reason for wetland drainage is the cutting of peat as a fuel and for horticultural purposes (Green 1985: 143–145). As the result of wetland destruction, runoff in many rivers has increased, aquifer recharge rates have diminished, and average dry-weather stream flow has declined.

Wetlands occur in relatively quiet shoreline waters or where the soil is waterlogged for some portion of the year. Reedy plants and swamp grasses invade inundated soils close to shore and shorelines and rooted plants or free-floating plants settle in the shallows farther out. Where water levels are relatively stable and water flows limited, bog mosses (*Sphagnum spp.*) will invade, resulting in an accumulation of peat, increasing acidity, and the eventual filling in of water bodies. Because they are often fed by nutrient-poor streams or rainwater, bogs are normally nutrient-poor and contain species adapted to this condition, such as the insectivorous sundews (*Drosera spp.*). Where soils and waters are alkaline, nutrient-rich fens form, with a richer and more diverse flora than acid bogs (*ibid.* 147–154; Pye-Smith and Rose 1984: 106–111).

Bogs and other types of wetland provide habitat for a variety of invertebrate and vertebrate species, some of which are threatened by habitat decline. The losses of both peatlands and fens have been substantial in recent years (Table 4.1), and have been driven to a large extent by draining for agriculture. A variety of species are threatened by wetland losses, including a number of dragonfly species, a large number of flowering plants, and the river otter. Of the 149 native species showing 20 percent decline since 1930, 69 of them are wetland species, and of the 117 nationally rare species showing at least 33 percent decline since 1930, 21 are found in wetlands (NCC 1984: 62–64). In the U.K. as in many other countries, the loss of wetlands is playing a significant role in the process of species endangerment and extinction.

Riparian habitat modification and dam construction

A powerful influence on riparian areas that rivals and contributes to wetland loss is the construction of dams. Of all human-built structures, dams, such as the Hoover Dam on the Colorado and the Grand Coulee Dam on the Columbia River, are among the most visually impressive. Among all human-built structures, dams also rank very high as modifiers of the natural environment. Dams alter river hydrology, water quality, sediment flows, erosion patterns, floodplains, and the diversity and composition of plant and animal life.

Physical changes

The most significant physical change induced by dams is the alteration of water flow patterns. First and foremost, a dam converts a part of a river into a lake. The reservoir behind a dam is used to store water for electricity generation, irrigation, urban water supply, or flood control. In the process, the flow pattern of a river is significantly disrupted. On entering the reservoir, water velocity slows and suspended sediments drop out, causing the reservoir to become a sediment trap. This in turn reduces the sediment load of the river below the dam and increases the clarity of the water. The flow pattern of the river below the dam is also altered, depending on the purpose of the dam. If the dam is used for flood control, flooding below the dam is eliminated or at least mitigated; if the dam is used for electricity generation or irrigation, pulses of water flow from the dam according to peak load demands for electricity or irrigation requirements. The absence of flood waters below the dam shrinks the physical extent of the floodplain, the area previously inundated in flood episodes. The rate of erosion immediately below the dam often increases because of the absence of suspended sediment in the flowing waters and the attempt by the river to restore its equilibrium sediment load (Petts 1984).

The replacement of part of a river by what is essentially a lake reduces the flow rate of water in the river and increases the potential for biological production. In fast-flowing turbulent waters, which characterize the upper reaches of watersheds, free-floating planktonic forms of algae have difficulty surviving. In the quiet waters of a dam reservoir fed by nutrient imports from upstream, biological productivity can flourish. Given that reservoirs are thermally stratified, the cold lower layer often becomes depleted of oxygen by the decomposition of dead organic matter descending from the sunlit (photic) zones where plant growth takes place. In these waters various chemicals, such as iron, manganese, and hydrogen sulfide, become suspended, along with other toxins and plant nutrients. Water quality below dams that release from the bottom of the reservoir is, consequently, frequently impaired, while water quality below dams that release from reservoir surface waters will be relatively high, although such reservoirs may discharge significant volumes of algae into downstream waters (*ibid.*).

Biological changes

The physical changes to rivers caused by dams bring forth substantial biological changes. Dams eliminate important floodplain habitat, alter thermal regimes and thermal cues on which many species depend, change water flow patterns to which many species are adapted, and create barriers to migration for anadromous fish species that spawn in rivers and streams and spend their adult lives in ocean waters.

Naturally flowing rivers can be categorized as either floodplain or reservoir rivers. Reservoir rivers have a relatively stable year-round water flow and only infrequently overspill their banks. Floodplain rivers are characterized by a cycle of flood and drought, overspilling their banks during flood episodes, creating backwaters of residual pools and wetland areas. Dams tend to stabilize water flows and diminish flood episodes and in the process reduce the size of the floodplain. Dams essentially convert floodplain rivers into reservoir rivers. The loss of the floodplain results in the loss of backwater pools and the succession of wetlands to meadows. This in turn reduces habitat for waterfowl, muskrat, beaver, and moose (Petts 1984).

Diverse habitats create diverse niches for a variety of species. Dams simplify riparian habitats not only by reducing the extent of floodplains but in other ways as well. Dams simplify daily and seasonal thermal regimes, evening out temperatures and eliminating thermal cues to which a variety of aquatic insects and other invertebrates are adapted. Hatching, growth, and emergence for a variety of organisms depend on water temperature. Dams also often eliminate the pool and riffle habitat to which many invertebrates are adapted and change the substrate from rock and gravel, characteristic of fast-flowing waters, to sand and silt associated with slower water flows. Studies have found that while the biomass of invertebrates tends to increase on rivers with dams relative to their natural counterparts, the number of species present tends to diminish (*ibid.*). Reduced biodiversity is a central result of habitat simplification caused by the construction and operation of dams.

Riverine fishes have probably suffered the most of all biotic organisms from dam construction. River impoundment in all probability has markedly increased the rate of extinction of freshwater fishes. The central problem for fishes created by dams is the inundation of spawning grounds and the construction of barriers to migration. Trout and salmon, for example, spawn in relatively fast-flowing stretches of rivers with gravel-covered bottoms. Dam reservoirs often flood such habitats and inhibit migration upstream to remaining spawning beds. Not all fishes are harmed by dams, such as those that are adapted to slow-flowing waters and certain introduced exotics able to take advantage of increased food supplies in the tailwaters of dams. The elimination of floodplains, however, removes important spawning and rearing areas for a variety of fish species, and the variation in water levels below dams caused by dam operations can eliminate stable habitats for endemic species. Shifts in temperature regimes after dam construction have often harmed native fish populations whose spawning and growth patterns are temperature-determined.

The impact on migratory fish from dam construction is perhaps best illustrated by the historical experience with dams on the Columbia River in the Pacific Northwest region of the U.S. Chinook salmon runs into the mouth of the Columbia River – runs that historically were among the largest in the world – have declined significantly since the mid-1920s. Mature chinook salmon migrate upriver to the spawning grounds of their birth, lay and fertilize their eggs in gravel river and stream bottoms, and then die. Juvenile salmon or smolts emerge, spend up to a year in local waters, and then migrate downriver to the waters of the Pacific, where they remain until they mature and repeat the spawning cycle. The decline in chinook salmon runs are the result of both over-fishing and a decline in habitat conditions in the Columbia River and its tributaries.

The most dramatic alteration to Columbia watershed habitat has been the construction of numerous dams. While the construction of dams for irrigation and electric power generation on the smaller tributaries of the Columbia dates back to the early 1900s, mainstem dam construction on the Columbia and a major tributary, the Snake River, did not commence until the 1930s. Between 1933 and 1969, 22 mainstem dams were constructed on the two rivers. On the Columbia, the Grand Coulee Dam was constructed without fish ladders and thus blocked upstream migration of salmon to northern Washington state and Canada. The upper and middle reaches of the Snake River were also blocked off from salmon migration by dam construction. Even though fish ladders were installed at many dams, these structures are still formidable barriers to upstream and downstream migration of salmon. Both upstream and downstream migrants face the danger of nitrogen poisoning in the supersaturated waters just below spillways, and downstream juvenile migrants confront the additional danger of injury and death from passage through electrical turbines. The large reservoirs behind dams reduce spawning opportunities by inundating spawning beds where relatively cool, well oxygenated waters flowed across gravel bottoms. Normally downstream migrants face upstream and simply float with the current. In the stagnant reservoirs behind dams juvenile salmon are forced to expend more energy than otherwise swimming downstream, face increased exposure to predators, and sometimes have trouble discerning the appropriate direction in which to swim. Although mortality varies from one dam to another and with flow conditions, fisheries researchers have estimated that upstream mortality for each dam is roughly 5 percent, while downstream mortality is approximately 20 percent. A conservative estimate of the chinook salmon run lost because of dams is approximately 3 million fish out of a run of 3.5 million (Booth 1989). The impact of dams on fisheries is clearly a serious matter.

Habitat problems and development in the Yellowstone ecosystem

Unlike timber harvesting and dam construction, threats to natural habitats and species by industry can sometimes be more indirect. This is the case for new high-technology industries that permit population relocations to relatively remote areas, one of which is the Yellowstone region in the western U.S. The beauty of the 2.2 million acre Yellowstone National Park and the uniqueness of its biotic resources are legendary. Species and biotic communities outside the boundaries of the park, in what can be called the Greater Yellowstone ecosystem, are threatened by various forms of economic activity. Some of these, including hardrock mining, timber harvesting, oil and gas development, and grazing, have been carried out in the area for many years. The basic problems with mining are contamination of ground and surface waters with toxic heavy metals and the wholesale removal of plant and animal communities through strip-mining. Timber harvesting and associated road construction results in loss of old-growth forest habitat and removal of cover for large mammals such as bears, the loss of nesting sites for birds in snags, and erosion and stream sedimentation. Roads serve as a pathway for the introduction of exotic species into forests and increase both legal and illegal hunting. Roads and clearcuts fragment forests, increasing the amount of "edge" and reducing the amount of interior habitat for deep-forest dwelling animals, such as the pileated woodpecker and pine marten. Almost half of the public lands in the Yellowstone ecosystem are leased for grazing, an activity that is of great cultural importance in the area. Grazing has significant environmental effects, including the degradation of riparian areas, reduction of grazing habitat for wild grazing animals (ungulates), the removal of the wolf as a predator in the Yellowstone ecosystem, transmission of disease to bighorn sheep, the introduction of exotic grasses, and the trampling of soil crusts and mosses, altering nitrogen fixation processes (Glick et al. 1991).

While logging, grazing, and mining continue in the Yellowstone area, economic expansion is being generated by growth in tourism, increases in vacation and retirement homes, and an influx of new service-oriented footloose business activity, as outlined in Chapter 3. One consequence has been increased subdividing of rural ranch lands, particularly along river corridors. Approximately a quarter of Yellowstone's northern elk herd and mule deer herd migrate onto private lands in the winter, and their migratory patterns are disrupted and available habitat reduced by subdivisions and their accompanying fencing and harassing dogs. Stream-side housing construction is also causing a loss of prime riparian habitat and in some cases increased water pollution where inadequate septic systems are installed (Glick et al. 1991; Rasker et al. 1991). The proliferation of roads associated with subdivisions also increases the animal road kill rate and expands habitat access for hunters. Human settlement in wildlife habitat has also resulted in increased human encounters with wild animals, such as mountain lions and grizzly bears, which often result in the animal involved being destroyed (Snyder 1994). In the spring under certain conditions grizzlies find the riparian corridors, so attractive to human settlement, to be optimum habitat. Grizzly bear kills as the consequence of human encounters are the single largest threat to the survival of the Yellowstone area grizzly population (Mattson and Reid, 1991). Given that over a million acres, or one-third of the private rural land, in the Yellowstone ecosystem has been subdivided, the threat to wildlife habitat is substantial (Rasker et al. 1991).

As Richard Manning (1995) suggests, the grizzly, the elk, and the bison are creatures not of the mountains in their present home at Yellowstone, but of the grasslands. Human encroachment on their grassland habitat resulted in Yellowstone becoming their final refuge. Yet, because of advances in human technology, further encroachment in this remote area is occurring on the little lowland habitat remaining and may in the end eliminate this final refuge.

Conclusions

One of the consequences of economic growth is increasing threats to the continued survival of species and biotic communities caused by habitat destruction and deterioration. The emergence and growth of a variety of new kinds of economic activity in the U.S. and the U.K., including railroads, U.S. prairie state agriculture, the Great Lakes lumber and pulp and paper industries, motor vehicle induced urban construction, modernized agriculture and forestry in the U.K., hydroelectric power, and microelectronics, have played a significant role in the decline of a variety of natural habitats including the U.S. tallgrass prairie, Great Lakes forests, Pacific Northwest old-growth forests, U.K. woodlands, grasslands, heathlands, and wetlands, riparian areas on many rivers in the western U.S. and valley and riparian areas around Yellowstone. Economic growth processes as currently constituted result in reduced and altered natural habitats and threaten the continued existence of a number of species whose populations have been driven to relatively low levels. Notwithstanding their effect on our own self-interest, such events command our moral attention.

5

ECONOMIC GROWTH AND ENVIRONMENTAL CHANGE

Air, water, and pesticide pollution

In the last chapter, the significance of the habitat loss problem caused by the new industry creation process that underpins economic growth was documented. In this chapter the impacts of air, water, and pesticide pollution on human health and well being and the health of species and ecosystems are considered. As already noted, understanding the seriousness of contemporary environmental problems is essential to any judgement that economic growth fosters environmental deterioration. Such understanding is also essential to an ethical evaluation of the damage done by environmental problems, an evaluation that necessarily precedes determination of appropriate measures to forestall environmental decline. Again, the central thesis of this work is that new forms of economic activity create new kinds of environmental problems. This chapter is concerned with the seriousness of those problems. The next chapter addresses the question of resistance to resolution of environmental problems by vested economic interests. We will then be in a position to proceed to the final topic of this book, an ethical evaluation of environmental issues and, flowing from that, a presentation of economic reforms that will satisfy environmental standards based on ethical norms.

Air pollution

Conventional air pollutants

Emissions of air pollutants don't automatically translate into environmental harm. For harm to occur, concentrations have to be high enough, or certain atmospheric conditions must prevail, in order for harmful chemicals to form in sufficient concentrations to do damage. Pollutants either have the potential to do damage directly (primary pollutants), or else serve as precursors to the formation of other pollutants (secondary pollutants). Pollutants in the presence of sunlight, for example, often undergo oxidation reactions that lead to the formation of still other harmful pollutants. Nitrogen oxide and hydrocarbons react with sunlight to form ozone, a highly erosive form of oxygen. Sulfur dioxide and nitrogen oxide react with water vapor to respectively form sulfuric and nitric acids. These are only some of the possible products of atmospheric reactions involving the interactions of pollutants, sunlight, and water vapor (Stern *et al.* 1984: 161–174; Harrison 1975: 5–53).

Primary and secondary pollutants in sufficient concentration first and foremost are harmful to human health. Carbon monoxide, a primary pollutant emitted from the burning of fossil fuels, reduces the ability of the human circulatory system to transport oxygen, impairing motor functions, aggravating cardiovascular disease, and causing death at high exposure levels. The fossil fuel generated primary pollutants sulfur dioxide and particulates can increase chronic and acute respiratory disease, and excessive exposure to nitrogen oxide, another primary pollutant from fossil fuel combustion, can increase human susceptibility to respiratory pathogens. Finally, the secondary pollutant ozone, whose precursors orginate in fossil fuel combustion, can reduce pulmonary functioning and increase asthma attacks (Stern *et al.* 1984: 110–111; McGrath and Barnes 1982).

In addition to harming human health, air pollutants can cause damage to materials and structures. Exposure of metals to sulfur dioxide accelerates corrosion, and sulfur dioxide and moisture react with limestone to form calcium sulfate which eats away at limestone blocks and mortar between them in buildings. Sulfur oxides cause the tensile strength of materials to decrease, dyes in materials to fade, and deterioration in paint, paper, and leather. Similarly, ozone increases the fading of dyes and causes rubber to crack. Not only is air pollution damaging to human health and the well being of plants, animals, and ecosystems, but it can harm the materials and structures that underpin our economic life. Moreover, air pollutants often create hazy conditions that interfere with visibility and offend our aesthetic sensibilities (Stern *et al.* 1984: 130–153).

Emissions of conventional pollutants continue to be a serious problem in both the U.S. and the U.K., as suggested by the data presented in Chapter 3. In the U.S., emissions manifest themselves in the violation of ambient air quality standards in many metropolitan areas. The U.S. Clean Air Act establishes ambient standards for carbon monoxide, ozone, sulfur dioxide, particulates, nitrogen dioxide, and lead, and the standards that are most frequently violated are for carbon monoxide and ozone (Stern *et al.* 1984: 357). In 1991, 16 metropolitan areas in the U.S. violated carbon monoxide ambient standards, while 63 violated ozone standards. The worst case, Los Angeles, violated carbon monoxide standards on 41 days of the year, and ozone standards on 91 days (U.S. Department of Commerce 1993: 226). Regulation and slower growth in energy consumption have reversed the growth of air pollution emissions in the U.S. (Figure 3.2), but very serious problems remain.

Evolving quite differently in the U.K. than the U.S., the lynchpin of the British approach to air pollution regulation is the use of the "best practicable means" to control emissions. This concept was codified relatively early in U.K. history, making its first appearances in the Smoke Nuisance Abatement Act of 1853 and the Alkali Act of 1874 (Ashby and Anderson 1981: 19, 32). The watershed event for air pollution in U.K. history was the London killer smog of 1952, during which as many as 4,000 premature deaths occurred as a consequence of smoke (Brimblecombe 1987: 124). Following calls for public action after the killer smog, the National Clean Air Act was passed, replacing all existing laws and containing provisions for prohibiting the emission of dark smoke, limiting grit and dust, and the creation of smokeless zones where the use of smokeless fuels in home heating is required. Under the Act, the regulation of air emissions from industrial sources was largely left in the hands of the Alkali Inspectorate, which continued the "best practicable means" tradition of control (*ibid.*: 104–119). The British system of control has thus relied primarily on limiting emissions, and until recently lacked specific ambient standards (Wood 1989: 98).

Since the passage of the U.K. Clean Air Act, smoke levels have declined dramatically in London and elsewhere not only because of control measures, but also as a consequence of a changeover from coal to gas and electricity as energy and heating sources, the spread of central heating, and shifts in population from city to suburb (Ashby and Anderson 1981: 116). As a consequence of control measures instituted by the Alkali Inspectorate (now known as Her Majesty's Pollution Inspectorate), sulfur emissions have also dropped in the past two decades and tall chimney-stacks have been used with increasing frequency to disperse emissions over a wider area, reducing local ground-level concentrations (Figure 3.3; Park 1987: 14–21). With the decline of the smoke problem and the limiting of local sulfur dioxide concentrations, air pollution has not appeared to be an immediate threat to U.K. residents. Up to the 1980s, for example, motor vehicle emissions in the U.K. did not constitute a visible problem in urban areas and went unregulated, resulting in an absence of progress in reducing nitrous oxide and carbon monoxide emissions (Figure 3.3).

This lack of visibility does not mean that the U.K. is free of air pollution problems, however. The U.K. tall chimney-stack policy, for example, has simply transmitted pollutants downwind, worsening acid rain problems, much to the consternation of other European countries, and as recently as 1990 the U.K. continued to be the second largest source of sulfur dioxide emissions in Europe after the former East Germany (World Resources Institute 1996: 331). Scandinavian countries, which suffer from acid deposition problems that are not of their own making, have been particularly vocal critics of upwind countries such as the U.K. which use tall chimney-stacks to inject sulfur dioxide into the upper atmosphere (Park 1987: 157–188). Moreover, since the decline of smoke pollution in London and growth in the number of sunny days, photochemical smog has increased, and with increasing motor vehicle traffic, Londoners are encountering higher levels of carbon monoxide (Brimblecombe 1987: 175–177). Under some protest, the U.K. has agreed to abide by European Community directives on limiting vehicle exhaust emissions, lead in petrol, and sulfur emissions (McCormick 1991: 128–148). Although sulfur dioxide is the overriding U.K. air pollution emissions problem, the country is not completely immune from the urban air pollution problems caused by carbon monoxide and ozone that plague so many U.S. cities (Royal Commission 1995: 21–37).

The acid rain problem originating with sulfur dioxide and nitrous oxide emissions pointedly illustrates that many of the same pollutants that are threatening to human beings are also harmful to the health of plants and animals. The loss of fish life as a consequence of acidification in Scandinavian, U.S., and Canadian lakes and acid-induced tree death in the Black Forest of Germany illustrate the significance of air pollution problems for the health of aquatic and forest ecosystems (Park 1987; Gould 1985). Because it is a major environmental threat in both northern Europe and the northeastern U.S., the problem of acid rain deserves more detailed attention.

Acid rain and aquatic ecosystems

The primary sources of acid deposition are emissions of sulfur and nitrogen oxides. When sulfur and nitrogen dioxide mix with moisture in the air, they are oxidized respectively to sulfate or acid sulfate and nitrate or acid nitrate, increasing acidity. Acidic moisture can be carried hundreds of miles downwind before being deposited on land or water surfaces as precipitation. Dry deposition of sulfur dioxide and acid sulfate as well as nitrogen dioxide and its other oxidized forms also occurs, increasing acidity through absorption by materials or moisture. Much of the acid deposition in the eastern U.S. is thought to originate from large coal-fired electric generating plants in the Midwest, while deposition in the Scandinavian countries originates from electric generating and industrial facilities in the U.K. and other western European countries (Gould 1985; Howells 1990; Park 1987).

Because rainfall is naturally somewhat acidic, biotic systems are adapted to a certain background level of acid deposition. However, sulfur or nitrogen oxide emissions in sufficient volume can raise the level of acidity from wet and dry deposition well above background levels. When soils contain buffering agents, such as calcium carbonate (found in limestone), acid deposition will be neutralized and not cause any damage. If soils are derived from bedrock, such as granite, which lacks buffering agents, elevated acid levels are potentially threatening to terrestrial and aquatic life (Gould 1985; Howells 1990).

Where buffering agents are in short supply, as in the Adirondack Mountains in New York State and the lakes of Scandinavia, acid deposition has resulted in serious harm to biotic communities in lakes and streams. Of 1,000 lakes sampled in the Adirondacks, 25 percent have acidified to the extent that they no longer support game fish, and fish have disappeared from 20 percent of 5,000 lakes in southern Norway (Gould 1985; Park 1987: 84).[1] While high acidity does not necessarily preclude the presence of fish, it does reduce their numbers and diversity. Salmonids (trout and salmon), for example, are highly sensitive to acidity. The level of acidity itself may not be so much the problem for aquatic life as are the heavy metals liberated by acids from the soils and bedrock (Park 1987: 87–89). As acidified water runs through the upper layer of soils before reaching lakes and streams, it dissolves aluminum and other heavy metals harmful to fish gills and reproductive processes (Howells 1990: 134–150). The loss of fish populations has larger ecological effects, such as the reduction of local populations of birds, including loons, gulls, kingfishers, and mergansers, that in turn feed on fish.

While the loss of game fish is of the most interest and concern to humans, other aquatic organisms are acid-sensitive as well, including freshwater clams, snails, crayfish, and other bottom-dwelling organisms (Gould 1985: 18–19). Although acidification does not seem to alter basic ecological processes, such as productivity and nutrient recycling, it does substantially reduce biotic diversity. Acid-tolerant species replace those that are intolerant, and the ecosystem continues to function, but at a much reduced level of complexity. Acidity fundamentally alters the composition of the biotic community, causing one assemblage of species to be replaced by another (Howells 1990: 151–165).

Unfortunately, the effects of acid rain may not be very easily reversed. Years of deposition have built up acids in the soils and depleted stocks of buffering materials. While emissions reductions are essential to halt the acid buildup, a substantial lag between the time at which emissions and the acidity of lakes and streams are reduced is likely (Gould 1985: 94; Howells 1990: 183). The acid deposition problem is in part cumulative. The final answer to the problem is a significant reduction of both sulfur and nitrogen oxides, although much time will pass before the damage is reversed.

Air pollution and forests

Acid rain constitutes a threat not only to aquatic ecosystems in the northeastern U.S. and Scandinavia, but to the forests of the eastern U.S. and northern Europe. Both acid rain and other forms of air pollution can do substantial harm to forest ecosystems, even at long distances from emission sources. Forests are susceptible to damage not only from the wet or dry deposition of acids, sulfates, and nitrates, but from direct contact with gaseous sulfur and nitrogen dioxide as well as ozone.

Forest damage from air pollution is most obvious near point sources of heavy emissions, such as in the Sudbury, Ontario, area, where fumigation of the surrounding landscape with sulfur dioxide and other pollutants by three large nickel and copper smelters has resulted in 25,000 acres of barren land and 36,000 acres of stunted woodlands. Exposure to high ambient concentrations of sulfur dioxide inhibits photosynthesis and tree growth in some species and causes significant damage to foliage. Because of selective damage from pollutants to the more sensitive species such as the white pine, simplification and reduced biodiversity of the mixed boreal forest ecosystem surrounding Sudbury has resulted. Similar problems have occurred around other smelters in Canada and the U.S. as well (Smith 1990: 486–493).

Beyond such obvious cases, much uncertainty remains in the scientific literature on the complex relationships between air pollutants and forest ecosystems (Smith 1990). However, there are a number of pathways by which air pollutants are likely to harm forest ecosystems. One pathway is through the leaching of soil nutrients and reductions in fertility as a result of acidification. Another is through the mobilization of heavy metals damaging to plants. Excess acidity in the soil dissolves aluminum, which is in turn absorbed by red spruce roots and interferes with nutrient uptake in high mountain spruce forests found in the eastern U.S. (*ibid.*: 260). Tree death in the Black Forest of Germany has been attributed to reduced soil fertility caused by acid-induced nutrient leaching and tree root uptake of dissolved aluminum (Park 1987: 100–105).

Although receiving less attention, British forests have not been free of the effects of acid rain. Perhaps the most acid-sensitive of plants are lichens, and studies of the distribution of epiphytic lichens that grow on the surface and branches of trees indicate that they have disappeared from about a third of England and Wales. While the results have been controversial, research studies have found evidence of acid-induced tree damage to beech, yew, fir, oak, spruce, and pine in U.K. forests (*ibid.*: 96–98, 106–108).

Acid rain is not the only air pollution problem faced by forests. Ozone has been shown to reduce plant growth at levels commonly experienced in the summer months over much of the eastern U.S. Ozone damage may be shifting the composition of eastern forests by selectively reducing white pine populations (Smith 1990: 339, 460). Ozone has been implicated in the decline of ponderosa pine in the San Bernardino Mountains on the eastern edge of the Los Angeles Basin. Ozone trapped in an inversion layer over Los Angeles is funneled into mountains from radiant heating on the south-facing slopes. The level of ozone in parts of the San Bernardino forests reaches as much as 120 ppb, an amount just equal to the EPA upper limit for urban areas. Ozone exposure inhibits tree growth and increases susceptibility of ponderosa pine to bark beetle infestations. If the air pollution problem continues, a transformation of the forest will occur from one that is well stocked and dominated by ponderosa pine, to one that is poorly stocked with less susceptible species such as white fir, incense cedar, California black oak, and various shrubs (*ibid.*: 467–474). In essence, air pollution will have significantly transformed the original forest ecosystem, replacing one ecosystem type with another.

These are the clearest cases of possible linkages between air pollution and damage to forests. Forest growth over much of the eastern and southeastern U.S. has declined in recent years and this has yet to be fully explained. While other stresses have occurred, this was a period of time during which both acid rain and ozone pollution increased (*ibid.*: 447–458). A similar story can be told for the forests of Germany. When the evidence is viewed as a whole, the consequences of air pollution for the health of forests in both the U.S. and Europe are a matter of serious concern.

Greenhouse gases and global warming

Perhaps the most serious air pollution problem of all is the emission of greenhouse gases, of which carbon dioxide is the most important, and the potential of such gases to cause global warming. Since the beginning of the fossil fuel era in the mid-nineteenth century, about 60 percent of all carbon dioxide released through fossil fuel burning has remained in the atmosphere while the rest has been absorbed by sinks. The specific rates at which this extra carbon is absorbed into the oceans, soils, and plants are unknown. The amount of time before a given surge in atmospheric carbon is absorbed by sinks could be anywhere from 50 to 200 years (National Academy 1992: 93). Cline (1992) suggests that deep ocean mixing won't begin to significantly offset the carbon buildup until 2275. At the current rate of increase in carbon dioxide concentrations (0.5 percent per year) and concentrations of other heat-trapping gases in the atmosphere (methane, 0.9 percent, and CFCs, 4 percent), greenhouse gas concentrations equivalent to the doubling of pre-industrial carbon dioxide will occur by the middle of the next century (National Academy 1992: 27). This could ultimately increase the average global temperature by somewhere between 1 and 5°C, with a likely figure of 2.5°C. We are already committed to around 1.7°C of warming from the existing accumulation of greenhouse gases, and warming could increase to 10°C or more, if nothing is done to alter likely fossil fuel consumption patterns (Cline 1992).

Forecasts of increasing global temperatures are based on calculations from complex climate simulation models that may be subject to significant error. The central difficulties in accurately simulating global climate patterns include correctly characterizing feedback effects and properly accounting for all variables that can significantly influence climate. Global warming would initiate a number of positive and negative feedback effects that can alter the extent to which warming occurs. In the absence of any feedback effects, a doubling of atmospheric carbon dioxide would cause a 1.3°C increase in the average global temperature. A warmer climate will in turn result in a damper climate as a consequence of the increase of evaporation. Since water vapor traps heat and absorbs solar radiation, the increase in temperature from a CO_2 doubling would rise to 2.1°C, taking into account higher evaporation levels. A warmer climate will also result in less ice and snow cover, causing the planet to be darker and absorb more solar radiation, rather than reflecting it off into space. The most uncertain feedback effect occurs as a consequence of cloud formation. Clouds increase warming by acting as a greenhouse gas, but they also reduce warming by reflecting solar radiation back into space. While there is general agreement that clouds on balance cool the climate, there is little agreement about the changes that would result in clouds from additional warming. Warming could increase cloud altitude and reduce their ability to reflect solar radiation because of cloud cooling. Warming could also increase the water content of clouds, making them brighter and better able to reflect solar radiation (National Academy 1992: 100–109).

Warming can facilitate other positive biotic feedback mechanisms as well, although their magnitude is uncertain. A 1°C increase in mean temperature in the middle latitudes is equivalent to a 100 to 150 kilometer northward shift in climatic latitude. In general, forests would be forced to migrate northward as a consequence. However, tree death on the southern boundary would likely occur more rapidly than migration on the northern boundary. The result would be an added release of carbon as trees died, and increased warming. Warmer temperatures could also increase the rate of plant matter decay more rapidly than photosynthesis, resulting in a net increase in carbon emissions (Woodwell 1989).

While positive feedback mechanisms accelerate global warming, certain pollutants emitted into the atmosphere may be counteracting global warming. For example, the emission of sulfates into the atmosphere from power plants and other sources may reduce temperatures by the direct back-scattering of solar radiation, the brightening of clouds, and increasing cloud formation (Balling 1992: 130). Of course, if sulfate emissions are reduced in order to reduce acid precipitation, then this source of cooling will be removed.

What can the climate record tell us about the actual extent of global warming? The record suggests that the average global surface temperature has risen somewhere in the range of 0.3 to 0.6°C since the last century. This is somewhat less than the 1°C increase predicted by climate models. The disparity could be a consequence of a lag in ocean thermal uptake, or it could be explained by increased sulfate emissions (National Academy 1992: 117–129; Balling 1992: 130). Or the observed warming could be the consequence of normal fluctuations in temperature. Only time will tell whether global warming is a reality.

While the extent of global warming is uncertain, because the environmental changes it could bring are of such a large order of magnitude, it cannot be ignored. Global warming threatens the well being of human societies because of possible sea level rises, damage to agriculture and industrial forests, harm to urban vegetation, increased summer cooling costs, and damage to natural ecosystems. Ecosystem damage in turn could threaten rare species and plant and animal communities and dramatically accelerate an already unprecedented rate of species extinction. Because of the potential seriousness of each of these problems, they deserve more detailed attention.

Climate change and a rising sea level

On a geological time scale, sea level appears to be linked to average global temperature. In the last ice age when the average temperature was 5°C cooler, sea level was approximately 100 meters lower than it is today. In the last interglacial period when temperatures were 1–2°C higher than today, sea level was approximately 5 meters higher (National Academy 1992: 583). Global warming is projected to increase sea levels because of the thermal expansion of the oceans and the melting of glaciers. While predictions are highly uncertain, an equivalent doubling of CO_2 is likely to cause up to a 60 centimeter increase in sea level by the end of the next century (*ibid.*: 583), with a high probability of a greater increase (Titus 1989). Over the last century, sea level has increased by 10–15 cm.

An increase in the sea level could cause an inundation of some lowlands, accelerated coastal erosion, increased coastal flooding and storm damage, damage to coastal structures, and saltwater intrusion into freshwater estuaries and aquifers. Because bridges and harbor facilities are designed for certain water levels, some will be rendered useless and some will have to be modified as a consequence of a sea level increase. Because beach profiles tend to be flatter than the land just above sea level, a rise in the sea level will cause erosion of a land area several times the area initially inundated, and the inundation of entire barrier islands off coastlines. Needless to say, beach resort areas will suffer significant losses of buildings. With a higher sea level, storm surges will operate from a higher base and do significantly more damage. Higher sea levels will also force the groundwater table upwards, adding to flooding problems, and cause salt water to extend farther up into estuaries and intrude into groundwater sources. The economic cost of damage from and adapting to a sea level increase is difficult to predict, but could easily amount to billions of dollars annually for the U.S. alone (Titus 1989). According to Cline (1992), the annual U.S. cost for construction of protective structures and loss of land would amount to $7 billion (1990 $) for short-term warming (2.5°C) and $35 billion for long-term warming (10°C).

Climate change and agriculture

The CO_2 buildup in the atmosphere could actually benefit agriculture because it results in an acceleration in photosynthesis in certain types of plants such as wheat. While photosynthesizing, plants take in atmospheric gases through stomata in their leaves. At the same time, moisture escapes from the plant through the stomata. Enrichment of CO_2 permits a narrowing of the stomata openings, reducing the amount of moisture that escapes. Laboratory experiments suggest that plant growth increases with CO_2 enrichment, even if other growth factors are limiting. The results of field experiments have been more ambiguous. Enrichment caused photosynthesis to accelerate and then return to normal in an experiment in the northern tundra, while a similar experiment in a coastal wetland resulted in a permanent acceleration.

Despite the possibility of benefits from CO_2 enrichment, the potential for damage to agriculture from global warming is substantial. Not considering CO_2 enrichment, computer simulations suggest yield losses of 18–25 percent in the Great Lakes, Southeast, and Great Plains areas of the U.S. from greenhouse warming. However, these losses are significantly mitigated when CO_2 enrichment is considered, and when adaptions are taken into account, such as altered planting dates, moisture conservation tillage, and the use of longer-season plant varieties. These simulations do not consider new pest problems that could arise from new temperature regimes, nor the reduced availability of irrigation water as a consequence of diminished summer stream flows. The uncertainties in agricultural losses have led one economist, W. D. Nordhaus, to estimate an approximate $12 billion loss of U.S. GNP as a consequence of greenhouse warming (National Academy 1992: 506–568). Cline (1992: 92–101), however, disagrees with this relatively benign treatment of damage to agriculture from global warming, suggesting that droughts will be increasingly frequent and damaging, and that significant CO_2 fertilization is doubtful. In his view, the annual cost of U.S. agricultural losses for short-term global warming will be $18 billion (1990 $), and for long-term warming, $95 billion.

Climate change, commercial forests, and other problems

Managed forests will suffer as well from greenhouse warming. The projected climate change will move temperature isotherms to higher latitudes several times faster than forests are able to move on their own. The potential northern range of forest species is expected to shift by as much as 600 or 700 kilometers northward in the next century and the southern boundary by as much as 1,000 kilometers (Cline 1992: 101–103). The actual pace of migration for some species could be as low as 100 kilometers over the same period of time. In a given tract, species unsuited to a warmer climate will suffer, and slow seed dispersal will limit their ability to migrate northward. The result could be the loss of species with limited ranges and dispersal ability, and even deforestation. Managed forest can be adapted by planting species appropriate for a warmer climate, but adaption is limited by the difficulty of forest regeneration on exposed dry sites. Pest problems may multiply, and controlling fires will be more costly under a warmer climate regime (National Academy 1992: 569–575). Forests in the U.S. could lose anywhere from 20 to 50 percent of their standing biomass in the next 100 years. According to Cline (1992: 102–103), the annual loss from forest decline will amount to $3.3 billion (1990 $) for short-term warming, and $7 billion for long-term warming.

Other costs to human society from global warming will occur as well. Additional cooling will require increased electricity generating capacity. Because of coastal inundation and local climatic shifts, migration at a global level will increase, undoubtedly increasing U.S. immigration pressures. The severity and frequency of hurricanes and the damage that results from them are likely to increase, and water supply problems are likely to be magnified. Urban ozone problems will be worsened by increased temperatures, increasing human health problems over and above the increased death rate that normally correlates with increased summer warming (Cline 1992). Cline estimates that the annual aggregate cost for the U.S. from short-term global warming will amount to $61.6 billion (1990 $), and the figure for long-term global warming will be $335.7 billion.

Climate change and natural ecosystems

Humanized landscapes and ecosystems to a certain extent can be adapted to rapid climate change through human action. Natural landscapes and ecosystems, however, have a more limited capacity to adapt to rapid changes in climate. On a geological time scale, plant and animal species have migrated and resorted themselves at a community level in response to significant climate changes on the North American continent. While the magnitude of climate change likely to occur from global warming is not unprecedented in geological time, the pace of

Table 5.1 Some potential ecological consequences of global warming

---

Vegetation
Northward 300–800 km shift of vegetation zones
Decline of plant populations with low dispersal rates
Decline of plant populations confronting human barriers to northward migration
Decline of tundra vegetation type
Vertical 500 m shift of vegetation zones in mountains
Reduction in vegetation ranges for upper elevations in mountains; decline of subalpine
  vegetation type
Increased fire frequency in western forests

Animals
Loss of species dependent on habitat fragments (e.g. Kirtland's warbler; Yellowstone
  grizzly bear)
Loss of shorebirds from disruption of migration timing
Loss of species in coastal areas of Florida vulnerable to sea level increases (Everglades
  mink, Florida panther, key deer, American crocodile, sea turtles)
Loss of butterfly species because of temperature changes

Marine ecosystems
Loss of sea ice and marine mammal habitat
Reduction of Arctic Ocean primary productivity
Up to 60 percent loss of coastal wetlands
Altered coastal upwelling patterns and reduced fish productivity, prey for California sea
  lions

Sources: Peters and Lovejoy (1992); Cline (1992).

change is. The impacts of rapid global warming on natural landscapes and eco-systems are difficult to predict but are likely to be substantial. A partial list of possible consequences is presented in Table 5.1.

Different species respond differently to climate change. Highly mobile species, like birds and large mammals, can, in the absence of barriers to migration, adapt to climate change simply by moving to more suitable habitats in more northerly latitudes. Less mobile species, such as small mammals and plants, may not be able to respond so readily to shifts in temperature regimes. For plants, temperature changes under global warming may be simply too rapid for migration. Warming of 3°C will shift vegetation zones northward in the temperate zone by 300–800 kilometers. Some temperature-sensitive plant species will simply die out in warmer latitudes and be unable to gain a foothold in cooler latitudes because of slow seed dispersal. As a consequence, species found in a relatively narrow latitudinal range may be threatened with extinction. Northern hardwood forest species such as sugar maple, yellow birch, northern hemlock, and beech may disappear from the U.S. Great Lakes area. Because of a slow dispersal rate, genotypes of beech needed for survival in a more northerly range may not arrive in time to assure survival of the species (Peters 1989; National Academy 1992: 576–581; Peters and Lovejoy 1992). Climate change does not bode well for U.S. prairie species confined to small, fragmented habitats because of massive agricultural land barriers to species migration (Peters 1989). The northerly movement of vegetation ranges will also result in a substantial range shrinkage for the most northerly tundra vegetation type (Peters and Lovejoy 1992).

The movement of vegetation zones will not only be in a northerly direction, but in mountainous landscape it will be upwards as well, by as much as 500 meters. Just as a northerly movement of vegetation zones squeezes out tundra, a vertical movement of vegetation zones shrinks high-elevation subalpine vegetation habitats. In many areas, the lower timberline will move upwards as well, shrinking the total area devoted to forests. A drier climate in western U.S. forests would also increase fire frequency, shifting forest age in the direction of youth and reducing old-growth type habitats (Romme and Turner 1991). The net result will be a reduction of species diversity in mountainous landscapes (Peters and Lovejoy 1992).

Changing climate regimes and landscape patterns will have significant impacts on animal species as well. The probable disappearance of jack pine stands under global warming from northern Michigan in the U.S. will probably mean the extinction of Kirtland's warbler, a species dependent on jack pine stands for nesting (Peters and Lovejoy 1992). Global warming and the upward migration of forest zones will reduce whitebark pine stands in the Yellowstone area, causing a decline in whitebark pinenuts, a critical food resource for the local grizzly population (Romme and Turner 1991). A shift in the climate regime in the direction of earlier spring warming in tundra habitats could result in migratory shorebirds arriving after the peak of insect food availability, reducing their reproductive potential. Temperature regime shifts will also be damaging to temperature-sensitive butterfly species. In Florida, a number of species, including the Florida panther and key deer, are currently squeezed by human development into coastal habitats that are likely to be inundated as a result of rising sea levels (Peters and Lovejoy 1992).

While terrestrial biota will be dramatically affected by global warming, those ecosystems most likely to be altered by warming are those found in a marine or coastal environment. Coastal wetlands are among the most biologically productive ecosystems, serving as nurseries for numerous marine and terrestrial species and as important habitats for migratory and shore birds. As much as one-half of all fish caught spend part of their life-cycle in coastal wetlands. Large areas of coastal wetlands have already been lost as a consequence of economic development, and much of the remaining wetlands are threatened by a sea level increase induced by greenhouse warming. Wetlands can keep pace with normal rates of sea level rise through sedimentation and peat formation. However, a greenhouse-induced sea level rise will likely exceed the ability of wetlands to keep up. Human barriers, such as coastal highways, in some cases will prevent the inland migration of wetlands as sea levels rise (Titus 1989; National Academy 1992: 584–591). A 1 meter rise in the sea level could cause a 30–70 percent loss of coastal wetlands.

Global warming will have other consequences as well for marine biota. Marine ecosystems are highly sensitive to temperature changes and temperature-induced changes in ocean currents. Shifts in ocean currents could alter patterns of upwelling that bring nutrients to the ocean surface and support algae blooms that serve as the food base for numerous fish populations. Because of shifts in upwelling patterns, California sea lion populations may lose critical fish resources near their rookeries. Slight increases in temperature can also disrupt coral reef ecosystems by causing bleaching of the coral. Coral exists in a symbiotic relationship with algae that appear to be highly temperature sensitive. Increases in air temperatures may compress the intertidal zone by causing the desiccation of organisms living at the high end of the zone (Titus 1989). Climate shifts may also reduce the volume of Arctic sea ice, reducing habitat for marine mammals, and alter Arctic upwelling patterns, reducing the production of phytoplankton, the primary food source for Arctic marine food webs (Peters and Lovejoy 1992).

In sum, global warming has the potential not only to do costly damage to human societies, but to significantly alter and harm natural landscapes and ecosystems. While human benefits frequently accrue from those natural landscapes subject to harm from global warming, they may be seen by many as having value in their own right. If they do, the problem of global warming is a serious matter not only for economic reasons, but for ethical reasons as well.

The effects of water pollution

While water pollution in prosperous industrialized countries is today less directly a human health problem than air pollution, water pollution problems, particularly those resulting from nonpoint emissions, nonetheless seriously threaten aquatic ecosystems in both the U.S. and U.K., as suggested by the data presented in Chapter 3. In particular, aquatic species top the list of those at risk of extinction in the U.S., and water pollution is partly the cause (Nature Conservancy 1996; Adler *et al.* 1993). The key water pollution problems that are substantially nonpoint in origin are suspended solids, reduced oxygen levels, excessive nutrients such as phosphorus and nitrogen, and pesticide concentrations.

The effects of water pollutants vary considerably, depending on the characteristics and flora and fauna of the receiving water body. Suspended solids from urban runoff, agriculture, and logging operations, for example, increase the turbidity of the water in both lakes and streams, but are a special problem in trout and salmon streams where such materials can plug up gravel spawning beds and inhibit fish reproduction (Welch 1992). Suspended solids in such streams can also inhibit feeding activity by trout and salmon, which visually stalk their prey. Suspended solids are also an indicator of other pollution problems because they are often carriers of toxic heavy metals, pesticides, pathogens, and nutrients (Meybeck *et al.* 1989: 99).

Fish such as salmon and trout are also susceptible to reduced oxygen levels that result from pollution emissions. As a consequence of oxygen consumption by bacteria attacking organic matter, the emissions of biochemical oxygen-demanding materials (BOD) from point or nonpoint sources can reduce the level of dissolved oxygen in the water, threatening fish that are intolerant of low oxygen levels. The effects of increased BOD differ for lakes and rivers. In rivers, stretches immediately downstream from the point of discharge will experience oxygen sag. That is, dissolved oxygen will decline with distance from the discharge as the organic matter is broken down. At some point downstream from the discharge, a minimum level of dissolved oxygen will be reached, and the oxygen level will recover as a consequence of absorption at the air–water interface. Fish and invertebrates that are intolerant of low oxygen levels will be killed or, if able, they will vacate the area. Only species, such as the carp, that are tolerant of low oxygen levels will remain. If the waters become anoxic (devoid of oxygen), bacterial processes will become anaerobic, and hydrogen sulfide gas will be given off. The rapidity of re-oxygenation will increase with the turbulence of the water and as the temperature of the water declines (Welch 1992).

The emission of BOD from point or nonpoint sources also contributes to oxygen depletion in lakes, although the more serious problem in most lakes is the BOD created by excessive algae blooms caused by nutrient enrichment. Point and nonpoint discharges contain both organic and inorganic nutrients that stimulate algae production. Runoff containing fertilizers directly provides inorganic nutrients to algae, such as phosphorus and nitrogen. Since phosphorus tends to be the limiting nutrient[2] in freshwater, biological productivity will increase as phosphorus emissions increase, and large blooms of algae can occur, especially in lakes where phosphorus loading is large relative to the size of the lake and to the rate at which it is flushed out. High phosphorus load in lakes will favor the production of blue-green algae in mid- to late summer, a plant type that is generally unpalatable to grazing aquatic organisms.[3] Mats of blue-green algae will form and ultimately die, and in the process consume oxygen. The result can be a depletion of oxygen in the lake waters, threatening fish populations (*ibid.*).

Most lakes in temperate climates stratify in the summer, with warmer layers of less dense water near the surface and colder denser layers at greater depths. The deeper waters in highly productive (eutrophic) lakes often become anoxic as a consequence of excessive bacterial action on large volumes of dead organic matter descending from the surface waters where algae are going through their cycle of life and death at a relatively high rate. Deep lakes, or lakes with limited nutrient input (oligotrophic), are less likely to face this problem because of low algal productivity. In the summer, cold-water fish, such as trout and other salmonids, favor the cooler deeper waters. However, if deeper waters are anoxic, then cold-water fish may be trapped in a wedge of water where oxygen is available but temperatures are excessive. The result may be the loss of cold-water fish species in eutrophic lakes (*ibid.*).

Over-enriched or eutrophic lakes generally experience a succession of algae, beginning in the spring with diatoms, followed in the early summer by greens, and in late summer by blue-greens. Diatoms and greens are subject to control by zooplankton grazers, but the blue-greens are not because they are filamentous and colonial, making them impossible for filter-feeding grazers to digest. Blue-greens not only are unpalatable to grazers, but may also be toxic and can cause swimmer's itch, and they are generally visually displeasing to the human eye. The loss of top predators in lakes from anoxic conditions may actually increase the early-season algae problem because of population explosions in small predators that feed on grazing zooplankton. Top predators normally control smaller fish that feed on zooplankton, permitting larger zooplankton populations and increased grazing. With less algal production, the succession process will be extended in time and less production of undesirable blue-greens will result (*ibid.*).

Even if phosphorus inputs are reduced because of the control of point and nonpoint sources, the recovery of eutrophic lakes may be slow because of phosphorus buildup in bottom sediments. Under conditions of low oxygen, phosphorus is released from bottom sediments, some of which will find its way to surface waters and become available to algae. Lake pollution problems in some cases thus may be difficult to reverse because phosphorus emissions accumulate (*ibid.*). In the U.S. 70 percent of a sample of 493 lakes were classified as eutrophic in a 1979 study, while 65 percent of a sample of 101 lakes in OECD countries were classified as eutrophic in a 1982 study (Meybeck *et al.* 1989: 115).

While nitrogen is not typically a limiting nutrient in freshwater, the buildup of nitrates in freshwater is nonetheless a matter of concern. Through the nitrification process, nitrate is transformed first to nitrite and eventually to nitrogen gas, completing the nitrogen cycle. At sufficiently high levels nitrate can be acutely toxic to human individuals, especially babies, and nitrates have been implicated as a cause of stomach cancer (*ibid.*: 126–127). While nitrate infrequently plays a role in freshwater eutrophication, it constitutes a significant threat to coastal and estuarine waters, where it is a limiting nutrient instead of phosphorus. Toxic algae blooms in coastal waters known as red tide may be occurring with greater frequency because of excess nitrogen enrichment (Stevens 1996: B5). The single largest source of nitrogen is agriculture. Between 1965 and 1981, the use of nitrogen fertilizer per hectare of land increased threefold in the U.S. and in the U.K. by a factor of two and one-half. Between 1970 and 1985, the concentration of nitrate in the Mississippi River increased more than threefold from an annual average of 0.36 mg per litre to 1.23 mg per litre, while concentrations approximately doubled between 1960 and 1980 in the River Thames (Meybeck *et al.* 1989: 127–129).

Pesticides

Although the use of pesticides leads to nonpoint water pollution problems, pesticides as such constitute a larger environmental threat that deserves separate treatment. DDT and other pesticides were once thought to be wondrous products, capable of controlling insect-borne diseases and fostering substantial increases in agricultural productivity. This view came under challenge with the publication of Rachel Carson's *Silent Spring* in 1962. The central message of the book is presented in a parable of a town where the normal signs of spring – the drone of insects, flowers blooming, and birds singing – fail to arrive, and where vegetation, wildlife, and even human beings mysteriously sicken and die. The purpose of the parable was to dramatize the potential impact of the increasing use of powerful pesticides (Carson 1962; Hynes 1989). Carson's goal was to carefully explain the serious consequences of pesticide use for the health of plants, animals, human beings, and ecosystems in terms understandable to the lay public. In doing so, she marshaled the best scientific evidence available to explain and support her position. Many of her conclusions have stood the test of time, and her book is probably responsible for the ultimate bans and restrictions placed on the use of some of the most persistent and dangerous pesticides such as DDT.[4] Although the organochlorine pesticides Carson wrote about have largely been withdrawn from use, their replacement, the organophosphate-based pesticides, have a higher acute toxicity and create serious problems of their own for human beings and other organisms (Pimentel *et al.* 1992).

The purpose of broad-spectrum pesticide applications is to kill insects that are a threat to crops or human health, suppress weeds that compete with crops or are otherwise viewed as undesirable, or control fungal diseases that can threaten crops or ornamental plants. The fundamental problem with such pesticides is that they are biocides, as Carson puts it, and have the potential to harm biotic organisms other than their intended victims. In sufficiently large doses, both the chlorinated hydrocarbon and organic phosphate insecticides are immediately toxic to human beings. Handlers of pesticides have suffered serious illnesses and even death from accidents. Each year approximately 67,000 nonfatal pesticide poisonings are reported in the U.S., and approximately 27 pesticide-related accidental fatalities occur (Pimentel *et al.* 1992). Exposure to high doses of insecticides has the capacity for disrupting the functioning of the human nervous system and has been linked to a variety of other health problems such as liver disease, high blood pressure, and sterility (Carson 1962; Pimentel and Perkins 1979: 102–107). Chronic human health problems associated with low-level exposure to pesticides include cancer, sterility, immune system dysfunctions, and neurological disorders. While less than 1 percent of all cancer cases each year in the U.S. are attributable to pesticides, this still amounts to 10,000 cases (Pimentel *et al.* 1992).

Pesticides are directly and indirectly responsible for harm to an array of nonhuman biotic organisms. Approximately 6–14 million fish are killed annually in the U.S. as the result of pesticides that either drift or leach into waterways, and this estimate is probably low because of difficulties in determining the size of fish kills. Although annual bird kills from pesticides are also difficult to estimate, they are no doubt substantial. Carbofuron alone is estimated to kill 1 to 2 million birds each year in the U.S., and use of diazinon at just three golf courses killed one-quarter of the wintering population of Atlantic brant geese. The total annual U.S. bird kill from pesticides may be as many as 67 million (*ibid.*).

Low-level pesticide exposure also has chronic effects for fish and wildlife. The chlorinated hydrocarbon insecticides, of which DDT is the most well known, are highly persistent in the natural environment, taking years to decompose. Because of their ability to dissolve in fatty substances, these pesticides have the capacity to bioaccumulate. While they may exist in very low concentrations at the base of the food chain, they may be found in much higher concentrations in the fatty tissue of animals farther up the food chain. The spraying of DDT in the U.S. to control the Dutch elm disease in the 1950s and 1960s resulted in high mortality among robins and other birds because of the accumulation of DDT in earthworms eaten by the birds. The bioaccumulation of DDT was found to be a cause of reproductive failure in eagles, peregrine falcons, and other birds because of egg-shell thinning (Brown 1978). Concentrations of DDT and other chlorinated hydrocarbons have been found in human as well as animal populations, although concentrations in the U.S. have been declining since many of these chemicals were banned or restricted in use in the early 1970s. The long-term health consequences of such concentrations are unknown. They can cause mutations in genetic material and the growth of cancerous cells. Because many of these chemicals are still in use outside the U.S., at a global level their concentrations are continuing to increase (Davies and Doon 1987).

Since the placing of restrictions on the use of chlorinated hydrocarbons, the popularity of organic phosphate insecticides has increased significantly. While they are acutely toxic and are implicated in fish and bird kills as described above, the big advantage of these insecticides is their lack of persistence. Birds, however, may suffer long-term negative health effects from exposure to organic phosphates, such as changes in behavior, cold tolerance, growth, and embryo development. Reptiles also suffer from applications of certain organic phosphates. Parathion is also poisonous to some fish species, salmonids in particular, and may have sublethal negative effects on fish health (Brown 1978). Low-level pesticide doses also kill sensitive fish fry, and may kill key food sources, such as insects and invertebrates, for fish (Pimentel *et al.* 1992).

A general problem with insecticides is their unintended effects on nontarget insects. For instance, the pesticide poisoning of honeybees and wild bees needed for pollination is a serious problem (*ibid.*). Frequently, predators and parasites of the pest insects will be eliminated because of susceptibility to the insecticide or because they are simply starved out. The pest insect will recover more rapidly than its predators or parasites and will achieve much greater population levels. Competitors of the pest may also experience population explosions and themselves become a pest. Insecticides can also harm the soil microfauna that is so important in nutrient cycling. The problem with broad-spectrum pesticides is that they fail to take account of the complexity of ecological interactions, both above and below ground (Brown 1978). The other problem with such pesticides is the ability of target pest species to develop resistance to pesticides through genetic selection. As a consequence, new pesticides must be under constant development, creating pressure to bring them into use before their environmental consequences are fully understood.

Agriculture itself is not free of problems from pesticide use. Animal poisonings and product contamination from pesticides are relatively common. Pesticide resistance and the destruction of beneficial parasites are continuing problems, as are crop losses from the drifting of pesticides to nontarget crops, improper doses, excess soil residues harmful to rotated crops, and crop destruction because of failure to meet regulatory residue requirements. Farmers also face the problem of well water contaminated by pesticides (Pimentel *et al*. 1992).

The decline in bird populations resulting from the use of DDT and similar persistent pesticides in the 1950s and 1960s was brought to swift public attention in the U.K., as it was in the U.S., and the use of such pesticides was restricted as a result. A continuing less dramatic but perhaps more far-reaching effect of pesticide use in the English countryside is a reduction in floristic species diversity. Because they are not selective, herbicides eliminate numerous wildflowers as well as noxious weeds from arable fields and meadows. As a consequence of indiscriminate application and effectiveness at relatively low levels, herbicides often eliminate plants at considerable distances from targeted farm fields. The disappearance of plant species because of herbicides has resulted in the decline of insect populations, especially butterflies, and in some instances bird populations have declined because of the reduced availability of certain insects (Green 1985: 87–89).

To summarize, the pesticide industry and pesticide use in both the U.S. and the U.K. grew rapidly after World War II through the 1970s. In the 1950s and 1960s pesticides were applied indiscriminately without much thought to their environmental consequences or effects on human health. Rachel Carson changed all that with the publication of her book, *Silent Spring*, the primary consequence of which was the banning of DDT use in the U.S., as well as restrictions and bans on the use of other chlorinated hydrocarbons. While significantly reducing dangers to human health and the environment, these changes did not totally eliminate them. Although DDT use was banned in the U.S., production for export and consumption overseas was not. Chlorinated hydrocarbons, such as DDT, are still finding their way into the U.S. from atmospheric deposition. The total global environmental load of such chemicals is still increasing as a result of continued use outside the U.S. This has manifested itself in continued increases of DDT and other chlorinated hydrocarbon concentrations in fatty tissues of marine mammals and birds since the oceans are the ultimate repository of waterborne chemicals. DDT residues in marine mammals have reached dangerous levels and may be inhibiting reproduction (Brown 1978). DDT and other chemical residues (PCBs and heavy metals) are posing a major threat to wildlife in the Great Lakes region and at numerous other locations throughout the world (Behm 1994). In the Great Lakes area, both DDT and PCB concentrations in the environment and in the milk of nursing mothers have dropped significantly since they were banned in the U.S., but environmental concentrations may be turning up again, possibly because of atmospheric deposition and seepage from toxic hot spots where sediments have been heavily contaminated (Schneider 1994). Although they do not persist in the environment, the organic phosphates that have become the insecticides of choice in the U.S. are nonetheless themselves highly toxic and cause extensive human health and environmental problems.

Conclusion

After considering the role of industrial life-cycles in environmental problems, one might jump to the conclusion that over time, environmental problems become disconnected from economic growth. Fossil fuel energy consumption in the U.S. appears to have entered a period of very slow growth, if not stability. Absent regulation, this suggests that environmental problems associated with fossil fuels would experience a significant retardation of growth. As we have seen, the emission of a number of air pollutants was actually reduced somewhat in the 1970s, 1980s, and 1990s under the force of regulation. All this has occurred while the U.S. economy has continued to grow, although at a reduced rate relative to the 1950s and 1960s.

If we take a longer view of the growth and development process, a rather different conclusion follows. The development of Midwestern agricultural areas in the nineteenth century permanently eliminated the tallgrass prairie and altered for all time the structure of the Great Lakes forest ecosystem. Even if agricultural production and land use in the Midwest declined substantially, the prairie ecosystem could not be easily restored. The results of agricultural settlement in the Midwest are permanent and irreversible. The loss of old-growth forests from timber harvesting to feed housing construction and suburbanization cannot be reversed for several hundred years. Even if there are no further emissions of greenhouse gases, the prospect of global warming remains. The length of time for the extra carbon that has accumulated in the atmosphere to be absorbed in the oceans or other sinks is uncertain, but probably is of the order of centuries. Even though regulations have been instituted and fossil fuel use has stopped growing at a very rapid rate in the U.S., significant air pollution problems remain. Similarly, urban and rural water pollution problems remain, although urban and rural growth has slowed somewhat and regulations have been put in place. Even though pesticide use has stopped growing, a legacy of DDT and other chlorinated hydrocarbons remains in the environment threatening human health and the health of wildlife populations.

The point of industrial life-cycle analysis is simple. Aggregate growth is driven by the creation of new technologies, new products, and new industries. Most, if not all, create new environmental problems. Consequently, as growth occurs and new industries are added, new kinds of environmental problems appear. Old environmental problems are often mitigated through regulation, but more often than not they do not entirely disappear. Once a new industry is created on the basis of new technologies and products, a strong vested interest results that benefits from the externalization of environmental costs. As will be discussed in detail in Chapter 6, such interests will often be strongly opposed to environmental regulation.

To repeat the central point, growth is fed by new industries that create new environmental problems. As a consequence, environmental change is a cumulative process related to aggregate economic growth through the addition of new kinds of industries. Some might argue that industries of the future, such as microelectronics, information processing, communications, and biotechnology, are likely to be more environmentally benign than industries of the past. Such a claim is purely speculative. Scenarios that suggest the opposite are equally possible. While the horrors suggested by the book *Jurassic Park* seem extreme, very little is really known about the possible consequences of genetic engineering. Even the information age may not be as environmentally innocuous as it seems. The ability to communicate vast amounts of information rapidly and cheaply could cause work to be detached from offices, and population to spread away from urban centers to remote areas of natural beauty, a phenomenon that is already occurring around the Yellowstone National Park in the U.S. This in turn could result in land use developments that infringe upon and fragment the few remaining intact natural ecosystems left on the North American continent. Whether such problems will occur remains to be seen, but at this point their possibility cannot be ruled out.

The point of describing the consequences of environmental decline here in some detail is not to provide the last word on the subject, nor is it to focus exclusively on the strictly human consequences. The point, rather, is to suggest that something beyond a strictly human material interest is lost as a consequence of environmental decline. Landscapes not dominated by human activity have a life of their own in the sense that they evolve and change through time along particular paths. The message of this and the previous chapter is that human economic activity significantly bends if not truncates these paths. Whether this matters is the subject of Chapter 7. First we must try to understand why the process of economic growth impinges upon the political process and prevents significant mitigation of environmental problems.

6

ECONOMIC GROWTH AND THE LIMITS OF ENVIRONMENTAL REGULATION

The roots of environmental problems, and the failure of environmental regulation, are deeply embedded in the processes that generate economic growth according to arguments and materials presented thus far. The logic of the basic argument presented to this point takes the following form: long-run economic growth relies on the creation of new industries and new forms of economic activity; these new forms of economic activity create new kinds of environmental problems; and new forms of economic activity foster vested political interests that oppose environmental regulation. Previous chapters have addressed the first two components of the argument; the purpose of this chapter will be to address the final component. If it is the case that the economic system automatically creates vested interests opposed to regulation, then one cannot be very optimistic that regulatory processes in their current form will be the answer to our environmental problems.

Vested interests and environmental regulation

The problem of political organization plays a key role in explaining the limited effectiveness of environmental regulation. In general, small groups with large per capita interests have much less difficulty organizing politically to pursue their interests than large groups with small per capita interest (Olson 1971). Consider a group of 10 businesses that stand to lose $10 million dollars apiece from environmental regulation, and a group of one million individuals who stand to gain $40 million collectively in reduced external costs from regulation. The loss per business from regulation is $1 million, while the gain per person is $40.

The business group is going to be relatively easy to organize. If a single business fails to voluntarily participate in an interest group, the total amount of interest group activity would be reduced by 10 percent, a significant amount. Consequently, each business will have a strong incentive to participate. Transactions costs in forming a voluntary political lobby against regulation will be relatively low.

The group of individual citizens to the contrary will have great difficulty organizing. The nonparticipation of any one individual in the group will reduce the total effort by only 0.0001 percent, a trivial amount. Hence, individuals will be tempted to act as free riders, hoping to benefit from group efforts while avoiding membership costs. Transactions cost for a joint agreement on voluntary participation will be very high. Environmental problems tend to affect very large numbers of individuals, while industries that externalize costs tend to be composed of relatively small numbers of businesses. Consequently, the opposition to regulation is likely to have an easier time organizing than the proponents of environmental regulation.

As already outlined, industries are born, grow rapidly, and experience a retardation of growth as they age. These same industries create new environmental problems that are usually dependent in some way on production levels. As such industries emerge and grow, they create benefiting vested industry interests – managers, workers, stockholders, customers, and local communities where production is located. Each industry, with its relatively small number of firms, forms a natural political interest group that can organize relatively easily to fight regulation. The economic growth process, which depends on new industries, thus creates vested political interests opposed to regulation.

Despite the large-number problem, well organized environmental groups have emerged and have become effective advocates of environmental regulation in the U.S. and other prosperous countries. In the U.S. these groups include the Audubon Society, Environmental Defense Fund, National Wildlife Federation, Sierra Club, and Wilderness Society. All major environmental lobbying organizations together had over three million members in 1990 (Mitchell *et al.* 1991). These groups have been very active in lobbying for environmental legislation since the 1960s.

Why have they been able to successfully organize in the face of free rider and large-number problems? Part of the reason may be the value orientation of the movement. Most in the movement see humanity as ethically responsible for the world's ecological integrity, and ultimately vulnerable, like all other species, to the harms that humans inflict upon nature (Rosenbaum 1991: 21). In effect, the value foundations of the movement are ethical. Both human beings, who are ultimately dependent on nature, and nature itself are seen as valuable in their own right and deserving of ethical concern (Booth 1994). Members of and contributors to environmental groups may see their actions as a moral obligation. If so, then the free rider problem no longer applies (Ingram and Mann 1989). Support of environmental groups is seen as an end in itself.

Substantial support for such groups emerged only after environmental problems were brought to significant public attention. Environmental issues served as the central example for Anthony Downs's influential model of the "issue-attention cycle." According to Downs (1972), social problems proceed through a five-stage cycle:

1   the "pre-problem stage" where a social issue has aroused the interests of experts or interest groups but has yet to attract much public attention;
2   the "alarmed discovery and euphoric enthusiasm" stage where dramatic events or crises bring the problem to the public's attention, creating widespread enthusiasm for solving the problem;

3   a "realization of the cost of significant progress" stage where public enthusiasm diminishes;
4   a gradual "decline in intense public interest" stage where costs are recognized, the public becomes bored with the problem, and media attention to the problem declines;
5   the "post-problem stage" where the problem is forced off center stage by new problems and moves into "a twilight realm of lesser attention or spasmodic recurrences of interest."

Downs did note the possibility that interest in environmental issues might persist at relatively high levels because they affect a relatively large proportion of the population, unlike many other issues.

Perhaps the single most important event in mobilizing the environmental movement and bringing environmental issues into Downs's stage 2 of "alarmed discovery" was the publication of Rachel Carson's *Silent Spring* in the 1960s, where the dangers of emitting toxins such as DDT into the natural environment were established in a manner that was at once eloquent and convincing, and yet frightening. With the publication of this book, greater interest in environmental regulation by key political leaders, and increasing media attention to environmental problems, public support in the U.S. for environmental preservation grew rapidly, peaking in the early 1970s (Bosso 1987: 115–120; Mitchell *et al.* 1991; Dunlap 1991).

Beginning in the mid-1970s, environmental issues were forced out of the limelight by the energy crisis and resulting economic problems and were moved to the latter stages of Downs's issue-attention cycle. However, U.S. public support for environmental issues grew in the 1980s with Reagan administration threats to turn back the regulatory clock and publicity from a lengthy list of newsworthy environmental disasters, such as Bhopal, Chernobyl, and Times Beach. By 1990, public support for environmental regulation in the U.S. had reached unprecedented levels, exceeding those achieved in the wake of Earth Day in 1970 (Dunlap 1991). Downs (1972) was right in suggesting that the environmental issue may prove to be the exception to the issue-attention cycle.

Nonetheless, the intensity of public support for solving environmental problems has never been very deep, except among a significant minority of the population. When asked an open-ended question about the most important problems facing the country, the most who have ever included the environment in their list has been 22 percent (Dunlap 1991). For most people, other problems, such as crime or threats to economic security, take precedence over the environment. When push comes to shove, for many people the economy comes first. This in all probability has permitted vested interests in the U.S. to limit and inhibit environmental regulations.

The combined economic and political cycle can now be summarized. Specific industries emerge and grow, creating new environmental problems. Inside interests, or, as Bosso (1987) calls them, subgovernments, rule the regulatory process in the early stages of industry development before environmental issues enter the glare of wide public awareness. Problems are quietly solved by concerned parties and a few affected politicians. When publicity brings environmental problems to broad public attention, new interests favoring regulation organize and win legislative and legal victories against industry interests. When the issues recede from public attention and concern, the newly organized environmental interest groups remain, but vested industry interests are able to recover, and regulatory stalemate results. The regulatory war continues, battles are won and lost, but the rate of real regulatory change slows dramatically. Evidence for this process is provided by the U.S. political history regarding air pollution, water pollution, and pesticide regulation as well as management of the national forests.

The U.S. Clean Air Act and resistance to regulation

The first serious attempt at air pollution control in the U.S. was manifested in the passage of the Clean Air Act Amendments of 1970, passed under the highly effective tutelage of Senator Edmund Muskie of Maine and pro-environment congressional staffers. The Natural Resources Defense Council and other environmental groups lobbied for passage of the Clean Air Act. Public opinion was strongly in favor of doing something about air pollution. Industry interest groups that had prevented the passage of clean air legislation in the past, such as the National Coal Association, leading auto makers, and the American Petroleum Institute, were shut out of the decision-making process by Muskie, and suffered a major defeat (Melnick 1983: 24–52). In the early 1970s, clean air and other environmental issues were at the peak of the "alarmed discovery and euphoric enthusiasm" stage of the Downsian issue-attention cycle.

As a consequence of intense public interest and support, environmentalists were successful in obtaining relatively stringent provisions in the Clean Air Act and were able to toughen regulations through legal action in the courts. Unlike past regulatory measures, specific standards and regulatory requirements were written directly into the legislation with the hope of avoiding domination or "capture" of the regulatory agency by industries being regulated (Ackerman and Hassler 1981: 1–12; Rosenbaum 1989). In the Clean Air Act, ambient standards for the purpose of protecting public health were set for sulfur oxides, particulates, carbon monoxide, ozone, nitrogen dioxide, and lead, and states were required to implement these standards. The EPA was charged with defining and enforcing emission standards for all new sources, and new motor vehicles were required to achieve a 90 percent reduction in emissions. Emissions limits were enforceable by both state and federal governments, and citizens were given the right to sue the EPA if provisions of the Act were not enforced. The Sierra Club successfully sued the EPA on the grounds that the agency was required by law to prevent any significant deterioration of air quality in addition to enforcing ambient standards (Tietenberg 1994: 229–295).

Despite a regulatory framework containing stringent measures to regulate air pollution, the goals of the Clean Air Act have yet to be met. Industries subject to regulation have found means to delay and limit measures to control emissions and reduce air pollution. This has been accomplished by getting Congress and the EPA to interpret Clean Air Act measures in a manner favorable to the economic interests of specific states and industries, by limiting the EPA enforcement budget, and by obtaining favorable regulatory rulings from local courts. Successful resistance to clean air regulations coincided with the fading of the air pollution issue from public attention in the 1970s. While public support for environmental cleanup recovered in the 1980s in the face of retrenchment in the Reagan years, it was not until 1990 that new air pollution measures were passed.

The prevention of significant deterioration (PSD) ruling obtained from the courts by the Sierra Club is one example of a measure weakened in the face of pressure from economic interests. A literal interpretation of PSD would mean that no new sources of air pollution would be allowed to locate in an area, even if ambient air quality standards were not violated, unless there were offsetting reductions in pollution from other sources. Such an interpretation of PSD would have inhibited economic growth, especially in sparsely settled western states where the air was relatively clean. Western states would not stand for this, and even the Sierra Club backed away from a strict interpretation of PSD, since the Club's main interest was protection of air quality in national parks and wilderness areas. A weakened version of PSD was instituted by the EPA and written into law by Congress, permitting states to establish their own zoning scheme where only Class I areas would be subject to a relatively strict PSD interpretation allowing for virtually no decrease in ambient air quality. Otherwise, new sources could locate in Class II or III PSD areas if they installed the best available control technology and if ambient concentrations of pollutants did not exceed predetermined limits. Ironically, heavily industrialized eastern states, facing substantial emissions control costs, supported PSD regulations because of their potential to inhibit competition from new production facilities in western states that could otherwise meet ambient standards at relatively low costs (Melnick 1983: 71–112).

Another example of bending regulations to the interests of a particular industry occurred in the establishment of new source performance standards for coal-fired electric utilities. The lowest-cost and most effective method for reducing emissions from coal-fired plants was to switch sources from eastern high-sulfur coal mines to western low-sulfur coal. This, however, meant a reduction in use of eastern coal and shutdowns of eastern mines. The alternative was to require the installation of costly scrubbers to remove sulfur from powerplant emissions. Scrubbers in the 1970s were based on relatively new technologies and were not as effective as using low-sulfur coal. Under pressure from the eastern coal industry, the EPA required the use of scrubbers. Given that scrubbers were required, utilities found it cheaper to buy local high-sulfur coal, rather than imported low-sulfur western coal. As a result, sulfur emissions were greater than otherwise, and the cost of control was higher than otherwise (Ackerman and Hassler 1981).

Congress and presidential administrations in formulating and implementing air pollution control regulations faced strong, diametrically opposed interests.

Environmental groups pressed for strong air pollution regulations and rigorous enforcement procedures, while affected industries sought limitations on regulations and delays of their implementation. In the end, Congress and presidential administrations balanced the interests of these two groups by initially passing strict regulations but by subsequently allocating limited funds to the EPA for enforcement and by providing deadline extensions. The EPA lacked adequate staff resources in the 1970s to come anywhere near implementing the Clean Air Act under the original deadlines (Melnick 1983: 48, 168). In the early 1980s, the EPA budget for all its activities was used as a tool by the Reagan administration to cut regulatory efforts (Bartlett 1984). In 1974 and again in 1977, Congress extended the deadline for motor vehicle emission standards and has repeatedly extended deadlines in meeting ambient air quality standards for nonattainment areas. Given the importance of the auto industry in the aggregate economy, Congress had but little choice in extending the deadline, particularly in a climate of increasing concern over energy issues and economic stagnation (Melnick 1983: 35; Tietenberg 1994: 276–277). Deadline extensions continued in the 1980s for both motor vehicle regulations and State Implementation Plans (SIPs) to meet ambient air quality standards (Rosenbaum 1991: 180–182).

The combination of limited budgets for enforcement and courts friendly to local polluters created a serious problem for the EPA in implementation of the Clean Air Act. The goal of the EPA was to institute uniform emission standards for comparable sources. Federal District Courts looked upon pollution control quite differently, taking into consideration the economic impact of control measures on the local community. The concern of the courts was the local impact, not whether standards were uniformly applied. Consequently, regulations required by courts varied substantially from case to case (Melnick 1983: 193–238).

Because of limited enforcement resources, the EPA had to select its court cases very carefully for maximum impact. Also, the EPA had strong incentives to settle out of court or to negotiate enforcement orders that often involved variances in meeting deadlines. Polluters knew they could put off regulations for years by simply stalling. Consequently, the EPA often had little choice but to accept deals that involved relatively lenient interpretations of regulations. Environmental groups lacked the resources to fight hundreds of polluters in local courts. Industries could thus delay and weaken regulation by simply stalling and waiting until they were brought to court, or by negotiating a favorable deal with the EPA (Melnick 1983: 155–238).

In sum, environmentalists succeeded in obtaining relatively strict regulations for air quality from both Congress and the courts at a point of high public concern in the Downsian issue-attention cycle. However, once public attention turned to other issues, such as the energy crisis in the 1970s and economic problems in the 1980s, industry interests were able to turn some of these regulations to their advantage, to extract delays from Congress, and to take advantage of the EPA's limited enforcement budget and the friendliness of local courts to weaken and forestall air pollution regulations.

Resistance to U.S. water pollution regulation

The U.S. Clean Water Act of 1972 was approved over a presidential veto in the same climate of environmental enthusiasm that brought forth the Clean Air Act. As with the Clean Air Act, Senator Edmund Muskie was a pivotal figure in the passage of the Clean Water Act (Adler *et al.* 1993: 5–12). With the conflagration of pollutants floating in the surface layer of the Cuyahoga River and other reports of serious water pollution problems, the issue of water quality was at the peak of the issue-attention cycle in the early 1970s.

The Clean Water Act was even more ambitious than the Clean Air Act, calling for the total elimination of pollution emissions into navigable waters by 1985. In the interim, all waters were to be swimmable and fishable by 1983. The goals of the Clean Water Act were to be met by a system of technology-based emission standards augmented by state-level water quality standards and a system of emission permits. All point sources of pollutants were required to apply for emission permits. To get permits, municipal sewage treatment plants were required to undertake secondary treatment of their sewage flows by 1977, while industrial sources were required to meet emission standards based on the "best practicable control technology" (BPT). By 1983 industrial sources were required to meet emission limits based on more stringent "best conventional technology" (BCT) for pollutants such as suspended solids and nutrients and "best available technology" (BAT) for toxins.[1] To reach the zero discharge goal, the EPA was to update and tighten the standards periodically and through technology forcing achieve the final target of zero discharge (Tietenberg 1994; Goodstein 1995).

Under the 1972 Clean Water Act, the focus of attention shifted from a decentralized system of ambient water quality standards determined by states, to nationally determined emission standards. Nonetheless, where state-determined ambient water quality standards are violated as a result of pollutant outflows, permit requirements can be more stringent than the Clean Water Act technology-based emission standards (Adler *et al.* 1993; Goodstein 1995). States were required by the earlier 1965 Water Pollution Control Act to categorize their surface waters according to use, set ambient water quality standards, and to devise plans to meet those standards. The ambient standards approach originating in the 1965 Act continues to be a part of water quality law, but it has not been implemented very effectively and has not been the central focus of water pollution control policy (Adler *et al.* 1993: 158–164).

The regulatory process set in motion by the Clean Water Act thus involved two critical steps. First, the EPA was to write the technology-based standards for broad industry categories. The purpose of uniform standards within industries was to create a level playing field, so that no individual polluter would have a unique cost advantage. Second, permits were issued to individual businesses with emission limits determined by the technology-based standards. The permitting process was delegated to the states (33 in total), except where states lacked adequate administrative institutions (Adler *et al.* 1993; Goodstein 1995).

Industries and businesses have resisted implementation of clean water regulations, both at the rule-writing stage for emission standards and at the permit issuance and enforcement stage. Industries initially took the EPA to court on the basis of procedural challenges, forcing it to slow down its rule-writing process (Wenner 1989). Industries then challenged the EPA in court on the substance of its rules (*ibid.*). Court challenges have contributed to the relatively slow pace at which the EPA has written BAT/BCT regulations. It took until 1988 to complete effluent guidelines for 51 industries, well beyond original target dates, and at that time it still had 22 new and revised guidelines to write (Goodstein 1995: 221; Adler *et al.* 1993: 142–143). The process of moving from the older less stringent BPT standards to the new BAT/BCT standards has been relatively slow, with only one in three permit holders operating under a BAT/BCT standard as of 1991 (Adler *et al.* 1993: 141).

The permitting process itself has also been slow and subject to relatively weak enforcement. While over 64,000 permits have been issued, as many as 10,000 point sources may still lack permits. Budget cuts in the 1980s at both the state and the federal level have slowed both the rule-writing and the permitting process (Adler *et al.* 1993: 151; Ingram and Mann 1984: 256–257). As with other environmental legislation, Congress writes tough laws but then is reluctant to allocate sufficient funds for their full implementation. The Clean Water Act requires that permits be issued for more than a five-year period. Permit renewal affords an opportunity to update and tighten standards, an opportunity that has largely been forgone. Because of a permit renewal backlog, permits have been automatically extended without review, leaving outdated permit requirements in place for many dischargers (Adler *et al.* 1993: 158).

Enforcement of permit requirements has been relatively limited in scope, possibly because of inadequate enforcement budgets and perhaps because of political pressure. A study of EPA enforcement practices found that they rely heavily on informal enforcement actions, such as a simple comment on violations, a telephone call, an enforcement notice, or a notice of violation. Very seldom does the EPA resort to civil or criminal court actions in the enforcement of permit requirements. The study suggests that EPA personnel in the West and Midwest will not undertake enforcement action at all unless a very serious violation of the law has occurred (Hunter and Waterman 1992). Even when court actions are undertaken and are successful, fines and prison terms for criminal violations are not very severe (Adler *et al.* 1993: 168). The lack of EPA enforcement may have fueled an increase in citizen suits in the 1980s against private industry for Clean Water Act violations (Schwartz and Hackett 1984).

The regulation of urban and industrial storm water has also been plagued by resistance and delays. While the Clean Water Act recognizes storm water as a point source of pollution, the EPA has been reluctant to write regulations because of the vast number of outfalls. Nonetheless, with prodding from court suits, the EPA wrote storm water regulations only to have them challenged in court by industries and cities as too burdensome. Even though Congress put the EPA on a strict schedule for writing storm water emission guidelines, the process of writing storm water regulations had yet to be completed as of 1992 (Adler *et al.* 1993: 151–154).

The largest remaining source of water pollutants, nonpoint rural runoff, remains to be effectively addressed by the EPA. The 1972 Clean Water Act contained language in section 208 requiring that nonpoint pollution problems be addressed. A relatively large number of watershed nonpoint control plans were formulated at the state and regional level in the 1970s, but most were shelved in the 1980s because of inadequate funding, jurisdictional conflicts, and poor management by the EPA. The 1987 Clean Water Act Amendments again addressed the nonpoint problem, requiring states to implement nonpoint control programs. However, a lack of funding has been a principal barrier to implementing the 1987 nonpoint program, and the EPA has simply not enforced requirements of the law (Adler *et al.* 1993: 171–191).

In the end, it is not too surprising that a nonpoint program has been slow in coming. Because the writing of enforceable emission standards for diffuse nonpoint sources is virtually impossible, land use controls in some form are required to reduce polluted runoff. Land use regulations run against the grain of rural property rights traditions and are anathema to farmers and other rural landowners. Powerful agricultural property interests are strongly opposed to the imposition of any kind of land use regulations. The few successful nonpoint programs in existence have relied on voluntary landowner compliance and significant subsidization of capital costs for changing land use practices (Adler *et al.* 1993: 185–188). A successful nonpoint program will require substantially more funds than are currently allocated.

Resistance to pesticide regulation

The one issue that mobilized the environmental movement in the U.S. more than any other was the question of pesticides. The watershed event for the pesticides issue, and the environmental movement, was the publication of Rachel Carson's *Silent Spring*. Carson's book not only revealed the dangers of pesticides in terms that the lay public could easily understand, but also provided an alternative framework for evaluating environmental issues rooted in the science of ecology. This framework, the "ecological approach," suggested that all living things, including human beings, form a web of interdependencies and that this web was subject to disruption by the excesses of industrial progress.

Silent Spring marked the beginning of the "alarmed discovery" phase of the pesticide issue-attention cycle. Carson found the smoking gun needed to mobilize media attention and public concern – bird deaths and reproductive failures in raptors caused by pesticides. In the pre-problem phase of the pesticides issue-attention cycle, pesticide regulation was under the control of a "subgovernment," as Bosso (1987) calls it, composed of the chemical industry, agriculture, the U.S. Department of Agriculture, and key members of Congress. This subgovernment quietly negotiated and formulated pesticide policy. The product of their efforts was the passage of the Federal Insecticide, Fungicide, and Rodenticide Act (FIFRA) in 1947. Farmers wanted to be assured that insecticides were unadulterated, and the industry wanted fly-by-night operators screened out. As a result, the original FIFRA was little more than a truth-in-labeling law. Registration of new pesticides was required before introduction, but testing was not (Bosso 1987: 45–60).

In the 1950s and 1960s, growth of pesticide consumption in the U.S. was explosive (Pimentel *et al.* 1991). Farm policy that placed lands in reserve to avoid surpluses resulted in farmers pushing for maximum yields on nonreserve lands and unwittingly encouraged increased pesticide use for the purpose of pushing up production levels (Bosso 1987: 29). Extensive use of pesticides was also undertaken by the government in pest eradication programs (*ibid.*: 79–90). Pesticides were viewed as miracle chemicals, essential to a prosperous and growing agricultural sector. In the 1950s, voices of opposition were overpowered by advocates of the pesticides paradigm who saw chemicals as the centerpiece of an emergent industrial agriculture.

While Rachel Carson was the single most powerful force in bringing the pesticides issue to public attention, it was large-scale pest eradication efforts by the federal government that provided the most convincing evidence of harm to wildlife (*ibid.*: 79–108). Attempts to eradicate gypsy moths, fire ants, and other pests with large-scale spraying raised public health concerns and brought complaints about crop damage, fish kills, and increased bird mortality. The National Audubon Society membership were shaken by what they saw in the wake of spraying, and the Society was transformed into a political force opposed to damaging pesticide use. With the publication of three articles in the *New Yorker* in 1962 on the pesticides question, and the subsequent publication of *Silent Spring*, pesticides became an issue of broad public concern. Industry attacks on Carson's integrity as a scientist backfired, garnering public sympathy for her and increased support for her position (*ibid.*: 115–120).

A wave of public support for restricting pesticide use and for environmental regulation in general, resulted in significant revisions of FIFRA, a transfer of pesticides regulation from the U.S. Department of Agriculture (USDA) to the newly formed Environmental Protection Agency (EPA), and the cancellation of registration for DDT and other organochlorine pesticides that persist in the environment for lengthy periods of time. As a consequence of these cancellations, the volume of pesticide use declined significantly. This was less of a blow to the pesticides industry than it may seem, because many pests were becoming resistant to DDT anyway and 79 percent of DDT production was exported and was thus not subject to regulation. The result has been a greater reliance on new, less persistent but more specialized pesticides. The new products, however, tend to be more highly toxic (*ibid.*: 143–177).

By the mid-1970s, the pesticides issue lost public visibility and became the purview of experts and interest groups. Although the old pesticides subgovernment was dead, the industry was able to regain some of its influence in Congress and the regulatory process, helped by the Reagan administration anti-regulatory phi-losophy (*ibid*.: 178–233). While environmental groups made limited gains in their goal of restricting pesticide use, by 1986 only 16 of some 600 active ingre-dients requiring re-registration under the 1972 amendments to FIFRA had been fully tested, and the health and environmental effects of some 40,000 products on the market remained largely unknown (Bosso 1988; Nownes 1991). Even though environmental groups remain heavily involved in lobbying efforts to accelerate pesticide regulation, the industry has been able to exercise veto power over many changes in the regulatory process inimical to its interests.

U.S. national forest policy and timber exploitation

Unlike privately owned industries that degrade the environment through emis-sions of pollutants, the national forests are in public hands and thus managed under governmental control. This does not mean, however, that management of the national forests has necessarily been environmentally benign. As noted in Chapter 4, suburban expansion in the 1950s and 1960s increased the demand for timber, a significant portion of which was fulfilled by increased harvesting of virgin timber from the national forests. The U.S. Forest Service was thus highly responsive to demands for increased timber harvesting, but it was resistant to growing demands for wilderness preservation in areas that included marketable timber stands. Why did the Forest Service express a stronger interest in forest exploitation than forest ecosystem preservation?

Three views of U.S. Forest Service behavior have been offered by different observers and include the sustaining of fundamental organizational value com-mitments, arbitrating compromises between contending interest groups, and budget maximization.

The Forest Service's professed value commitments were founded historically on the notion that private sector timber harvesting practices would ultimately lead to a "timber famine" preventable only by adopting the principles of sus-tained yield forestry on national forest lands under the management of a scientifi-cally trained professional elite. Gifford Pinchot, the principal promoter and founding head of the Forest Service, was trained in European forest management princi-ples and imparted the values of sustained yield forestry to the agency. The spe-cific goals the Forest Service derived from the Pinchot tradition are to manage the national forests for the purpose of producing a steady flow of wood fiber for the consuming public, to maintain a stable wood products industry, and to promote the stability of local communities economically dependent on wood products (Nelson 1985). This value orientation is sustained by a variety of internal bureau-cratic mechanisms and rules according to Ben Twight (1983), a principal advo-cate of the value commitment view, as well as by recruitment of personnel from forestry schools that internalize the Forest Service's value commitment. Twight argues further that the Forest Service is willing to sacrifice portions of its juris-dictional domain when necessary, rather than give up its value commitment, and that it is largely insulated from the external influence of interest groups that have values and goals counter to its own.

An alternative view is that the Forest Service is responsive to client group interests in order to sustain political support for Forest Service activities. In the absence of contending interests over the use of national forest resources, the Forest Service would essentially be a client of the wood products industry. The Forest Service and the timber industry would constitute a subgovernment, as Bosso (1987) defines it. However, because of growing conflict between wilderness preservationists and wood products industry groups, the Forest Service, according to the proponents of this view, has become essentially an arbitrator forging compromises over land use policy between conflicting groups. The Forest Service has thus avoided capture by any particular interest group and can play one group off against another to limit the influence of any individual group (Culhane 1981).

A third view is that the Forest Service behaves in a manner that will result in the maximization of the size of its budget. It will allocate lands and carry out timber harvesting decisions in such a way as to bring the largest possible budget. Proponents of this view argue that policies such as timber harvesting on the basis of sustained yield can be explained as the result of budget maximization. Under the principle of sustained yield forestry, timber harvesting can be increased only by increasing the overall productivity of a forest through improved silviculture practices that require added budgetary expenditures (Johnson 1985; O'Toole 1988: 144). The Forest Service would thus be in a position to trade increases in the allowable timber harvest based on sustained yield for increases in its budget. Oversight committees for government agencies, such as the Forest Service, are often dominated by members of Congress whose constituents benefit from agency output. Consequently, oversight committees for the Forest Service would generally favor budget increases that expand timber harvesting and timber industry employment. Sustained yield principles are therefore consistent with the pursuit of higher budgets.

Because of the strong emphasis the Forest Service has placed on timber harvesting over other goals, such as wilderness preservation and the protection of natural plant and wildlife habitats, it is hard to argue that it serves as an arbitrator between conflicting interests. Compelling evidence has been presented by Randal O'Toole (1988) that the Forest Service operates in a fashion that maximizes its budget. He points out that various laws allow the Forest Service to retain a portion of timber sales revenues for brush disposal, reforestation, and timber salvage sales (O'Toole 1988: 112). O'Toole notes that because of these budgetary kickbacks, the Forest Service has a strong incentive to undertake timber sales that cost more than they generate in revenues, and he finds that many national forests undertake below-cost timber sales, a practice that is consistent with budget maximization (O'Toole 1988: 112–171). Below-cost timber sales are possible because timber sale preparation costs and road engineering costs are not charged against timber sale revenues, but are funded through budget allocations.

If indeed the Forest Service attempts to maximize its budget, it will have little interest in establishing wilderness areas in order to protect natural and old-growth forest habitats. Wilderness generates little in budgetary revenues. The historical record clearly suggests substantial resistance by the Forest Service to wilderness preservation (Booth 1994; O'Toole 1988: 160–166). In its two studies of roadless areas, RARE I and RARE II, the Forest Service was reluctant to allocate areas with significant exploitable timber to a wilderness designation. For the RARE II study published in 1979 by the Forest Service, only 16 percent of roadless areas in western Oregon and Washington were given a wilderness designation, while approximately 72 percent were designated non-wilderness where timber harvesting would be permitted. Under pressure from wilderness advocacy groups, the proportion of western Oregon and Washington roadless area that was actually designated wilderness by Congress was more than double the original assignment by the Forest Service (Booth 1994: 159–161). The Forest Service has also strongly resisted policies to protect spotted owl habitat in the Pacific Northwest (Booth 1994). Only federal court rulings that halted timber harvests were able to get the Forest Service to take spotted owl habitat preservation seriously.

Advocates of wilderness have managed to win protection for some natural forest habitats, although initially much of this was confined to higher elevations that are less biotically diverse and contain little valuable timber. In recent years wilderness advocates have been more successful in winning protection for lowland old growth, although there isn't much left to protect. Their biggest victory has been a dramatic reduction in old-growth logging in the Pacific Northwest, resulting from a lawsuit to protect the habitat of the endangered spotted owl. This lawsuit was promulgated under the wildlife protection requirements of the National Forest Management Act of 1976, and was later supported under the Endangered Species Act once the spotted owl was declared by the U.S. Fish and Wildlife Service to be threatened (Sher and Stahl 1990; Booth 1994).

Unlike other environmental issues, wilderness and old-growth forest protection has not received as much public attention and does not appear to fit the Downsian issue-attention cycle explanatory scheme. Rather, the wilderness movement has been driven since the 1950s by a comparatively small group of highly committed grass roots activists and outdoor organizations, such as the Sierra Club and the Wilderness Society, which have lobbied hard in Congress to bring about wilderness protection (Roth 1984; Allin 1982). The organizational free rider problem has apparently been overcome by these groups as a consequence of wilderness and ecosystem preservation being viewed by supporters as a moral quest (Booth 1984: 173–221). The act of contributing resources and effort is probably seen by many who belong to wilderness preservation groups as the fulfillment of an ethical commitment.

Just like private industry, the U.S. Forest Service went through a period of rapid expansion in its activities, followed by a period of growth retardation. And just like private industry, the Forest Service politically resisted efforts to curtail its activities in the name of environmental protection. Wilderness preservation groups experienced some success in curtailing Forest Service timber sales and preserving natural forest habitats, but a significant decline in old-growth forest stands has nonetheless occurred. Forest Service behavior fits the Schumpeterian cycle, and, although the Downsian model of political behavior doesn't seem to apply, political resistance to protecting the natural environment is clearly part of the story.

Resurgence of the U.S. environmental movement

In reaction to the anti-environmentalism of the Reagan administration and publicity indicating continued environmental deterioration, public sentiment in favor of more extensive environmental regulation in the U.S. reached a new high by 1988 (Dunlap 1991). Up to 1986, environmental and pesticide industry interests were deadlocked over reforms to FIFRA. In that year a coalition of environmentalists and industry representatives worked out a compromise on FIFRA reforms. Industry was worried about recent bad publicity and growing environmental sentiment. It was not until 1988, however, that Congress finally took the initiative and passed a new FIFRA amendment setting targets for re-registration of pesticide ingredients (Nownes 1991).

In 1990, support for new clean air measures from the new "environmental President," including the control of the emission of air toxins and of acid rain, resulted in the passage of the 1990 Clean Air Act amendments. Attempts to reform the Clean Air Act had languished in the 1980s because of strong opposition by the Reagan administration and business interests to increased regulation. In the 1987 election, presidential candidate Bush recognized growing public sentiment for reform and embraced environmentalism. President Bush's environmentalism, however, was short-lived, and he soon drew the line against further regulation of industry, and opposed international measures to curb CO_2 emissions and global warming (Vig 1994; Kraft 1994). As Anthony Downs (1972) noted, the environmental issue may be the exception to the standard issue-attention cycle because it affects a wide cross-section of the population. Problems of this nature are able to recapture the public concern from time to time. However, with economic issues receiving increasing attention in the early 1990s, environmental issues have again faded from public attention.

Environmental regulation in the U.K. and the Schumpeterian cycle

The history of environmental regulation and activism in the U.K. is remarkable for its contrasts to the U.S. experience. The regulatory process in the U.S. features intense conflict between the regulators and businesses subject to environmental regulation, heavy involvement by environmental groups, and extensive public mistrust of business motives relating to environmental issues. These patterns are almost entirely reversed in the U.K., at least for air and water pollution regulation. Until very recently, the U.K. regulatory process has been character-ized by a high degree of cooperation between government regulators and busi-nesses, limited involvement by environmental organizations, and a presumption by the public that businesses will behave in a socially responsible manner. With the exception of the killer smog of 1952 and certain "countryside" issues, the Downsian issue-attention cycle does not seem to accurately describe the politics of regulation in the U.K., at least prior to the 1980s and 1990s.

Nonetheless, the Schumpeterian cycle of industry creation fostering vested interests opposed to economically threatening environmental regulation still serves as a reasonable description of the U.K. regulatory process. Regulators have in-deed pushed industries to clean up the worst of their pollution problems, but they have been reluctant to require industry to take on costly emission control mea-sures, particularly for pollutants that cause problems beyond Britain's borders or problems that are not immediately visible to the public. Pollution control in the U.K. historically has been left to the quiet management of a subgovernment com-posed of regulators and industries. In this setting, regulators have been reluctant to press industries for the rapid adoption of stringent pollution control measures, as we will see in the discussion below.

In recent years, however, U.K. environmental policy has been transformed by European Community politics. The emergence of the Green Party as a major political force in Germany, and the growing influence of the European Commu-nity together altered the environmental policy dynamic in the U.K. beginning in mid-1980. While U.K. environmental groups and the public at large have given only limited attention to air pollution issues, at a larger European level the opera-tion of the Downsian issue-attention cycle is more apparent, particularly on the acid rain question. U.K. environmental groups have instead focused their ener-gies on countryside preservation issues, although the political power of the farm lobby and the exclusion of agriculture from the land use planning process have been an inhibiting force. These points require further elaboration and justifica-tion, a task to which we now turn.

The politics of air pollution regulation in the U.K.

As anyone who has read Charles Dickens knows, air pollution in the form of smoke, particularly in London, was a longstanding problem in the U.K., as old as the use of coal for industry and the domestic fire. It was not only the growth of industry that brought forth the London smogs, but the English attachment to the hearth and its open fire as well (Brimblecombe 1987: 63–92). Efforts to address air pollution prob-lems in the U.K. are also longstanding (*ibid.*: 92–106). A Smoke Nuisance Abate-ment Act applying to the London area was passed in 1853, requiring furnaces and steam boats to have smoke consumption devices, although polluters could avoid pen-alties if they used the "best practicable means" to abate smoke (Ashby and Anderson 1981: 15–19). The concept of "best practicable means" was also embodied in the Alkali Act of 1874, an extension of the 1863 Alkali Works Regulation Bill which

sought to regulate hydrochloric acid emitted in the process of producing sodium carbonate used in soap, glass, and textiles (*ibid.*: 20–43). To enforce the Bill, the Alkali
Inspectorate was appointed and became the forerunner of modern environmental protection agencies. Although its regulatory responsibilities were expanded to include
noxious fumes generated by other industries, the Inspectorate failed to gain control
over smoke pollution from industry until after the 1952 killer smog and passage of
the Clean Air Bill in 1956. Local authorities could proceed against emitters of black
smoke under the Public Health Act of 1875, but violators could avoid legal consequences by employing the best practicable means to abate emissions. Because of this
escape clause and lax enforcement, little progress was made in controlling smoke
pollution until the 1950s (*ibid.*: 44–123). While the Alkali Inspectorate was reasonably effective in using moral suasion to achieve reductions in noxious fumes in the
late nineteenth and earlier twentieth centuries, the industrial revolution was built on
coal and smoke, and a stricter, more confrontational approach to regulation threatening to industrial activity was not forthcoming, nor were English households ready to
give up their coal fires. The Smoke Abatement Society, an organization devoted to
reducing smoke pollution, came into existence in 1899 but could not overcome the
problem of public apathy until the 1952 London smog.

Air pollution regulation up to the 1950s was left in the hands of local authorities, the Alkali Inspectorate, and industry, and kept out of public view. In terms of
Downs's issue-attention cycle, air pollution was in the "pre-problem stage" where
it was dealt with by subgovernments of immediately interested parties. The 1952
London smog with its approximately 4,000 excess deaths brought air pollution
into the "alarmed discovery" stage and was followed by the Clean Air Bill containing many of the provisions supported by the National Society for Clean Air,
the successor of the earlier Smoke Abatement Society (*ibid.*: 104–119). As discussed in Chapters 3 and 5, the smoke pollution problem disappeared soon after
this, partly as the result of legislation, but partly as the result of fortuitous changes
in home heating fuels and technologies. In the 1970s and early 1980s, the air
pollution issue fell back into subgovernment hands, with the Alkali Inspectorate
relying on persuasion, education, and steady pressure to get industries to restrict
emissions of smoke and sulfur dioxide. While the Inspectorate has been accused
of being too friendly to industry, it has met with some success, judging by the
large sums spent on pollution control measures by industry (*ibid.*: 140). The
specifics of air pollution regulation agreements have been kept out of the public
view, and the British environmental lobby has given little attention to air pollution issues (McCormick 1991: 91–95).

While air pollution has not been a burning public issue inside the U.K., it has
elsewhere in Europe. By 1972 researchers in Sweden concluded that precipitation over large areas of Europe was unusually acidic and that acid rain was damaging lakes and forests. Over the next decade evidence mounted that acid pollutants
were being transported long distances, with up to half of Britain's sulfur dioxide
emissions being exported to other European countries. According to this evidence, Norway and Sweden were respectively receiving 92 and 82 percent of

their acid deposition from other countries, while the U.K. was receiving only 20 percent from external sources. As might be expected, the importing countries expressed much more concern about the acid rain problem than the exporters, at least initially. The Scandinavian countries took the lead in calling for reduced acid emissions, while the acid exporters, the U.K. and Germany in particular, viewed the problem with less urgency (Park 1987: 158–169).

The turning point on the acid rain issue came in 1982 when Germany did an about-face and decided to embrace a call for reducing emissions by at least 30 percent. The Germans by this time had discovered that their own beloved Black Forest was suffering tree deaths from acid rain, and the popularity of the environmentally oriented Green Party pushed the German administration in a direction more friendly to environmental issues (McCormick 1991:140–147; Boehmer-Christiansen and Skea 1991: 185–204). European environmental groups began to mount campaigns bringing attention to the acid rain issue and public awareness began to increase (Park 1987: 173–176). Both France and Germany announced programs to reduce emissions unilaterally by 50 percent. In the meantime the U.K. government (along with the U.S.) resisted membership in the so-called 30 percent club that included countries agreeing to at least that amount of emissions reductions.

In the U.K. opposition to acid pollution controls came primarily from Britain's largest electricity producer, the state-owned Central Electricity Generating Board. The Board was the central source of research on acid rain issues in Britain and it was unwilling to concede that a link existed between sulfur emissions and acid rain damage. Controls on sulfur emissions would be costly and result in substantial electricity rate increases. The government of Prime Minister Margaret Thatcher wanted to sell and privatize electricity production and desired more generally to reduce regulation. Increased regulation and regulatory costs were not only contrary to the government's free market philosophy, but would reduce the amount private investors would be willing to pay the government for government-owned electric production facilities (McCormick 1991:140–147; Boehmer-Christiansen and Skea 1991: 205–220).

In 1987 the European Community issued a directive on large-plant combustion emissions, and in 1988 the Thatcher administration reversed course, approving the directive and committing the U.K. to a 60 percent reduction in emissions by 2003. By this time evidence of acid damage in the U.K. was growing, domestic environmental groups such as the Friends of the Earth were becoming increasingly active on the issue, a House of Commons Select Committee had issued a report condemning past policy on acid rain, the government needed to clarify future regulatory requirements in order to successfully privatize electricity production, and Britain was the last European holdout on controlling acid emissions. Finally, the U.K. could hardly go against European Community directives if it wanted to maintain its standing as a major player in the Europeanization process (McCormick 1991: 140–147; Boehmer-Christiansen and Skea 1991: 220–221). The Downsian issue-attention cycle explains why the U.K. ultimately took action, but the stage on which the cycle played itself out was a larger European one. Advocates of acid controls gained public attention and political support primarily outside of the U.K., and by virtue of its membership in the European Community Britain had to go along with the Community's efforts to limit environmental damage.

The U.K. has also agreed to other European Community directives on the environment, such as one requiring the installation of catalytic converters on new automobiles from 1992 on. It did not do so without a fight, however. Because of acid rain and the growing power of the Green Party, Germany threatened to go it alone and require U.S.-style emission controls on motor vehicles. To preserve the idea of a single European market, individual countries could not unilaterally set their own emission requirements without inadvertently excluding others from their markets. The U.K. auto industry had invested heavily in "lean burn" technology and was opposed to the catalytic converter requirement because of lack of experience with it. The German auto industry, on the other hand, was much more familiar with catalytic converters because of its presence in the U.S. markets where such devices are a regulatory requirement. In the end, the U.K. was forced to accept the German view, and, again, the intensity of public awareness of the air pollution issue in Germany played a significant role in determining environmental policy in the U.K. (Arp 1993).

While regulatory measures for utilities and motor vehicles will indeed reduce emissions, they do not mean that U.K. pollution problems have been solved. Under new regulatory arrangements instituted since the privatization of electricity generation, the industry has been resisting the installation of costly flue gas desulfurization technologies and the government has negotiated lower targets on emissions reductions than desired by many of its European neighbors to offer some protection to the coal industry and large electricity producers (Skea 1995). Because of growth in motor vehicle traffic and reduced use of public transportation, emissions of nitrous oxides and volatile organics are increasing rapidly and will not be curtailed sufficiently unless other measures are undertaken (Pearce 1993: 51–59, 150–164). As in the U.S. and many other countries, the U.K. has yet to adequately confront the greenhouse warming problem. While the U.K. will probably meet its targets for greenhouse gas emission reductions under the Rio Earth Summit Climate Convention, those targets are insufficient to reverse warming trends (*ibid*.: 170–175). To its credit, the U.K. has instituted an energy tax for the purpose of reducing carbon emissions, although politically the real goal of the tax appears to be reductions in the government deficit (Maddison and Pearce 1995).

The politics of water pollution regulation in the U.K.

Like problems with smoke, water pollution was a contentious political problem early in Britain's history. As early as 1824 Parliament investigated the plight of the salmon fishery on the Thames and other rivers and concluded that little could be done to improve conditions in light of the substantial investments that had been made in the polluting riverside industries. In the 1850s cholera was recognized as a waterborne disease and Parliament pressed water companies to avoid use of the polluted lower Thames for supply purposes. Industy found waterside sites to be advantageous for waterpower, supplies of water, transportation, and waste disposal, and nineteenth-century industrial progress was not about to be inhibited by concerns over declining water quality (Clapp 1994: 71–76).

After a serious and rather extensive investigation of water pollution by a parliamentary commission, the Rivers and Pollution Prevention Act was passed in 1876 (*ibid.*: 80–83). The new law made it illegal to discharge sewage or industrial or mining wastes into rivers and established municipal councils as enforcement authorities. Polluters could satisfy the law, however, if they used the best practicable and available means for controlling discharges. Because pollution control technology was virtually nonexistent at the time, the force of the law was significantly weakened by this measure (Kinnersley 1988: 51–52). Moreover, local authorities were much more interested in promoting economic growth in their own areas, and were reluctant to constrain industry with pollution control requirements. Consequently, little progress on pollution control occurred until well into the twentieth century, and at the end of World War II many British waterways continued to be highly polluted (Clapp 1994: 84–88).

The modern history of water pollution control began with the 1951 Rivers (Prevention of Pollution) Act, requiring new sources of emissions, but not existing sources, to apply to River Boards for consents that limit the amount of pollution. River Boards were established in 1948 to regulate water withdrawals and were governed by a mixture of elected officials from local municipal councils and representatives appointed by the central government. Exemptions from obtaining consents for sources existing prior to 1951 and for sources discharging to estuaries were ended by the 1974 Control of Pollution Act. Using the excuse of maintaining trade secrets, the emission limits established under consents and their enforcement were undertaken confidentially and kept out of the public view. River Board members were also frequently local council members charged with the management of sewer systems, and River Boards were pressured to ignore consent violations by local sewer systems short on financial resources to upgrade facilities. The 1974 Act required the elimination of secrecy in the consent-setting and enforcement process, but a decade passed before secrecy completely disappeared (Kinnersley 1988: 76–78). During the 1970s, the River Boards were consolidated into 10 areas organized by river basin, taking water supply, sewage, and pollution control out of local hands, although the Regional Water Authorities (RWAs) still contracted with municipalities for sewer services. The 1980s was a period of tight capital spending budgets for sewage authorities, causing a deterioration in sewage treatment systems that probably contributed to a decline in water quality for some rivers (Kinnersley 1994: 46–48). In the 1980s the system was again changed with the privatization of water supply and sewer services. The National Rivers Authority (NRA) was created in 1989 to regulate water withdrawals and pollution emissions and implement water quality objectives for specific lengths of rivers (*ibid.*: 51–93, 145–168).

Under the old systems of River Boards and Regional Water Authorities, water pollution control was in the hands of a relatively small group of interest parties and was kept from public view. Judging from recent deterioration in water quality (see Chapter 3), control efforts were not very successful in the past. Water pollution control regulatory arrangements, however, appear to be improving under the new NRA. Ironically, this improvement is a product of the Thatcher administration policy on privatization of water and sewer utilities. In the original proposal for privatization, water companies were to be self-regulating, but this caused such a stir among environmental groups, and even business organizations, that the idea was quickly withdrawn. In its place the NRA emerged with strengthened regulatory powers in comparison to the RWAs and environmental groups as a part of its constituency of interests, marking a sharp break with historical practice (Winter 1996: 260–262).

One of the most profound changes that has occurred under the NRA is in the control of nonpoint agricultural runoff. In response to an EC directive on nitrate pollution, the Ministry of Agriculture established a Code of Good Agricultural Practices in 1985. Because the Code protected farmers who followed it from prosecution for water pollution, it may have done more harm than good. The 1989 Water Act that established the NRA, however, removed this protection from liability, and the NRA was possessed with full enforcement powers against farmers. As the result of new directives from the EC, Nitrate Sensitive Areas in the U.K. have been established where farmers sign voluntary agreements to reduce fertilizer use and farm animal stocking densities in return for subsidy payments. Possibly because mandatory regulations are available if voluntary participation is not forthcoming, participation rates by farmers in pilot programs have been high and fertilizer application levels have dropped. Farm pollution incidents have also fallen because of increased enforcement actions by the NRA (*ibid.*: 264–277). Unlike the U.S., the U.K. has implemented new arrangements that may go a long way toward reducing rural nonpoint pollution problems if fully implemented. Resistance of the farm lobby has been overcome by the establishment of a pollution control authority relatively free of dominance by farm interests and responsive to environmental group concerns. On this issue, organizations such as Friends of the Earth have gained influence, capitalizing on recent growth in public concern in the U.K. with environmental deterioration. The NRA has, however, met resistance from the Office of Water Services (OFWAT), the agency that regulates prices charged by the privatized water and sewer companies, to its efforts to reduce water pollution emissions. Wanting to avoid price increases for sewer services necessitated by stricter pollution controls, OFWAT has attempted to focus public attention on the costs of such measures (Maloney and Richardson 1994).

The politics of countryside issues

Unlike the problem of nonpoint water pollution, progress on other countryside issues has been more limited. The preservation of semi-natural habitat and a relatively diverse array of native species in the U.K. countryside was largely compatible with the system of mixed farming that existed before World War II, as already noted (Chapter 4). The industrialization of agriculture after the war, however, meant the elimination of many hedgerows (120,000 miles), draining of wetlands, cutting down of forests, and plowing up of meadows and rough grazing land (Chapter 4). All this plus industrial forestry's replacement of native woodlands with conifer plantations has dramatically reduced semi-natural habitat and caused population reductions for rare and endangered species (Chapter 4). The policy of agricultural intensification under an umbrella of various subsidy programs continued well after the war and was encouraged from 1970 on by the European Community's Common Agricultural Policy, which provided guaranteed prices and permitted farmers to sell whatever they could produce, irrespective of demand (McCormick 1991: 71). Farmers and their principal lobbying group, the National Farmers' Union, have gained a privileged relationship with the primary regulator of farm policy, the Ministry of Agriculture, Fisheries and Food, and farm policy has been largely administered by this closed subgovernment of narrow interests (ibid.: 79; Winter 1996: 100–128).

Farmers were protected politically not only by their special relationship to government, but also by the exclusion of farmland from the land use planning process. In marked contrast to property rights in the U.S., all land in the U.K. is ultimately owned by the Crown. Under the 1947 Town and Country Planning Act, individual freeholders have the right to use their land as they have in the past, but any new developments must be approved by a local planning authority and such developments must be in conformity with local development plans. In 1947 agriculture was still seen as the natural conservator of the countryside and was exempted from provisions of the Planning Act. As a result, farmers could alter their agricultural practices as they saw fit, although they were constrained in terms of buildings they could put up or from converting the land to nonagricultural uses (McCormick 1991: 76; Pye-Smith and Rose 1984: 55–56).

Even though the emergence of industrial agriculture and forestry has resulted in substantial declines in semi-natural habitat, natural areas have been protected under several conservation programs. Conservation programs directed exclusively at preserving natural habitat features include National Nature Reserves and Sites of Special Scientific Interest (SSSIs), both of which are under the administration of the Nature Conservancy Council (now called English Nature), a government agency established by the 1949 National Parks and Access to the Countryside Act. By 1992, 297 nature reserves had been established covering 1,763 square kilometers, and 5,852 SSSIs had been designated on 18,161 square kilometers. While National Parks have broader goals than natural habitat preservation, they do serve to preserve significant natural habitats and promote wildlife protection. By 1992 National Parks had been designated for approximately 9 percent of the total land area in England and Wales (13,729 square kilometers) mostly in upland areas (Pearce 1993: 108–109; NCC 1984: 15–36). The designation of SSSIs involves notification of landowners and planning authorities, but has been of limited effectiveness because of the exclusion of agriculture and forestry from the planning process and the resulting need to rely on voluntary compliance. Some funding is available for compensation to farmers in SSSIs whose income is reduced through conservation efforts, but they can get the funding by simply threatening to undertake land use practices damaging to natural habitat features (Pearce 1993: 111–112; McCormick 1991: 78). The designation of National Parks has also been of limited effectiveness because much of the land remains in private hands and planning for the parks is under the control of local authorities (Green 1985: 44–51). While these and other conservation efforts undertaken by various private groups in the U.K. are laudable, they have been insufficient to prevent habitat decline and the endangerment of species resulting from the industrialization of agriculture and forestry.

The U.K. has a large and active environmental lobby, one that is strongly focused on countryside issues. The roots of environmental concerns go back to the natural history clubs, footpath protection groups, and bird protection societies of the nineteenth century. As in the U.S., increased awareness of environmental issues in the 1960s prompted substantial growth in environmental organizations. Between 1967 and 1980 the Royal Society for the Protection of Birds alone increased its membership from 38,000 to 321,000, and new groups, such as Greenpeace and Friends of the Earth, became established. Between 1980 and 1989 Greenpeace expanded its membership from 10,000 to 320,000, while Friends of the Earth grew from 12,000 to 120,000. Between 1980 and 1989 total membership in environmental and amenity groups increased from about 3 million to around 4.5 million or 8 percent of the total population in Britain (McCormick 1991: 28–38, 152).

Environmental groups have focused their efforts primarily on the planning system with the goals of limiting local pollution, protecting areas of natural beauty, and preserving natural habitats.[2] Air and water pollution regulation has received less attention by the environmental movement, perhaps because of the secretive and closed nature of the regulatory process and the limited visibility of problems such as acid rain or excessive nitrates in rivers. The planning system, by contrast, is open and public, although its structure is favorable to developers. Anyone wishing to develop their property in any way must apply to the planning authority for permission. Plans must be publicized and comments in writing must be considered by local authorities. For controversial developments, government ministers can order planning inquiries to gather information from concerned parties. The process is favorable to developers because they can appeal refusals at the local level to the central government, where larger economic interests are more likely to be favorably considered. Developers whose activities will create employment can also gain the support of local interests in favor of economic expansion (Vogel 1986: 125–127). Because of developer advantages, environmental groups have experienced mixed results in the efforts to oppose various kinds of development (*ibid.*: 107–142; Blowers 1984). Environmental groups were, however, successful in stopping mining in Snowdonia National Park and the construction of oil production platforms in a Scottish deep-water loch (Vogel 1986: 118–125).

In light of the numerical strength of advocacy groups involved in countryside issues, their lack of effectiveness in limiting rural habitat decline caused by agricultural and forestry practices at first glance might seem surprising, but a little reflection suggests that the deck is stacked against them. The primary problem is that agriculture and forestry are outside the planning system. In short, the planning system cannot be used to restrict agricultural or forestry land use practices.

The power of agriculture was demonstrated in the political lobbying preceding the passage of the 1981 Wildlife and Countryside Act. The Royal Society for the Protection of Birds was successful in influencing the content of a 1979 European Community directive on the conservation of wild birds that had been motivated by public concern for the annual slaughter of migratory birds in southern Europe, and the purpose of the Wildlife and Countryside Act was to fulfill the conditions of the directive in the U.K. Ironically, environmental groups were virtually excluded from initial consultation on the Act, which was confined to the Department of the Environment, the Ministry of Agriculture, the Country Landowners' Association and the National Farmers' Union. Although subject to intense lobbying on behalf of environmental groups in the House of Commons, the final provisions of the Act were favorable to agriculture and were flawed from the perspective of preserving wildlife habitat features. Under the Act, landowners were to receive compensatory payments for management practices beneficial to wildlife that in turn caused economic losses. Subsequent to passage of the Act, local and central government funding for compensation has been inadequate and landowners have been able to receive payments simply by threatening to alter land use practices. Partly in response to the failures of the Wildlife and Countryside Act, as well to public concerns about the taxpayer cost of farm programs, the farm lobby experienced diminished influence, while the political strength of environmental groups increased in the 1980s.

Recognizing the growing power of the environmental movement and increasing public antagonism to costly farm programs, the Ministry of Agriculture embraced nature conservation in the 1986 Agriculture Act. As a result of the Act, a system of so-called Environmentally Sensitive Areas (ESAs) was established that included 15 percent of agricultural land by 1995. Within these areas, agreements were negotiated with farmers who received payments in return for engaging in or refraining from certain land management practices, including restrictions on fertilizer use and stock densities, prohibitions on the use of pesticides and herbicides, restrictions on land drainage, and the maintenance of certain landscape features such as hedges and woods. A cynical view of the ESA scheme is that it constitutes another means for legitimizing the continuation of subsidy payments to farmers and it permits continuing farm lobby control over countryside environmental issues. Under the program farmers are often paid for practices they would have undertaken anyway, grazing is frequently intensified elsewhere to compensate for reduced stocking in ESAs, conservation tree planting in woodlands is often undertaken to create commercial monocultures, and the budget for providing conservation advice to farmers is extremely small (Winter 1996: 225–256). Despite this and other conservation programs, damage to SSSIs continues and progress in reversing habitat deterioration has been limited (Young 1995).

The U.K. issue-attention cycle

Just as George Bush became the environmental President in the late 1980s, Margaret Thatcher became the "environmental Prime Minister" in a series of speeches in 1988 professing concern for the problems of overpopulation, global warming, ozone layer destruction, and acid precipitation (McCormick 1991: 60). Before this, the Thatcher administration had been notably unsympathetic to environmental issues. While the subsequent benefits to the environmental movement from this conversion have been questioned, it does signify growing public support for environmental issues (*ibid.*: 48–68; 107–127). In the 1980s, U.K. environmentalism appears to have moved from the "pre-problem stage," where subgovernments of narrow interests deal with problems, to the state of "alarmed discovery," where the problem comes into public view and a wider array of interests become involved in the regulatory process. While progress indeed has occurred on such issues as acid rain and water pollution control, resistance by economic interests continues to inhibit the preservation of semi-natural habitat, the reduction of pollution emissions from privatized sewer plants, and further reductions in sulfur emissions from electric generation facilities.

Conclusion

A narrowly economic approach to the environmental problem suggests that environmental decline is the result of cost externalization and the solution is to simply internalize such costs through appropriate voluntary negotiations, court action, or regulation. A broader approach to the environmental problem suggests that environmental decline is inherent in the capitalist economic growth process. Economic growth requires the creation of new industries and new forms of production that bring with them new kinds of environmental destruction. These new industries also foster the formation of organized political interests opposed to environmental regulation. Initial regulatory victories are won by environmentalists at the peak of the Downsian issue-attention cycle, but industry interests recover as public interest in environmental issues wanes, and regulatory gridlock results. The problem of environmental decline remains. To bring about true environmental protection requires changes in the economic system that are more profound than the existing scheme of regulation introduced in the 1970s and 1980s. To this subject we now turn.

7

ETHICS AND THE LIMITS OF ENVIRONMENTAL ECONOMICS

Environmental change is depicted so far in these pages as an inevitable result of the economic process as currently constituted. Economic growth is rooted in the creation of new industries, and new industries in turn create new environmental problems and politically resist regulations that would resolve those problems. Accepting that this is a reasonable description of the way the world works, the next step is to address questions of valuation. To what extent and in what sense does environmental decline matter, and how far should societies go in protecting the natural environment? Once these questions have been answered, then the practical question of reforming economic institutions can be addressed. The final purpose of this chapter is to address the question of how far societies should go in protecting the natural environment. The goal of subsequent chapters is to address the practical question of how to get there.

Should damage to the natural environment in any form be permitted so long as the resulting additional benefits exceed the additional costs? Many, if not most, environmental economists would answer with a resounding "yes." Some, however, would respond with skepticism, suggesting that the cost-benefit approach is deeply flawed because of methodological and measurement problems, while others might respond by arguing that the cost-benefit approach is wrong-headed to begin with on philosophical grounds, even if measurement and methodological problems could be resolved (Norton 1987: 25–45; Kelman 1981; Sagoff 1988). The goal of this chapter is to develop a philosophical framework for evaluating environmental change based on an ethics of environmental concern and to use this framework to investigate the limitations of cost-benefit analysis as applied to environmental issues.

The central proposition put forth here is that under an ethics of environmental concern the scope of possible cases where cost-benefit analysis can be legitimately applied from an ethical point of view is narrower than commonly believed by environmental economists. In order to evaluate this proposition, an ethical framework applicable to environmental issues is needed, one that takes into account key findings of environmental ethics (Callicott 1989; Rolston 1988; Taylor 1986; Fox 1990; Brennan 1988; Norton 1987). After presenting the general features of an ethics of environmental concern in the first section of this chapter, the next step will be to explore the theoretical limitations of environmental economics under the assumption that human beings are subjects of moral concern and that nature is instrumentally valuable. This amounts to the application of human ethics to environmental problems and assumes that the environment is of ethical concern indirectly because of its effects on human well being. The second step will be to explore the theoretical limitations of environmental economics under the assumption that the nonhuman natural world is also a subject of moral concern in its own right apart from its effects on human well being. The chapter will conclude by suggesting an ethical standard for evaluating environmental issues, one that will be applied in Chapter 8. The primary task of Chapter 8 will be to argue that a steady-state economy is a sufficient means for satisfy the ethical standard established in this chapter.

Valuing the natural environment

Ethical concern for the environment can be based on the idea that the natural environment is of instrumental value to human beings or on the idea that the natural environment is noninstrumentally valuable, meaning that it is valuable in its own right independently of any benefits it confers on human beings. If the environment is solely of instrumental value, then it becomes an object of ethical concern indirectly when environmental destruction threatens instrumental values received by human beings, including members of future generations. The essence of ethical behavior in this context is a willingness on the part of one individual to defend the existence and well being of others for their own sake. The object of direct moral concern here is human beings; the natural environment is of indirect moral concern because it is instrumental to human well being. Nature is defended in this set of circumstances by human individuals for the sake of instrumental values, not because of any value it has for or in itself.[1]

If elements of the natural environment are also seen as noninstrumentally valuable, then they have the potential to be objects of moral concern directly rather than indirectly. If the environment is noninstrumentally valuable, then it is valuable for or in itself independently of any instrumental values it provides to human beings (Goodpaster 1978; Plumwood 1991). This implies that the realm of moral concern extends beyond human society to the world of plants, animals, biotic communities, and ecosystems. In this situation human individuals are willing to defend the existence and well being not only of one another, but of nonhuman natural beings as well, and to defend them for their own sake, not for the instrumental value they deliver.

While many environmental philosophers agree on extending the realm of direct moral concern beyond human beings to the rest of nature, there is extensive disagreement over the philosophical foundation for doing so. Some environmental philosophers are skeptical that reasonable philosophical foundations can be worked out for the idea of direct moral concern and suggest that an expanded instrumentalist approach to environmental ethics is the best we can do (Norton

1987: 151–182; Norton 1989). The large array of views on environmental ethics can by no means be easily summarized. Consequently, three different positions that seem to be fairly representative of differing perspectives will be presented for the purpose of suggesting that they lead to a similar conclusion – the human species has a conditional moral obligation to preserve the natural environment. The three positions are the following:

1   an objectivist view of noninstrumental value;
2   a subjectivist view of noninstrumental value; and
3   an extended version of instrumental value.

An objectivist environmental ethic

An objectivist environmental ethic claims that something should be morally considerable if it has a certain characteristic, such as the capacity to reason, sentience, the ability to self-replicate or self-organize, or the capacity to pursue some end (Fox 1990: 161–196). The existence of value, in this view, is the result of an objective feature of the natural world and is thus independent of the valuer (Regan 1981; Goodpaster 1978; Rolston 1981). Value is nonanthropomorphic because it exists independently of the human valuer. The essence of Homes Rolston's argument on this subject is that natural beings pursue valued ends and thus possess value for themselves. Trees seek light as a part of their quest for growth, reproduction, and a genetic legacy in future generations. Because they seek such ends, they are valuable in their own right.

Values may exist in nature as Rolston suggests, but to say that entities having value for themselves are objects of moral concern does not necessarily follow. Some other argument is required. The usual approach is to argue by analogy. Human beings have value for themselves; therefore human individuals are morally worthy; consequently, other natural beings that have value for themselves are also morally worthy (Regan 1981).

Since humans are not exactly like other species, not all environmental philosophers are convinced that the argument by analogy is acceptable (Callicott 1985). In a recent article, Keekok Lee (1996) suggests an alternative interpretation of the objectivist approach to environmental ethics. Human beings not only have value for themselves, but have value in themselves as well. That is, they not only unconsciously pursue certain ends, but have the capacity to consciously reflect on their lives and to formulate specific goals. Human beings are unique because of their capacity to generate their own scheme of values and create their own plan of action in the world. Because humans have the capacity for conscious reflection, they in turn have the ability to recognize the presence of intrinsic value in nature in the sense that natural beings pursue unconsciously determined ends. This capacity of recognition in Lee's view is the source of human moral concern for beings that have intrinsic value (Lee 1996). It is not argument by analogy that sustains moral concern; rather it is the recognition of intrinsic value in nature.

A subjectivist holistic environmental ethic

The objectivist environmental ethic can still be criticized on the grounds that the logical act of recognizing intrinsic value does not necessarily lead to moral concern for it. Just because we observe the presence of intrinsic value doesn't mean we will attribute moral standing to it. Contrary to the objectivist view, a subjectivist approach relies directly on the human capacity to emotionally identify with entities outside the self. Through such identifications external beings are brought into the realm of moral concern (Callicott 1985: 260–266; Brennan 1988: 186–200). While in this case value is anthropomorphic, in the sense that it lacks existence apart from the human valuer, it is not anthropocentric because of the human capacity to value something in nature independently of any instrumental values it may have. While choices of the objects of moral concern are subjective, they will not necessarily be totally arbitrary. The capacity to identify with something requires some sort of connection to it, such as being a member of a particular family or society, belonging to a particular species, being a member of a given biotic community, or being a product of some biophysical process (Callicott 1985).

An environmental ethic can in theory either be holistic in its focus, with species and ecosystems being the objects of moral concern, or be individualistic, with individual organisms being morally considerable (Taylor 1981). While there is a natural human tendency to identify with the individual organism in nature, the functioning of ecosystems raises problems for a strictly individualistic environmental ethic. Natural processes often dictate the sacrificing of individual organisms. Overpopulation of rabbits, for example, may be resolved by increased predation of rabbits by wolves. To protect individual organisms in many instances would require their removal from their ecological context. To do so for all organisms would be an overwhelming task (Norton 1987: 166–168). On the other hand, ecosystems and species can be protected from human disturbances. Not all rabbits can be saved from premature death, but by preserving the ecosystem in which they are embedded we can preserve them as a species. Even though human sentiments for wild animals are often individualistic, the actions that can be taken to preserve individuals are for all practical purposes restricted to protecting ecological wholes.

While ethical theory tends to focus on moral norms that apply to individuals, in practice there are dimensions of moral behavior that are holistic in their focus, such as patriotism and institutional loyalty. The human capacity for emotional identification is thus not totally individualistic. The human species evolved as a consequence of the interaction of geophysical and ecosystem evolution, and an understanding of this phenomenon can result in the human capacity to emotionally identify with other species as fellow life forms and with ecological wholes as creators of order and producers of life forms (Rolston 1988: 186–189; Oelschlaeger 1991: 281–353). Such identifications make possible the human treatment of ecosystems and species as valuable for themselves. A holistic subjectivist environmental ethic thus can be supported on the grounds that human beings have the capacity to emotionally identify with environmental wholes.[2]

An instrumentalist environmental ethic

Some remain skeptical of the concept of a noninstrumental environmental ethic. Bryan Norton (1987), for example, argues instead for a nonutilitarian instrumentalist approach. In his view, the preservation of natural ecosystems is essential not only for the physical well being of human beings, but also for the value-shaping function of experiences in the world of nature. If we are so lucky as to spend time in a tropical rain forest or in the Arctic National Wildlife Refuge, our view of the world will change forever. Our values will be transformed for the better. We will want such places preserved not only for our sake, but because they will have similar transformative effects on others, in both current and future generations. Values are not fixed and predetermined as a utilitarian would argue; rather, they can be shaped by experience, suggesting an obligation to preserve opportunities for potentially valuable and value-determining experiences. A decent human life requires not only a basic standard of material consumption, but also the opportunity for significant experiences in the natural world.

An obligation to preserve the natural environment; cost-benefit analysis

All three views of environmental ethics suggest a moral obligation to preserve naturally occurring species and ecosystems. The objectivist and subjectivist ethics argue that to the extent possible, natural beings ought to be preserved for their own sake, while extended instrumentalism suggests that natural beings ought to be preserved for the values they instill in human beings. As such, none of these views suggests anything about the depth of this obligation, but they do suggest a duty to preserve the natural environment. The depth and specific form such an obligation may take is spelled out in a later section. Before this, however, the conventional evaluation procedure used by environmental economists, cost-benefit analysis, needs to be judged in light of environmental ethics. If cost-benefit analysis satisfies the criteria of environmental ethics it should be used as the central evaluative criterion; if not, it should be rejected in favor of an ethical standard.

Evaluation of the conventional cost-benefit approach of environmental economics in the light of ethics will proceed here in two steps. First, an ethic of environmental concern that views human beings as valuable in their own right and nature as instrumentally valuable will be used to evaluate cost-benefit environmental economics. Here human beings are the direct objects of ethical concern and the nonhuman natural environment is of indirect ethical concern to the extent that it affects human well being as suggested by Norton's (1987) instrumentalist environmental ethic. Second, cost-benefit environmental economics will be evaluated assuming that nonhuman entities in nature are also morally considerable as argued in objectivist and subjectivist environmental ethics. The basic premise of this position will be that human individuals are willing to defend the existence or well being of nonhuman natural entities even when they are devoid of instrumental value. In this case, the natural environment is of direct ethical concern.

Human ethics and environmental economics

While the philosophical underpinnings of human ethics is by no means a settled matter, many environmental philosophers would accept the notion that human individuals have value in their own right and ought to be treated as ends in themselves. This position can be defended on either objectivist or subjectivist grounds along the lines discussed above. One can claim that human beings are valuable in their own right because of some characteristic they have, such as rationality or sentience or the capacity to pursue consciously or unconsciously determined ends, or one can justify such value on the grounds of a human capacity to emotionally identify and empathize with one's own kind. The idea that human beings are valuable in their own right independently of any instrumental values they provide to others seems to enjoy widespread support in western societies. Consequently, this idea is accepted as a basic premise of human ethics in the following evaluation of environmental economics. This idea is particularly important, because if it is accepted as a basic element of human ethics, then, as we will see, it contradicts the recommendations of cost-benefit analysis in certain situations. As Ellerman (1988) has pointed out, this very simple idea has surprising consequences for the moral evaluation of the capitalist property system in general.

While one need not accept Kant's objectivist justification for a human ethic, his categorical imperative that one should always treat other human beings as ends in themselves and not merely as means is compelling, as is his discussion of the obligations it entails:

> Every man seeks his own happiness as his natural goal. Perhaps humanity would survive even though no one helped others to become happy, as long as no one got in the way of another's happiness. But this would be only a negative kind of harmony with humanity as an end. A positive harmony requires each person to do as much as possible to promote the happiness of others. For since a person is an end in himself, then as far as possible *his* ends must become *my* ends too, if the idea of harmony with humanity as an end is to have any positive effect on me.
>
> (Liddell 1970: 160)

At the minimum we ought not to interfere with the happiness of others, and certainly we ought not to interfere with their capacity for moral self-development. Happiness is a natural end that all human beings seek, and the development of their moral capacities is an end that they ought to seek. While everyone is responsible for their own self-development, we all have a duty to promote the happiness of others insofar as we do not impair our own ability to develop as human individuals. While we cannot be responsible for the development of morality in others, we do have a negative duty not to impair the capacity of others for self-development (*ibid.*: 161). Because an ethic that treats individuals as ends in themselves has a strong Kantian flavor, the approach to human ethics taken here will be given a Kantian label.

What does this mean for the human treatment of the environment? Is a Kantian ethical approach consistent with the cost-benefit framework for analyzing environmental problems? Kantian ethics raises two questions, one that can be partly addressed in the context of the cost-benefit framework central to environmental economics, and one that cannot. The first question has to do with the obligation not to hinder the seeking of happiness by others, and the second has to do with the obligation not to prevent or hinder the capacity of others to develop their moral selves.

The goal of happiness is achieved in part through instruments provided by the natural environment. There are two ways in which such instruments can be used. A nonmaterial use of the environment tends to leave it unaltered and does not reduce the capacity of the environment to provide for the instrumental needs of others. Nonmaterial use is benign use. Examples would include the observation and aesthetic appreciation of nature and the use of natural entities as cultural symbols. Certain material uses can also be benign, such as the human use of air as a source of oxygen. It is benign because oxygen absorption in human respiration is balanced by oxygen production in photosynthesis. Hunting or fishing for organisms whose populations are regulated for sustained yield could also be a material but benign instrumental use of nature. On the other hand, the use of nature for material purposes can be harmful when either the extraction of a material or the emission of a waste byproduct reduces the capacity of the natural environment to provide other useful services to human beings. This would occur, for example, when wood fiber is extracted from nature through the clearcutting of old-growth forests, or when waterways are used as a waste sink. In the first instance old-growth forests would no longer be available for purposes of aesthetic observation or scientific investigation, and in the second, waterways may no longer be usable for fishing or swimming. Such material uses of nature are destructive, and they tend to drive out benign uses in the absence of legal recourse by damaged parties or government regulations. The essence of the problem is that benign users in many instances cannot appropriate for their own exclusive enjoyment the free goods of nature because of the impossibility of excluding others, while destructive users by their very acts of destruction are able to privately appropriate those qualities of nature that are valuable to them.

Under Kantian ethics, individuals would have a moral responsibility not to reduce the ability of others to seek happiness by damaging features of the natural environment instrumental to such happiness. Damage to the environment would not be ruled out, however, if those who would suffer as a result could be compensated for their losses in some fashion that would permit them to obtain an equivalent level of happiness by other means. In other words, if the incremental benefits of environmental damage equal or exceed the incremental costs, those who are carrying out environmentally destructive activities could do so as long as the damaged parties are appropriately compensated. For compensation to be feasible, the economic efficiency criterion – incremental benefits exceeding or equaling incremental costs – would have to prevail. If the reverse occurred, then damaging use of the environment could not be undertaken because compensation would not be fully covered out of the benefits received from use.

Under the conditions just outlined, the classic net benefits maximizing solutions to environmental problems suggested by environmental economics would be consistent with Kantian ethics. The utilitarian ethics that underpins cost-benefit analysis and Kantian ethics would lead to the same result. Maximizing society's utility and happiness are equivalent and are called for under both ethical theories. However, Kantian ethics would require that losers be compensated for environmental damage whereas a utilitarian ethic would not so long as total utility is at a maximum. Not only would polluters have to limit their pollution to efficient levels under a Kantian ethic, but they would have to compensate those who suffer from any remaining pollution damages.[3] Kantian ethics would thus require a specific position to be taken on a matter that is in its essence distributional, while the practitioners of environmental economics are generally unwilling to take positions on the distribution of benefits from the use of nature, focusing entirely on the issue of efficiency. In his classic paper, "The problem of social cost," Coase (1960) goes so far as to suggest that changes in the distribution of property rights do not alter the efficient level of environmental damage.

Moreover, the Kantian approach turns the usual distributional outcome on its head. Normally, in the absence of legal recourse and government regulation, destructive use of nature forces out benign use, as noted above. The destructive users of nature gain the benefits of use by default. The resources they use are typically not owned by anyone and cannot be owned because of exclusion problems, so access is open. Because damaged parties tend to simultaneously use the resources of nature and tend to be relatively large groups, they suffer from the free rider problem in the bringing of collective lawsuits or in pursuing collective political action to prevent damaging use (Olson 1971). In many instances, damage may be difficult to prove conclusively in a court of law. Destructive use in a gain-seeking society is motivated by the opportunity to externalize costs that would otherwise be internally borne. If wastes were not disposed of in the air or water, gain-seekers would otherwise have to bear the costs of waste disposal themselves rather than members of society as a whole (Kapp 1970; Swaney and Evers 1989; Bromley 1978).

The compatibility between Kantian ethics and environmental economics hinges on the possibility of substitution between instruments in the quest for human happiness. If such substitutions are not possible, then compensation is not possible and cost-benefit analysis fails in its ability to determine an ethically accept-able use of nature. This occurs when some instrument in nature is so essential for human happiness that compensation for its loss in the form of other instrumental values is not possible. No other instrument can be substituted for it. To conjecture about a famous case in wilderness preservation history, there is probably no ma-terial object that John Muir would have accepted in exchange for the damming of the Hetch Hetchy Valley (Nash 1982: 161–181). The area was in all likelihood so highly valued by him in its natural state that there was no amount of compensa-tion he would accept in return for its inundation by a dam. Kantian ethics requires that losers be compensated, and cost-benefit analysis requires that costs borne by losers in resource allocation decisions be calculable. Since the costs of damming Hetch Hetchy would be incalculable, given Muir's apparent attitudes, cost-ben-efit analysis could not be properly applied. What cases like Hetch Hetchy really constitute is a moral dilemma pitting the happiness of wilderness preservation-ists, such as John Muir, against the happiness of resource users, a dilemma not resolvable with reference to cost-benefit calculations.

This conclusion, as already noted, assumes that the John Muirs of the world are motivated by a utilitarian form of individual happiness. However, other interpretations of attitudes towards nature like Muir's are possible. Where na-ture is simply an instrument for which there are ready substitutes, a moral com-mitment to the happiness of others in both present and future generations does not necessarily imply an indirect commitment to preserve a particular biotic community or natural landscape. The happiness of others may be more readily achieved through other means. On the other hand, if one believes that the hu-man experience of a particular landscape or biotic community is essential for life to be worthwhile, as Muir might have thought for Hetch Hetchy, then there is indeed an indirect moral commitment to the landscape itself. Human happi-ness in this view ultimately depends on experiencing natural landscapes and having values shaped by them. If this were true, then there would be no substi-tute means for achieving human happiness and a moral commitment to the latter would imply an indirect moral commitment to preserving natural land-scapes. Norton refers to values underlying such a commitment as transformative values and notes that they invalidate cost-benefit analysis because of its fixed preference assumption (Norton 1987: 185–213). The experience of a natural landscape in this view has the capacity to transform preferences. Finally, Muir could have seen Hetch Hetchy as having value in its own right apart from hu-man use and contact. The consequence of this kind of an attitude for cost-benefit analysis will be taken up in the next section.

The most fundamental moral obligation of all according to Kantian human ethics, one that is even prior to promotion of human happiness, is not to harm human individuals and their capacity for moral self-development. Under certain circumstances, the acceptance of this obligation leads to the failure of cost-benefit analysis as a methodology for evaluating environmental resources. The following passage from Kant serves to illuminate this issue:

In a kingdom of ends, everything has either a *price* or a *dignity*. Anything having a price can be replaced by something else with an equivalent value. But if its value is priceless, having no equivalent, we say it has a dignity. Those things which relate to general human desires or needs have a market price. ... But that which is the fundamental condition for all value must be an end in itself, its value is not relative, but inherent. Such is its dignity.

(Liddell 1970: 172)

Because human beings are ends in themselves, there simply is no equivalent value for them. There is nothing that can be substituted for harm to a human individual. There is no compensation for the impairment of the health or the death of a human being. Because compensation is ruled out on ethical grounds, the costs of reduced health or deaths associated with environmental damage cannot be calculated, and cost-benefit analysis cannot be applied. Here the Kantian imperative that human individuals be treated as ends rather than means comes into direct conflict with the utilitarian ethical premise that argues for the maximization of society's total utility. If maximizing aggregate social utility results in the death of someone or the significant impairment of their health, then such maximization ought not to be undertaken. If it were, individuals would be treated strictly as means rather than as ends.

Each individual consequently has an obligation not to use the environment in such a way as to physically harm other individuals. Health-impairing environmental damage is ruled out. Emissions of pollutants must be kept below levels that are significantly harmful to human health, irrespective of the levels of measurable benefits and costs. The only possible condition under which health-impairing emissions may be permissible is if not undertaking them would bring on a greater harm to human health. The moral obligation not to harm others through damage to the natural environment would hold in the Kantian view even if those individuals willingly accept compensation for damage to their health. We are obligated as moral persons to avoid harming not only the self-development of others, but also the development of our own beings. To accept compensation for damage to our own selves would be contrary to the Kantian moral imperative of treating ourselves as ends rather than as instruments.

To summarize, the conventional cost-benefit approach to environmental economics is adequate from the perspective of Kantian ethics so long as the benign users of environmental resources can be and are compensated for any losses they suffer from environmental damage. If, however, features of the natural environment are so highly valued that nothing is acceptable in compensation for their loss, or if damage to human health is involved, then the cost-benefit approach is no longer consistent with Kantian ethics if it leads to a recommendation of damaging resource use in the first instance, and a deterioration of human health in the second instance. Damaging resource use and deteriorations in human health may be morally permissible, but determining whether this is the case would require

the resolution of moral dilemmas for which cost-benefit analysis is not appropriate as a decision-making process.[4] In short, cost-benefit analysis relies on all
values being measurable in monetary terms, a condition that is violated for beings that are valuable in their own right.

The moral considerability of nature and cost-benefit environmental economics

As already suggested, nonhuman entities in nature, such as individual organisms,
species, and ecosystems, can be viewed as morally considerable in the sense that
human individuals are willing to defend their existence or well being apart from
any instrumental value they provide. Given such an attitude, the moral sphere
would encompass not only human beings, but the world of nature as well. To
view old-growth forests or blue whales as morally considerable is to be committed to their continued existence and well being even if they will never be observed or provide any kind of benefit flow. The idea of commitment goes beyond
the notion of utility interdependence, implying an abstract commitment to a being of a particular kind, not just to an arbitrary individual that happens to generate a sympathetic emotional response (Sen 1977; Etzioni 1986). Judging some
being outside the self as morally considerable is the ultimate altruistic act, suggesting a willingness to defend that being's existence and make personal sacrifices in the process without expectation of reward.

Given the logical possibility that natural entities are morally considerable,
what are the consequences for cost-benefit environmental economics? The traditional goal of environmental economics is to discover those allocations of natural
resources that will maximize net benefits. By doing so the Pareto criterion can
potentially be achieved because those who received the benefits would be able to
compensate any losers and still be better off.[5] Once environmental ethics is ad-
mitted, however, compensation for losses is no longer possible where a particular
resource allocation results in the destruction of something in nature that is held to
be morally considerable by someone. Neither the destroyed entity nor the moral
agent who holds that entity to be worthy of moral consideration can be compensated. If one holds a particular species to be morally considerable, it is obvious
that the species itself cannot be compensated for its own destruction. If it could in
some way, the moral problem would disappear. If the moral agent could be compensated in some way, the moral problem would also disappear, at least for the
moral agent. To show that a moral agent cannot be compensated for such a loss is
the purpose of the rest of this section.

A moral position is defined here to be a commitment to some end that is not
readily given up by the holder. A true moral position in this view cannot be
bought off in exchange for something of instrumental value usable for strictly
nonmoral purposes (e.g. the pursuit of personal happiness) (Etzioni 1986: 168).
Attaining the moral end is always preferred to not attaining it, no matter what the
level of income received for instrumental uses in the pursuit of nonmoral goals.

In other words, no increase in income is sufficient to render the individual indifferent between the income gain and the loss of a moral end. Indifference between a moral end and an instrumental value is ruled out, and compensation for the loss of a moral end is not possible. A wedge is driven between personal well being and moral choice (Edwards 1986, 1987). Moral ends are commensurable, but moral ends and instrumental values are not, except to the extent that instrumental values can be a means of achieving moral ends (Sen 1977; Edwards 1986; Brookshire *et al.* 1986). The ordering of moral preferences, in this view, is independent of the ordering of preferences over instrumental values (Etzioni 1986: 166–170). If I view tropical rain forests as morally considerable, and if I control their fate, then no amount of money would convince me to permit them to be destroyed, unless doing so allowed me to achieve some more highly ordered moral end. Even if the latter were the case, it would not really be a form of compensation because it would force me into a moral dilemma, to choose one moral end over another.

In using cost-benefit analysis to determine the disposition of a publicly owned exploitable natural resource, the normal procedure would be to determine the sum total of the public's willingness-to-pay to have the resource preserved or willingness-to-be-compensated for the exploitation of the resource, and then compare that with the market value of the exploited resource. Willingness-to-pay is the maximum payment the public is willing to make for preservation of the resource and assumes the public has no prior right to use it. Willingness-to-be-compensated is the minimum amount the public is willing to accept for giving up the resource in a preserved state and presumes a prior right of use. If the market value of the exploited resource is larger than willingness-to-pay and if no prior use right is judged to exist, then the resource should be exploited rather than preserved. If there is a prior use right for the preserved resource, then the market value of the exploited resource would have to be greater than the willingness-to-be-compensated for cost-benefit analysis to support exploitation. If preservation is perceived as an instrumental value, then the maximum payment by each individual to preserve the resource in the willingness-to-pay case leaves the individual indifferent between preservation and the additional income available in the absence of the payment. In the willingness-to-be-compensated case, the minimum acceptable level of compensation leaves each individual indifferent between preservation and compensation for exploitation.

If preservation is instead a moral end, in the willingness-to-pay case the individual is willing to sacrifice income up to some maximum amount where other moral ends take precedence, such as the capacity of oneself and one's family to live decently (Edwards 1986: 147–149). If preservation requires such a payment, then the individual will be rendered worse off by the resulting loss of income, being forced in effect to pay tribute in order to preserve something that ought not to be valued in instrumental terms (Kelman 1981: 38–39). If exploitation prevails because of insufficient payments for preservation, those holding preservation to be a moral end will also be rendered worse off and cannot be compensated for their loss. Remember, moral ends cannot be bought off by instrumental values.

The question of a prior right of access is moot because access is irrelevant to the attachment of moral considerability to a natural entity. Thus the normal procedure of cost-benefit analysis cannot yield a Pareto optimum; resource exploitation will always cause someone to be worse off where at least one person views the resource destroyed to be morally considerable. In the willingness-to-be-compensated case, if the natural entity in question is morally considerable, then there will be no acceptable level of compensation, and the costs of resource exploitation cannot be defined.

The argument is commonly inferred in environmental economics that if all environmental resources could be claimed as property the environmental problem would disappear (Coase 1960). Benign users would be able to bid for resources on an equal footing with destructive users of natural resources, and if benign users bid at a higher level than destructive users, preservation would result. On the other hand, when benign users lose in bidding for resource preservation, they will not be worse off because each will be indifferent between their maximum bid and preservation of the resource. The Pareto principle will be preserved in either instance.

If components of the natural environment are morally considerable, this unfortunately would not be the case. The argument is exactly the same as the one presented above for cost-benefit analysis. Those who hold natural entities to be morally considerable will experience the loss of their objects of moral concern in the case of losing bids. Morally considerable natural entities will be destroyed. The amount of income retained as the result of the losing bid will not compensate for the moral loss. Thus as economic growth and any resulting destruction of the natural environment proceed over time, those who hold elements of nature to be morally considerable will suffer losses for which they are not and cannot be compensated. This will be true even if property rights could be extended to the whole of the natural world.

Whether nature is viewed by very many as subject to moral concern remains an open question, as does the question of whether many would accept Kantian moral principles for the treatment of human beings. However, the disparity between willingness-to-pay and willingness-to-accept in many contingent evaluation studies is consistent with the possibility that moral decision making is playing a role in evaluating resource use. Willingness-to-accept has been found to be up to four times as great as willingness-to-pay in some studies (Mitchell and Carson 1989: 30–38). Such a disparity would be consistent with moral commitments to the preservation of nonhuman natural entities. Willingness-to-pay may really be measuring willingness to sacrifice for the moral end of preserving a component of the natural environment, and willingness-to-accept may really be measuring the point at which the payment received in compensation for damage to the environment can be used to achieve some other moral end. The upper bound on willingness-to-pay is established by the minimum income needed to achieve other moral ends, such as supporting one's family at a decent standard of living. The lower bound on willingness-to-accept in such cases would be established by the point at which the added income could be used to achieve a moral goal ordered more highly than preservation of the component of the natural environment in question. A lower bound on willingness-to-accept in an imperfect moral world could also be established as a consequence of weakness-of-will at a point where the compensation is attractive enough to give up moral commitments. Up to half of the respondents in some contingent evaluation studies either refuse to sell or want an extremely large or infinite amount of compensation, a finding consistent with moral commitments so strong that nothing is acceptable in return for environmental destruction.

If human ethics as described in this paper reasonably approximates actual human behavior, or if components of the natural world are viewed as morally considerable, then the range of environmental issues to which cost-benefit analysis ought to be applied is limited. It is limited to those cases where elements of the environment are instruments for which there are substitutes. If an environmental problem involves damage to human life and health, or if there are no substitutes for the natural environment in the achievement of human happiness, then cost-benefit analysis ought not to be used in the determination of the permissible level of damage to the natural environment. Nor should cost-benefit analysis be used where nonhuman natural entities are valued noninstrumentally and viewed as morally considerable.

Does a noninstrumental evaluation of nature matter? The case of the spotted owl

Would acceptance of the idea that nonhuman components of the natural world are objects of direct moral concern alter resource decision making? The recent controversy over the spotted owl, a species that is currently threatened with extinction, provides an interesting case for addressing this and some of the issues discussed above. The controversy is basically over whether the spotted owl should be allowed to go extinct or whether it should be preserved as a species. The spotted owl has been shown to be dependent on old-growth forests in Washington, Oregon, and California (Thomas *et al*. 1990). Old-growth forests have largely disappeared on private lands in these states, primarily because of timber harvesting, and are now found almost exclusively on public lands. Preserving these forests would mean giving up a valuable timber resource and would reduce employment in a timber industry that has already experienced substantial job losses.

A cost-benefit study of spotted owl preservation has found that the present value of the net benefit of spotted owl preservation is approximately a negative $24 billion (Mead *et al*. 1990). In other words, costs exceed benefits by $24 billion. This study takes into account the dollar value of recreation and other benefits of preserving old-growth forests, the value of which is far exceeded by the costs of resulting timber and employment losses. The study does not take into consideration a variety of other possible benefits of old-growth forests, such as the preservation of species diversity and ecosystem services and the preservation of natural areas and species for future generations. A more complete cost-benefit study, however, could still yield the conclusion that old-growth forests ought to be harvested and the spotted owl ought to be allowed to go extinct. To find $24 billion of additional benefits from preserved old growth could be a very difficult task.

Would the application of Kantian ethical principles to the spotted owl issue possibly yield a different result? In terms of promoting human happiness, if there is a negative net benefit from spotted owl preservation, then the spotted owl should be allowed to go extinct so long as other goods are substitutable for it. What this suggests is that more effective means of achieving human happiness are available than preserving spotted owls, specifically the harvesting and use of the timber from old-growth forests. To show that old-growth forests and spotted owls ought to be preserved on the basis of Kantian human ethics, one would need to demonstrate that there is no substitute for them in achieving human happiness or that they are essential to the preservation of human life and health. For some the experience of contact with old growth and spotted owls may be essential for attaining human happiness. However, human individuals and cultures have flourished historically without much direct contact with wild nature, suggesting there may be sources of higher cultural values other than the natural world.

Apart from their role as a cultural resource, old-growth forests may provide essential global ecosystem services, such as carbon absorption and species diversity, that are ultimately necessary for the preservation of human life and health. But genetic engineering might be able to compensate for losses of genetic diversity, and younger replacement forests might do an adequate job in providing other global ecosystem services. The point is, the application of principles from an anthropocentric human ethics might not be enough to justify the preservation of the spotted owl and old-growth forests.

If the spotted owl as a species and old-growth forests as ecosystems are viewed as valuable for themselves independently of any instrumental evaluations, a moral commitment to preserve them follows. Where cost-benefit analysis and human ethics may yield one decision, a noninstrumental evaluation of nature that sees the nonhuman natural world as of direct ethical concern could well yield another.[6]

Conclusion: an alternative ethical standard

The rejection of a cost-benefit approach to evaluating certain environmental issues does not mean that environmentally destructive activities are always forbidden. The decision to undertake such activities, however, should be arrived at on ethical grounds rooted in moral orderings, not on the basis of cost-benefit analysis. Such questions as limiting health-damaging ozone pollution, restricting sulfur emissions that threaten aquatic ecosystems through acid rain, and preserving the spotted owl should be posed as moral dilemmas. Is the economic cost of pollution control or species preservation a greater or lesser evil than the damage caused by the pollution or the loss of a species? The answer to a question of this sort is not easily arrived at. Moral decisions are never as easy as calculating benefit–cost ratios. Ethical rules of conduct and priority principles of the type discussed by Paul Taylor (1986: 169–218, 256–313) are needed to illuminate questions involving conflict between human material well being and the preservation of nature. At the risk of simplification, a standard of behavior resulting from such an approach to environmental ethics would be something like the following:

> Destruction of the natural environment shall not be undertaken unless absolutely necessary to maintain the real incomes of all human individuals at a level required for the living of a decent human life.

If, for example, the costs of air pollution control needed to prevent the acidification of aquatic ecosystems or the income losses from preserving old-growth forests and spotted owls do not cause a reduction of individual incomes below the required minimum, then pollution control and old-growth preservation should be undertaken. Such a standard implies that human beings take priority when the income they require to live decently is threatened, but that ecosystems have priority over incomes above this level. A standard of this sort provides a reasonable alternative to cost-benefit analysis in the determination of the human use of the natural world.

Component parts of this standard are subject to interpretation, but this will be the case for any ethical principle. Clearly, there will be differences of opinion over what constitutes material well being adequate to the leading of a decent human life. We do devise such minimum income limits in the political process, however; the U.S. government, for example, has an official income level it uses in measuring the extent of poverty. Disagreement could also arise over defining morally relevant destruction of the natural environment. The discussion in this chapter suggests that such destruction would include actions that cause significant harm to human health, the endangerment of species, or threats to the continued existence of representative types of natural ecosystems. Some suggest that ecosystem preservation could be approached at a landscape level. This might mean that certain habitats could be exploited or altered within a landscape area so long as certain other habitats were left alone or allowed to return to natural conditions in order to maintain a diversity of ecosystem types (Norton 1991: 148–183). The point is, any morally rooted decision-making process will necessarily require participants to formulate appropriate definitions of the terms in the standard of ethical behavior employed.

Why accept the above ethical standard for determining whether an ecosystem should be preserved or exploited? The standard does provide a means for reconciling an individualist human ethic with a holistic environmental ethic, and it is consistent with the widely discussed idea of a safe minimum standard that calls for preservation of the natural environment unless the costs of doing so impose an unbearable burden on society (Norton 1987: 119–123). Deep ecologists might object to the standard on the grounds that it is anthropocentric, and indeed it is. It gives priority to human beings when their ability to lead a decent life is threatened. The standard is consistent with Baird Callicott's idea of a widening circle of moral concern featuring a greater intensity of obligation for human beings who occupy the inner circles than for species and ecosystems found on the outer circles (Callicott 1990). The standard does, however, recognize the moral standing of species and ecosystems. Some might argue that the standard is tilted excessively in favor of human individuals because in almost all cases someone's income will suffer excessively if ecosystems or species are preserved. On the other hand, some will argue that the standard is tilted excessively in favor of the environment for precisely the opposite reason – seldom will incomes be reduced by environmental preservation to the point where leading a decent life is impossible. The best way to judge an ethical standard is through its application, a task to which we turn in the next chapter.

Before we do this, a brief summary of key conclusions made to this point in the book is in order. Economic growth as historically experienced generates environmental change and resistance to environmental regulation, and something of significance has been lost as a result of environmental change. If human beings have an ethical obligation to limit environmental change, then cost-benefit analysis is an inappropriate tool for judging specific measures to forestall environmental deterioration and an ethical standard is needed. The ethical standard suggested here is that human societies are obligated to avoid environmental harm unless such harm is absolutely necessary to live decent human lives. While there is some evidence that individuals accept the idea of a moral duty to the natural world (Milbrath 1984), the argument here remains a contingent one, valid only if such a moral duty is accepted. If such a duty exists, what should we do? To this question we now turn.

8

THE STEADY-STATE
ALTERNATIVE

If we indeed have a moral obligation to avoid harm to the health of human beings, species, and natural ecosystems, as the previous chapter argues, then one method for doing so is to implement a steady-state economy as suggested by Herman Daly (1991a). The goal of a steady-state economy is to bring the global economy into balance with the global ecosystem. The central conclusion of the earlier chapters of this book is that economic expansion places increasing demands on a global ecosystem that has a finite ability to absorb wastes and provide ecosystem services. These growing demands also result in environmental threats to the health of human beings, plant and animal species, and ecosystems. Regulation has mitigated the effects of growth on the environment but has succeeded neither in stabilizing all significant environmental threats nor in reducing them to ethically acceptable levels.

The ethical standard of the previous chapter argues for full protection of human, species, and ecosystem health from environmental harm, given that living standards are not reduced below levels needed to live decently. The goals of this chapter are to suggest measures essential for achieving a steady state and to estimate the economic costs of such measures for the U.S. using existing studies. Doing so will allow us to determine whether or not the costs of a steady-state economy are so burdensome as to cause a larger moral harm. The specific steady-state measures chosen here are by no means intended to offer final answers on environmental policy. Not all environmental issues are addressed in this chapter, although the most critical are included. The central point here is to offer a methodology for constructing environmental policy founded upon the principles of environmental ethics. Another important goal is to suggest that the cost of each steady-state policy initiative cannot be evaluated in isolation. All initiatives must be considered as a package to determine if the sum total of their cost is excessive in the sense that a larger moral harm results when implemented as a group.

A steady state

While the concept of a steady-state economy in its early formulations by Daly (1991a: 31–48) referred to a stable stock of material wealth, the ultimate goal of a steady state is to establish sustainable throughput rates for matter and energy.

Consequently, a steady state can be just as readily defined in terms of energy/ matter throughput rates, a formulation that is more convenient for macroeconomic analysis since macro theory focuses on flows rather than stocks. Doing so also puts the focus of attention where it should be, on the scale of the economic system relative to the global ecosystem (Daly 1992).

The steady-state proposal offered by Daly emphasized energy/matter throughput and did not directly consider the impact of economic activity on ecosystem services or environmental health. Daly argued that limiting energy/matter throughput to a sustainable level would reduce waste flows into the environment and resolve the problem of environmental and ecosystem decline (1991a: 61).[1] In light of such problems as global warming and the destruction of natural ecosystems as a consequence of economic development, limiting energy/matter flows will not necessarily bring ecosystem destruction to a halt. For example, a sustainable steady-state use of fossil fuels at levels ultimately replaceable by renewable solar energy could result in excessive carbon dioxide emissions and global warming. Hence, the emission of wastes into the environment and various land and aquatic resource uses must be directly constrained so as to preserve ecosystems and ecosystem services. In fact, ecosystem destruction as a consequence of exploitive land use, toxic contamination, and growing imbalances in atmospheric gases appears to be a much more serious problem than any looming energy or materials scarcities (Daily *et al.* 1991; Abrahamson 1989; Wilson 1988).[2]

This suggests that the focus in formulating a steady state should be on waste emissions and natural habitat destruction, rather than energy and materials consumption. The steady-state proposal put forward for the U.S. economy here includes the following major components:

1   a reduction in CO_2 emissions by 90 percent of forecasted levels over the next century and emissions stability thereafter;
2   the preservation of all remaining undisturbed habitats and ecosystems on the national forests and the conversion of previously exploited national forest lands to natural habitat;
3   reduction of nonpoint pollution to levels sufficient to preserve and restore habitat for native aquatic life; and
4   reduction and elimination of pesticides harmful to human beings, species, and ecosystems.

In the following sections, arguments will be offered suggesting that these measures lead to ethically acceptable levels of air and water quality, natural habitat protection, and limitations on exposure to pesticides and are not so economically burdensome as to reduce living standards below a level that permits a decent human life. In addition, the adoption of strict carbon dioxide emission limits will foster a move to sustainable energy consumption from renewable sources. Daly's original formulation of a steady state will thus be turned on its head. Rather than controlling throughput, emissions will be controlled, and the result will a sustainable throughput for energy.

Acid rain control as a model

Provisions of the 1990 U.S. Clean Air Act establishing upper limits on sulfur emissions serve as a model for steady-state emission controls. The Act establishes an absolute cap on sulfur dioxide emissions by electrical utilities of 8.95 million tons per year after a reduction of 10 million tons by the year 2000.[3] Some scientists argue that a 50 percent reduction in emissions is enough to result in the eventual recovery of currently acidified aquatic ecosystems (Goodstein 1995: 293–296). If they are right, then the cap on sulfur dioxide meets the ethical standard of ecosystem health protection suggested in the previous chapter. The only acceptable reason for allowing more emissions, according to the ethical standard of ecosystem health protection, would be if the cost of control creates such a large burden on society that it renders impossible the achievement of a living standard needed for the living of a decent human life. The cost of emission controls is estimated to be $4 billion per year in 1989 dollars, or less than 0.2 percent of GDP. This would hardly affect even the poorest paid in society, and would certainly have little impact on our capacity as a society to provide an adequate standard of living for all.[4]

The means of achieving emissions reductions will also be innovative. Under the technology-forcing regulatory approach of the past, each utility would have been required to install a technology that reduces emissions by somewhat more than 50 percent to achieve the 10 million ton reduction. Economists have long argued that this results in higher control costs than necessary. Different utilities are likely to have different control costs because of age and technological differences in their facilities. One utility may have a much lower per ton incremental cost for emission reduction than another. If so, then to minimize control costs the low-cost utility should undertake emission control up to the point where its own incremental control costs rise to the level of the high-cost utility.

Under the 1990 Clean Air Act, utilities will simply be given permits equal to 30 to 50 percent of their emissions 10 years earlier. Some permits will be retained and sold at auction by the EPA to prevent monopolization of permits by existing utilities. Low-cost utilities can then control emissions beyond the level required to be within their permit holdings and sell surplus permits. High-cost utilities can reduce their control costs by simply purchasing permits from low-cost utilities. The end result is minimization of emission control costs.[5]

Some have objected to the whole scheme on the grounds that it is unethical to trade in permits to pollute, much like prostitution or the buying and selling of slaves is unethical. This view is valid if the absolute lid on emissions is insufficient to protect human and ecosystem health. If the scientists are right and the emissions lid is sufficient, then it is hard to see that emission trading is ethically problematic. Another more serious objection has been raised. Local emission hot spots could occur around high-cost utilities that fulfill their obligations by purchasing emission permits. If this happens, then the permit trading scheme would have to be augmented by the enforcement of local ambient standards. Whether hot spots will be a significant problem remains to be seen.

If properly implemented, acid rain regulations appear to satisfy the conditions necessary to meet ethically based environmental standards and to achieve a steady state. Hence, this regulatory scheme will serve as the model for regulatory measures in other arenas needed to achieve ecosystem-wide environmental protection and a macroeconomic steady state. The key features of the scheme are absolute caps on environmental damage and institutional measures that minimize regulatory costs.

Steady-state policies for global warming

Apart from an international treaty that attempts to freeze CO_2 emissions at 1990 levels, little has been done to address the problem of greenhouse gas buildup in the atmosphere and the global warming it may cause. Given the importance and political power of the fossil fuel and motor vehicle industries, and given the speculative nature of the problem, this is not too surprising. The position taken in this section is that global warming is a serious threat that needs to be taken seriously. While there is some probability that this position is wrong, the consequences of global warming are potentially so threatening to human and ecosystem health (Chapter 5) that we have an ethical obligation to do something about it. The goals of this section include providing a justification for reducing CO_2 emissions in order to limit the potential temperature increase to 1.7°C, establishing whether or not the costs of doing so will create a larger moral harm, and suggesting a regulatory scheme for achieving the CO_2 limitation.

Stabilizing climate

Because of the mysteries of the global carbon budget, little agreement exists on how much emissions reduction is required to achieve global climate stability. Around 7 billion tons of carbon is emitted from human sources each year, with about 6 billion coming from fossil fuel emissions and around 1 billion from deforestation (Abrahamson 1989: 7; Gillis 1991; Cline 1992). Roughly half of this release is being retained in the atmosphere, around 2 billion tons is being absorbed into terrestrial and marine carbon sinks (mostly the oceans), and the ultimate fate of the rest is unknown. The nature of the relationship between emissions and absorption into sinks is not fully understood. About half of carbon emissions remain in the atmosphere beyond a decade (Cline 1992: 16). An immediate reduction of approximately 60–80 percent in emissions would bring forth climate stability and limit warming to approximately 1.7°C (*ibid.*: 17). Cline (1992), who has undertaken the most extensive analysis and summary of the economics of global warming, argues that limiting emissions to 4 billion tons per year will ultimately limit warming to 2.5°C.

Carbon dioxide is not the only heat-trapping gas being emitted into the atmosphere. Other gases, such as methane, nitrous oxides, chlorofluorocarbons (CFCs), and tropospheric ozone, may account for as much as one-half of the possible surface warming between 1980 and 2030 (MacDonald 1989). A reduction in fossil fuel used to curb CO_2 emissions would also reduce ozone and nitrous oxide emissions. Although some methane emissions are related to fossil fuel use, many originate in agriculture. Since methane emissions are short-lived in the atmosphere, only around a 20 percent reduction would be required to bring them into a steady state that limits further warming (Cline 1992: 17). CFCs are being brought under control as a result of the Montreal accord to limit destruction of the ozone layer. The greenhouse benefits of reducing CFCs have been questioned because the repair of the ozone layer will to some extent offset the reduction in CFCs as a greenhouse gas (*ibid.*: 18). Together, all this suggests that for reducing global warming, the primary emphasis must be on carbon emissions reductions.

Costs of climate stability

If fossil fuel use and deforestation are not restricted in any way, global carbon emissions will grow from around 6 billion tons (gigatons, or GtC) currently to 57 billion tons by 2275 (Table 8.1). After that, carbon emissions decline as global fossil fuel stocks begin to run dry. Also, at that point the amount of carbon in the atmosphere will likely begin to decrease because by this time deep ocean mixing is projected to accelerate the absorption of carbon (Cline 1992: 46–50). The increase in average global temperature by 2275 under the "business as usual" scenario will be approximately 10°C (*ibid.*: 74).

Table 8.1 Global warming: options and costs, 2000–2275

Variable	2000	2025	2050	2100	2275
Carbon no limits	7.1	10.9	13.8	21.6	57.2
Warming no limits (°C)			3.1	4.7	10.1
Carbon Cap at 6 GtC	6	6	6	6	6
Warming 6 GtC (°C)			2.6	3.3	5.0
Carbon Cap at 4 GtC	4	4	4	4	4
Warming 4 GtC (°C)			2.3	2.5	2.5
GDP cost 4 GtC limit	3.5%	3.5%	2.5%	2.5%	2.5%
Carbon 90% decline		1.1	1.4	2.1	
Warming 90% decline (°C)		1.7	1.7	1.7	
GDP cost 90% decline		4.6%	3.9%	2.6%	

Source: Cline (1992).

A popular option for limiting global warming, one given consideration at the 1992 UN Conference on Environment and Development held at Rio de Janeiro, is to freeze emissions at the current level of roughly 6 GtC, limiting warming to roughly 5°C (Table 8.1). In perhaps the most comprehensive economic study of global warming, William Cline (1992) suggests that capping emissions at 4 GtC is a realistic alternative that will limit warming to 2.5°C. As already noted, an immediate reduction in carbon emissions by 60–80 percent would stop carbon accumulation in the atmosphere and limit warming to an unavoidable 1.7°C. A more feasible 90 percent reduction below forecasted use with a 25-year phase-in period would accomplish approximately the same limit to warming.[6] Emissions would drop to 1 GtC by 2025 under this scenario and rise to approximately 2 GtC by 2100 because of global economic expansion. Thereafter, emissions would be capped at 2 GtC.

To determine whether and to what extent carbon emissions should be limited requires us to have some idea of the cost of different control options. Cline (1992) has provided an excellent summary of carbon emission control cost studies by economists and others and has integrated those cost studies to come up with aggregate estimates of costs as a percentage of global GDP. Two types of study have been undertaken to estimate costs: one utilizing economic models, and another focusing on improvements in energy efficiency obtainable at relatively low costs. The top-down economic models rely on historical data, production functions that permit the substitution of labor and capital for energy, and cost estimates for backstop energy sources that can replace high carbon content fossil fuels. For a 90 percent reduction in carbon emissions from an unregulated baseline, these models estimate that the cost will initially be approximately 5.7 percent of global GDP and will decline to 3.7 percent by 2100 (Cline 1992: 229).

The top-down economic models neglect bottom-up engineering estimates of cost savings available from energy conservation. Engineering studies suggest that as much as a 20 to 25 percent reduction in carbon emissions can be obtained through energy efficiency improvements and substitution of renewable energy sources at zero net economic cost (Cline 1992: 197–202).[7] Such measures include the replacement of regular with compact fluorescent bulbs; window glazing, weather stripping, and increased building insulation; increased use of solar heating; installation of low-flow devices in showerheads and better insulation of water tanks; increased motor vehicle fuel efficiency; energy efficiency improvements in industrial processes; and increased use of geothermal, biomass, solar photovoltaic, and wind energy sources.

Even though many of these measures result in net cost savings, they have not been undertaken because of the lack of readily available information on energy conservation and energy supply alternatives, limited access to capital for financing energy investments, and excessive discount rates implicitly used by consumers in evaluating energy conservation measures. The problem of "bounded rationality" in itself inhibits the adoption of cost-effective energy conservation measures. Business managers have limited time and resources and focus only on those goals that are most important to them, and energy conservation may well be of secondary importance for most.

Cline (1992) adjusts the top-down cost estimates for bottom-up energy cost saving opportunities and finds that a 90 percent reduction in carbon emissions would cost approximately 4.6 percent of global GDP by 2025, which would fall to 2.6 percent of GDP by 2100. If reforestation and reductions in deforestation are also undertaken to curb atmospheric carbon, then the cost estimates are reduced to 3.2 percent of GDP for 2025 and 2.5 percent by 2100. For purposes of analysis, the higher, more conservative cost estimates excluding the forestry option but including bottom-up measures will be adopted here.

Various options for limiting global warming and their costs are presented in Table 8.1. Cline's preferred alternative is to cap global carbon emissions at 4 GtC, limiting warming to 2.5°C. The option selected here is the more stringent one of a 90 percent reduction in emissions from their baseline, no control level. The justification for choosing a relatively stringent measure is fundamentally ethical. As outlined in Chapter 5, global warming will seriously disrupt natural ecosystems and probably cause a wave of species extinctions. Also, global warming would result in increased mortality and reduced economic productivity, reducing the prospects for a decent life for future generations. Cline (1992) estimates that the loss of global GDP by 2275 will be somewhere between 5 and 16 percent if nothing is done about global warming. If we can avoid the destruction of key natural ecosystems, the extinction of species, and significant harm to future generations while still being able to live decently, then the ethical approach to evaluating environmental issues offered in Chapter 7 suggests that we should.

Climate stability and living decently

Because the U.S. share of global carbon emissions (17.52 percent) is less than its share of global GDP (25.74 percent), its cost of emissions reductions as a proportion of GDP would be less (0.68 × 4.6% = 3.1% for 2025). The European Community accounts for an even lower ratio of global carbon emission to GDP share (0.49) and would have an even lower cost as a proportion of GDP (2.3%).[8] However, in order to solve the problem of global warming, an international agreement will be needed that will doubtlessly require income transfers from poor countries to rich. Consequently, in evaluating whether the cost of forestalling additional global warming is consistent with a living standard in the U.S. that would permit a decent life, the larger 5 percent cost figure is used on the grounds that at least an annual transfer of 2 percent of U.S. GDP per year to poorer countries will be required to garner their support for carbon emission limits.[9] A similar amount would likely be required from the European Community, resulting in a total GDP decline of a little over 4 percent.

Would a 5 percent reduction of real income make living decently impossible in the U.S.? This is not an easy question to answer. It largely depends on the meaning of "living decently." Most would agree that the bottom fifth of the U.S. population in the income distribution, who received 4.5 percent of total income in 1991 (U.S. Bureau of the Census 1993), don't live decently by U.S. standards. The top two-fifths of the income distribution in 1991 received 68.3 percent of the total income in 1991 (*ibid.*). Doubling the income of the bottom fifth by reducing the income share of the top two-fifths from 68.3 to 63.8 percent would certainly enhance the prospects of the bottom fifth for living decently, without significantly altering the living standard of the top two-fifths. Reducing the income of society as a whole by another 5 percent to pay for greenhouse warming controls would not likely reduce the living standard of the poorest in society below a decent level, given the suggested income redistribution measure. For the U.S. at least, climate stabilization does not necessarily conflict with the attainment of decent living standards for all. A similar analysis would likely reveal a comparable conclusion for other relatively wealthy countries such as those in the European Community.

Reducing economic inequality, some would argue, would destroy economic incentives on which high output levels are based in the U.S. A 64 percent share of output for the top two-fifths of the income distribution is about equal to the actual historical figure in the late 1960s, a period of vigorous economic growth, suggesting that inequality is currently excessive for incentive purposes (U.S. Bureau of the Census 1975). As Herman Daly (1991a) emphasizes, a steady-state economy will be unacceptable to the public at large if gross economic inequities are allowed to persist. Issues of economic injustice and environmental decline are ethically inseparable and must be addressed together.

Marketable carbon emission permits

While many have suggested carbon taxes to achieve emissions reductions (Pearce 1993), a marketable emissions permit system has certain advantages. A permit system affords direct controls over total emissions. Permits could be domestically distributed annually on a per person basis equal in amount to existing emissions initially, and then reduced by 3.6 percent of the initial amount each year over a phase-in period of approximately 25 years to arrive at a 90 percent total reduction.[10] Individuals who don't need the full allocation for their own energy consumption could sell their surplus permits at the going market price. Such a system would tend to redistribute income away from industries and high-income families who are heavy consumers of energy to low-income families who tend to consume less energy. Because of the potential to sell surplus permits, the public resistance to a permit system would be less than to a carbon tax. The rising price of permits over time would provide the incentive needed for increased energy conservation and to shift to non-fossil fuel energy sources. As in the case of acid rain control, a marketable permit system for carbon emissions control results in control being achieved at the lowest possible cost.

The primary purpose of this chapter is to establish steady-state policies for affluent countries such as the U.S. and members of the European Community. Clearly, greenhouse warming is a global problem requiring global solutions. Because the U.S. share of global carbon emissions is 17.5 percent, it is a significant contributor to the problem, and elimination of 90 percent of U.S. carbon emissions is a significant part of the solution. Similarly, a 90 percent reduction of European Community emissions at 11.22 percent of the global total would be a major part of the solution. Nonetheless, action beyond the U.S. and European borders will be required. Given a program in place to cut emissions, the U.S. and Europe would be in a position to exercise considerable leverage on other countries, particularly their trading partners.[11] A global emissions trading system with emission permits partially distributed according to initial population levels would be very attractive to less developed countries, which are less reliant on fossil fuels than industrialized countries. These countries could earn foreign exchange by selling surplus permits and undertaking reforestation projects that sequester carbon. Given that carbon emissions from deforestation are counted in the emission permit system, less developed countries would have an added incentive to avoid deforestation. Under a global carbon emission permit system of this kind, the impact of emission control on GDP would be more heavily concentrated in the more energy-intense industrialized countries.[12]

Summary

Reducing carbon emissions by 90 percent is costly, but not so costly for the U.S. and other relatively wealthy countries as to make it impossible for its citizens to live decently. Doing so has considerable side benefits. Urban air pollution would be virtually eliminated, toxic air pollution emissions would decline, motor vehicle related urban runoff would be reduced, and, because of higher transportation costs, the tendency to urban sprawl and the traffic congestion that goes with it would diminish. The U.S. and other major fossil fuel importers would end up with energy systems based largely on renewables and thus achieve energy independence.

Nonpoint water pollution control

Despite the fact that most point sources of water pollution have been brought under some form of emission controls in the U.S. and other relatively affluent countries such as the U.K., water quality has experienced only modest improvement in terms of aggregate measures, although local success stories where water quality has been substantially improved in specific water bodies (e.g. Lake Erie) can be found (Adler *et al.* 1993; Freeman 1990). This is not surprising in the U.S., given that over 80 percent of suspended and dissolved solids, phosphorus, and nitrogen emissions and over half of biochemical oxygen demand came from nonpoint sources prior to the 1972 Clean Water Act (Freeman 1990) and given that nonpoint pollution has been subject to very limited control measures.

The technology-oriented philosophy of control adopted in the 1972 U.S. Clean Water Act is partly to blame. The earlier Water Quality Act of 1965 called for states to set ambient standards for interstate waterways and to develop programs to meet those standards. This approach to control was watershed-based and focused on ambient water quality. Because the capacity to measure and monitor water quality at the level of detail needed for a serious pollution control effort was unavailable at the time, an end-of-the-pipeline, technology-forcing approach was adopted instead.[13] Under the 1972 Clean Water Act, technology-based effluent standards were established by industry categories. These standards did not directly consider the quality of receiving waters, although the EPA could impose more stringent standards where designated uses of water bodies were not met because of poor ambient water quality (Freeman 1990; Adler *et al.* 1993). In practice, the ability to impose stricter effluent standards has seldom been used.

While point controls have undoubtedly improved water quality, to achieve the goals of the U.S. Clean Water Act, and to protect aquatic ecosystems, a watershed approach is needed that focuses on ambient water quality and the condition of aquatic ecosystems. First and foremost, a significant investment in monitoring capacity will be necessary (Knopman and Smith 1993). This will permit a more accurate assessment of nonpoint pollution problems, the presence of toxins, and any remaining harmful point sources of pollution. The critical water pollution problems remaining include excessive siltation and nutrient loading from nonpoint sources, runoff of toxic pesticides from farmlands, the emission of toxins from point and nonpoint industrial sources, and urban runoff (*ibid.*; Adler *et al.* 1993).

Under the 1987 Clean Water Act Amendments, the U.S. EPA is required to establish urban and industrial storm water emission limits and to implement a permit system for storm water runoff for municipalities and industries. In other words, storm water is to be treated like a point source, for regulatory purposes. Although the EPA has been slow to implement this program, once it has done so much of the urban runoff pollution problem will hopefully be resolved.

The nonpoint problems that remain largely unaddressed are excessive amounts of suspended solids, nutrients, and pesticides from agriculture runoff. The issue of reducing pesticide use will be considered separately in the next section. The regulation of agricultural runoff is politically difficult to achieve because it requires land use regulations that run counter to traditional Jeffersonian and Lockeian rural values (Hargrove 1980). By virtue of the labor they put into their land, their economic dependence on the land, and the traditional values of individual freedom they hold, rural landowners see themselves as the best and rightful judge of how their lands ought to be used. While landowners view regulation with trepidation, they are not opposed to incentives that result in changes in land use practices. The USDA Conservation Reserve Program, for example, pays farmers to keep some 35 million acres of land out of production (Licht 1994). Thus the path of least resistance for rural nonpoint pollution control is simultaneously to require rural landowners to adopt land use changes that improve water quality and to provide them with subsidies and economic incentives to carry out those changes. Such changes include contour plowing, no-till cropping, filter strips, crop rotation, reduced manure and fertilizer applications, stream buffer strips, manure storage tank and barnyard drainage control system construction, and the purchase of easements for wetlands and areas where wetland restoration can be undertaken (Adler *et al*. 1993: 183–189). Wetlands perform an important water-cleansing function in agricultural areas as well as providing significant natural habitat. The mixing of regulatory requirements with economic incentives has proven its value in the U.K.'s nitrate-sensitive areas pilot project (Winter 1996: 271–273).

The added costs of controlling urban and agricultural runoff are not fully known. Urban storm water controls generally involve rather low-technology measures such as more frequent street sweeping, installation of permeable parking lot pavements, construction of settling ponds, restricted use of road salts, construction site erosion control, and creation of streamside buffer strips, and in some cases retention and treatment of storm water. Controlling nonpoint loading of nutrients may actually be less costly than controlling point sources (Freeman 1990). The Conservation Reserve Program mentioned above inadvertently reduced loading of suspended solids, nitrogen, and phosphorus by 8–10 percent (*ibid*.). This program was undertaken at a cost of roughly $1.7 billion per year (Licht 1994) for the purpose of reducing agricultural production. Water pollution reduction and increased habitat for game were side benefits.[14] The same amount of reduced water pollution reduction could probably have been obtained at a lesser cost by reserving just those areas that contribute most heavily to pollution loading.

One source of nonpoint control cost information is existing state plans to control nonpoint pollution. The state of Wisconsin has instituted priority watershed projects for many of its rivers that takes a watershed approach to improving water quality and restoring aquatic habitat (Wisconsin Legislative Fiscal Bureau 1995). Each project involves a careful survey of nonpoint water pollution problems, an evaluation of the recreational and biological potential of streams and lakes, an assessment of threats to locally endangered species, and cost estimates for achieving feasible recreational and biotic potential use goals taking into account the protection of endangered species. Such goals involve anywhere from 40 to 90 percent reduction in pollutant loading. The goals are to be achieved by instituting changes in urban and rural land use practices through the reform of local land use ordinances and voluntary contracts between landowners and the state that include cost-sharing incentives for the landowner. The cost per stream mile for such a program in one of the most polluted watersheds in the state is approximately $300,000 per year for an eight-year abatement program (Wisconsin DNR 1992). Given that there are approximately 100,000 miles of impaired streams in the U.S. (Adler *et al*. 1993: 173), extrapolating the per mile cost in Wisconsin to the U.S. as a whole would yield an average annual cost for the first eight years of $30 billion per year. This figure is grossly overstated because it assumes that all watersheds in the U.S. are as polluted as one of the most polluted in Wisconsin.[15] Moreover, because most of these costs are one-time capital out-lays, the annual cost would tend to decline with time.

The annual cost of all U.S. water pollution programs in the 1980s was approxi-mately $30 billion per year, or, in 1989, around 0.6 percent of GDP (Freeman 1990). Suppose that at the outside, control costs doubled from 0.6 percent to 1.2 percent of GDP to take into account nonpoint control costs (around the $30 bil-lion figure estimated above). Even if this is added on to the cost of preventing global warming, the ability of the U.S. to provide all its citizens with a standard of living that permits a decent human life would be only moderately diminished. Changing the cost of reaching steady-state emissions goals from 5 percent of GDP to 5.6 percent would not really change the outcome of the argument pre-sented above in the global warming section on our economic capacity to provide the poorest members of society with a minimally decent standard of living.

In the case of global warming, a moral obligation to the health of present and future generations, nonhuman species, and ecosystems is a compelling justifica-tion to undertake the measures needed to bring about climate stability. Can we say the same for water pollution control? Nonpoint runoff poses a human health threat as a consequence of nitrate levels in local drinking water and concentra-tions of organisms originating from farm animals, such as cryptosporidium, that can get past water treatment systems and cause major public health crises like the one that occurred in the city of Milwaukee recently.[16] Although the subject has received little public attention, by far the most threatened categories of species are found in aquatic habitats. Over 30 percent of fish, 60 percent of crayfish, and 70 percent of mussel species are threatened in the U.S., and water pollution prob-lems are a central cause of the threatened status of many of these species (Adler et al. 1993: 59–69). Thus a clear ethical reason exists for addressing remaining water pollution problems.

The primary complaint of most economists about the Clean Water Act is its excessive cost (Freeman 1990). Excessive costs arise, according to economists, because effluent limits are more strict than necessary to achieve an adequate level of water quality and because facilities that control emissions at high cost and low cost on the same waterway are treated identically by technologically based effluent limits. While there is no evidence for the strictness argument, there is some evidence that a system of tradable effluent permits could reduce costs where a zero effluent standard is unnecessary to achieve an ambient water quality level that protects human and ecosystem health (ibid.). Low-cost polluters could control more effluent than required by permit limits and sell effluent allow-ances to high-cost polluters at an aggregate savings in control costs. Because most water pollution problems are highly localized, opportunities for such trades are probably limited and best discovered through a watershed-based approach to water quality management. While advantage must be taken of cost-saving opportunities, the central goal under an environmental ethic is to achieve an ambient water quality steady state that protects the health of humans, species, and ecosystems.

153

Pesticide regulation

In terms of total weight, U.S. pesticide use peaked in the 1970s and declined somewhat in the 1980s. However, this reduction can be explained in large part by the increase in toxicity and effectiveness of new pesticides (Pimentel *et al.* 1991). While the days of rapid growth for the pesticides industry are over, large volumes of highly toxic pesticides are still applied to agricultural croplands annually with serious environmental consequences, as noted in Chapter 5.

The use of pesticides in the U.S. causes damage to human health, animal poisonings and contamination of animal products, destruction of beneficial natural predators and parasites, resistance to pesticides in pests, bee poisonings and reduced pollination, crop losses from pesticide treatment, groundwater and surface water contamination and associated loss of fisheries, wild bird kills and reduced avian reproductive potential, and damage to soil microorganisms. The details of each of these problems were discussed in Chapter 5 and need not be repeated here. The estimated annual environmental and economic cost in the U.S. associated with these problems amounts to approximately $8 billion dollars per year (*ibid.*).

Pesticide use could be reduced by as much as 50 percent through modification of agricultural practices including increased crop rotation, closer pest monitoring and more discriminating pesticide applications, increased use of biological controls, decreased use of aircraft application (which wastes 75 percent of pesticide applied), and a variety of other techniques.[17] No-till cropping has become a popular means of reducing erosion and nonpoint water pollution from runoff, but it requires a substantial increased use of herbicides to keep weeds under control. One alternative to no-till that reduces herbicide use is ridge-till cropping, where crops are planted on 8-inch high permanent ridges. Ridge-till requires no herbicides and controls soil erosion more effectively than no-till (*ibid.*). Other erosion control alternatives that cut pesticide use include strip cropping, crop rotation, contour planting, terracing, windbreaks, mulches, cover crops, and green mulches. Using such methods to cut pesticide use in half would cost approximately a billion dollars a year (*ibid.*). Given the $8 billion dollar annual environmental and economic cost of pesticide use, a billion dollars would be a small price to pay. A reduction of pesticide use by 50 percent would most likely increase GDP as a result of reduced losses from pesticides in the agricultural sector alone.[18] Pesticide use could probably be reduced by as much as 75 percent over, say, a 25-year time horizon without any significant loss in GDP. Given the negligible costs of pesticide use reduction, and given the threats from pesticide use to human health, the health of wild bird populations, and the health of aquatic species, environmental ethics and steady-state economics suggest that pesticide use should be reduced and capped at approximately 25 percent of existing consumption.

One means for accomplishing this would be to issue or sell marketable use permits annually for each existing type of pesticide and reduce the number issued over time.[19] Use of those pesticides that pose a greater environmental risk could be reduced more quickly, and, if necessary, phased out completely. New pesticides not currently available could be assessed for risk, much as they are now, and brought into use through the purchase of use permits for existing pesticides of equivalent risk.

Preserving and restoring natural habitats: the U.S. national forests

The destruction and modification of natural areas has been a central element of the U.S. economic development process. Agricultural settlement in the Midwest fostered by the coming of the railroad caused the virtual disappearance of the tallgrass prairie; the mixed and shortgrass prairies to the west suffered as well from railroad-induced agriculture and grazing; prairie settlement was contingent on wood fiber extracted from the Great Lakes forests, a process that forever changed forest ecosystems; the housing boom of the 1950s and 1960s stimulated timber harvesting in the previously protected national forests and led to the decline and fragmentation of old-growth forests in the Pacific Northwest as well as the Rocky Mountain region; and dam construction on the Columbia River and other major waterways in the western United States for the purpose of generating electricity and providing irrigation water significantly reduced their suitability as fish habitat and salmon migration pathways. These are but a few examples of habitat modification induced by the pressures of agricultural and industrial development.

As already discussed in previous chapters, habitat destruction and modification threatens species, biotic communities, and certain types of ecosystems. Given a moral obligation to preserve these, remaining natural areas should be protected, and, where feasible and necessary, endangered habitat types should be restored. This should be done under an environmental ethic, so long as the cost is not so burdensome as to endanger the possibility of decent human living standards. So the purpose of this section is first to address the needs for habitat preservation and restoration on U.S. national forest lands, and then to consider the extent of the costs. The section will conclude with a brief discussion of other habitat preservation and restoration project possibilities.

Conservation biology and habitat needs

Conservation biologists suggest that the preservation of native species and biodiversity in a region requires habitat reserves that satisfy the following principles (Noss and Cooperrider 1994: 141):

1   Species should be well distributed in reserves across their native range because they are less susceptible to extinction than species confined to small portions of their range.
2   Large blocks of habitat containing large populations of a target species are superior to small blocks of habitat containing small populations.
3   Blocks of habitat close together are better than blocks far apart.

4   Habitat in contiguous blocks is better than fragmented habitat.
5   Interconnected blocks of habitat are better than isolated blocks.
6   Blocks of habitat that are roadless or otherwise inaccessible to humans are
     better than roaded and accessible habitat blocks.

Reserves conforming to such principles will generally support species
populations of sufficient size as to avoid endangerment, protect ecosystem
functioning, and assure the continuation of evolutionary processes. To fully
encompass a region's complement of native species, a reserve system would
also have to include all habitat types (Noss and Cooperrider 1994). In addition,
a system of reserves in a region would have to be sufficiently large to support
natural disturbance regimes, such as periodic fire. A given habitat type could be
wiped out by fire, for example, if a reserve system is insufficient in size. Because
many habitat types are adapted to natural disturbances and cannot exist without
them, disturbance processes, such as fire, should be allowed to function
uninhibited by human action. Prairie ecosystems, for example, are fire dependent
(Chapter 4).
    In absolute terms, a fair amount of land is already reserved from develop-
ment in the U.S. Around 27 million acres are currently reserved in designated
wilderness areas in the lower 48 states, while national parks and monuments
contain approximately 81 million acres of which around 4 million are designated wilderness (Wolke 1991: 63; U.S. Bureau of the Census 1993). Parks
and designated wilderness areas, however, were not designed according to
conservation biology principles. National parks and wilderness areas fail to
encompass all habitat types. National park lands exclude one-third of potential vegetation types (Noss and Cooperrider 1994), and designated wilderness
areas are heavily concentrated in relatively high-elevation mountainous areas
(Wolke 1991). National parks are too small to support populations of all their
native species. Species loss over time in national parks has been found to be
inversely correlated with park size. Similarly, designated wilderness areas
are often too small and too isolated to sustain all native species populations.
Both national parks and wilderness areas suffer incompatible uses, such as
logging, right up to their borders (Noss and Cooperrider 1994; Wolke 1991;
Foreman and Wolke 1992).

The national forests as biological reserves

The compelling need for biological preservation requires more and larger protected areas of natural habitat. A significant first step in this process would be to
designate the 191 million acre national forest system (8.4 percent of U.S. land
area) as a biological reserve and bring to a halt all uses incompatible with this
designation such as timber harvesting, mining, grazing, and oil and gas production. This would immediately assure the protection of an additional 54 million
acres of roadless area in the national forests currently outside of designated wil-

derness areas (Wolke, 1991). These roadless areas plus designated wilderness areas could serve as a core for relatively large-scale habitat reserves. Much of the forested area surrounding these core wildernesses has been highly disturbed and fragmented by timber harvesting and road building. Over the long run, many of these areas will recover if left alone and would serve to expand the boundaries of the original wilderness core areas.

A critical task in these recovery areas needed to protect biodiversity is the reduction of road density through road closures. Roads block the movement of small mammals; increase the hunting, poaching, and harassment of large mammals; cause erosion and stream sedimentation that harm aquatic species; lead to increased medium-sized mammal mortality as a consequence of roadkills; and are pathways for the invasion of pathogens and exotic species (Noss and Cooperrider 1994). In the Yellowstone area, for example, road closures are considered essential for reducing human–grizzly bear contacts that lead to the killing of bears (Mattson and Reid 1991; O'Toole 1993).

The one limitation of this proposal may be that not all vegetation types in a given region are represented in national forests. This would require careful region-by-region analysis using methods of conservation biology. Some ecosystems, however, would benefit significantly from national forest preservation. The northern Rocky Mountains ecoregion in the state of Idaho, for example, is 88 percent in public ownership, with most in national forests (Wright *et al.* 1994). Adding the national forests surrounding Yellowstone National Park to reserved status would significantly increase protection of the Yellowstone ecosystem, although large-mammal migrations to surrounding private lands need to be accommodated in some fashion (Noss and Cooperrider 1994; Berger 1991). And in northern Wisconsin, taking national forest lands out of timber production would markedly expand the potential for old-growth forest recovery needed to protect forest interior species (Alverson *et al.* 1988).

The economics of a national biological reserve

The annual net public subsidy for timber sales on the national forests is approximately $200 million per year, while the annual subsidy for grazing is approximately $20 million (O'Toole 1988: 11–12; O'Toole 1993). National forests with positive timber sale cash flows taking into account all costs are located only in the Pacific Northwest and the southern coastal plain (*ibid.*: 37). Pacific Northwest national forests are already under stringent timber harvesting restrictions to preserve spotted owl habitat. Taxpayers will thus gain on net by eliminating timber sales on the national forests. The national forests account for approximately 20 percent of total U.S. timber production (U.S. Bureau of the Census 1993). As a consequence of somewhat higher lumber prices from the elimination of national forest harvests, some of the decline in production would be made up by increased sales from private lands. The net costs, if any, of converting the national forests to a system of biological reserves is probably insignificant, once taxpayer savings are balanced against higher timber prices.

Randal O'Toole (1988, 1993) argues that recreation users of the national forests ought to be charged full market value for their visits, and that if this was undertaken, as much as $5 billion a year in revenues could be generated. While there is some danger that U.S. Forest Service bureaucrats would attempt to create outdoor "Disneylands" in order to maximize revenues, O'Toole's proposal has merit if land managers are placed under the right constraints. The first step would be to establish areas of national forests that should be put off-limits to human contact and to reduce road densities to levels that assure the preservation of species, ecological functioning, and evolutionary processes. Doing so would reduce the recreational potential of the national forests. Even if there was, say, a 50 percent reduction in road miles and a roughly proportionate decline in recreation visits, this would still result in perhaps $2 billion in revenues, certainly enough to fund ecosystem recovery and management activities. To assure that local forest managers focus on ecosystem preservation, periodic independent audits of habitat conditions and species populations could be undertaken, and the proportion of revenues retained for local use could be dependent upon the results of those audits.[20] Since the national forests don't cover all habitat types, some of the recreation revenues generated could be devoted to funding land acquisitions to fill in gaps.

Other measures to expand natural habitat

As already noted, national forest lands don't cover all habitat types, and are essentially absent from the Great Plains and old tallgrass prairie. Licht (1994) suggests creating a series of permanent grassland reserves in the tall- and mixed-grass prairie states totaling some 18 million acres. The reserve areas he suggests were selected for their potential for biodiversity preservation and ecosystem restoration. These reserves could permanently replace croplands in the USDA Conservation Reserve Program at a cost per acre that is probably lower than current taxpayer subsidies. This is another example of a biological conservation opportunity that will on net save money.

Converting the national forests to biological reserves and creating a system of reserves in the prairie states is not enough to protect all ecosystem types and assure the long-run survival of native species in the continental U.S. While instituting these two proposals would do much for biological conservation, other steps will be needed, including the preservation of key habitats on the Bureau of Land Management lands, purchase and preservation of wetlands and other critical habitats not represented on public lands, the control of invading exotic plants and animals, the restoration of riverine habitats destroyed by dams and channelization, and the protection of threatened coast fish stocks from overfishing. These measures are unlikely to be very costly as a percentage of GDP and are thus unlikely to impose a major economic burden on society as a whole.[21]

158

Conclusion

Surprisingly, key measures to achieve an environmental steady state are not very costly. A 50 percent reduction in CO_2 emissions can be obtained at roughly a zero cost because of the high return on energy conservation investments; a 50 percent reduction in pesticide use would probably increase GDP; and the national forests and large areas in the prairie states can be converted to biological reserves at a net saving to taxpayers. The most costly environmental measure suggested above is controlling the next 40 percent of CO_2 emissions, which will cost around 5 percent of GDP. Controlling remaining nonpoint water pollution may run another 0.6 percent of GDP. Even if these more costly measures are undertaken, they still would not make it impossible to provide everyone in the U.S. with a material standard necessary for a decent human life. Although the full cost of comparable measures has not been calculated here for European countries like the U.K., the order of magnitude is unlikely to be much different, and violation of the decent human life standard can probably be avoided in Europe as well under a steady-state economy.

The beauty of these proposals as a package is that they resolve the vast majority of our environmental problems. The elimination of CO_2 emissions, for example, serves as an umbrella for virtually all other air pollution problems, and eliminating such emissions will force us to turn to sustainable renewable energy sources. The result will be a steady-state energy supply system. Policies already in place in the U.S. and elsewhere should resolve the problem of a thinning in the protective stratospheric ozone layer. Other environmental issues not addressed directly or indirectly by the package of proposals in this chapter include the management of fisheries stocks, solid and hazardous waste disposal, and toxic emissions unrelated to fossil fuel use, but resolving these problems would probably not be very costly in terms of reduced GDP.

The only major natural resource issue ignored by the package of proposals is the continuing consumption of nonrenewable raw materials. Because of entropic processes, 100 percent recycling of materials is an impossibility (Daly 1992). As time passes, raw material reserves become increasingly inaccessible as the most easily exploited sources are utilized first. This means that over time the energy cost of resource extraction increases (Cleveland 1991). Real per unit extraction costs for raw materials historically have not increased over time because relatively cheap fossil fuel energy has been substituted for labor and capital. Once energy costs start rising, then extraction costs will start to increase for raw materials.

One measure that would encourage the conservation and recycling of materials is an *ad valorem* tax on the extraction of all virgin raw materials. Tax revenues could be used to fund energy conservation projects to offset the increasing energy consumption requirements for raw materials extraction. A sustainable steady-state consumption level for nonrenewable raw materials is a theoretical impossibility, but a tax and investments in energy conservation would increase future supplies and put off the day when a declining state becomes necessary.

Another issue not given serious attention here is the question of population growth. While U.S. and European fertility is at roughly replacement levels, U.S. population is still expanding because of immigration and disequilibrium in the population age distribution. Clearly, a stable or shrinking population would make the environmental preservation measures set out in this chapter much easier to achieve. Once we move outside U.S. and European borders, the population question becomes even more critical to attaining a steady state and a decent standard of living.[22]

Finally, the new industry creation process described in earlier chapters is likely to continue and create unforeseen environmental problems. This simply means that environmental policy must be a dynamic process. The central lesson of environmental history is that new technologies and industries must be scrutinized much earlier than in the past to determine and respond to their environmental consequences. This is particularly important because as new industries grow they become politically more powerful and are likely to oppose environmental regulation (Chapter 6).

Herman Daly's steady-state economy is not an idle dream; moral obligations to preserve the health of human beings, nonhuman species, and natural ecosystems can be fulfilled while at the same time assuring everyone a decent standard of living. Why don't we do it? This question has already been answered in Chapter 6. The economic development process as we know it creates vested interests able to block the substantial reforms needed to bring about an economy that is in a steady state relative to the natural environment.

If the economic process itself creates vested interests that oppose environmental regulation, then a steady-state economy is perhaps an idle dream. There may be, however, other trends in economic and political life that could assist in overcoming the vested interest problem. These possibilities are taken up in Chapters 10 and 11. First the nature of macroeconomic policy under a steady state needs to be spelled out.

9

THE MACROECONOMICS OF A
STEADY STATE

The central conclusion of this book so far is that environmental problems are fundamentally rooted in macroeconomic phenomena. Nonetheless, surprisingly little has been said by economists about the macroeconomics of modern environmental problems. Although such problems are seen by most economists as fundamentally microeconomic, there are dissenters, as noted in the introduction to this book and in the previous chapter. Herman Daly's (1991a, 1991b) formulation of a steady-state economy is in response to what he sees as a macroeconomic environmental problem of crisis proportions. The essence of his view is that the scale of the global macroeconomy is dangerously out of sync with the scale of the global environment. While he argues that scale is the essential macroeconomic problem (Daly 1991a), neither he nor others have explored in detail the macroeconomic consequences of a steady state. How does the fundamentally cyclical character of macroeconomic activity square with the notion of a steady state? What are the consequences of a steady state for macroeconomic policy? Is a steady state even consistent with a growth-prone economy based on capitalist forms of business organization? The goal of this chapter is to begin the task of addressing these and other issues related to the macroeconomics of a steady state, taking into account the specific steady-state policies put forth in the last chapter.

Macroeconomic consequences of a steady state

The focus of attention in high-growth macroeconomics is usually on the idea of labor productivity growth. In order for living standards for the average worker to increase, ultimately the output produced per unit labor (L), or GDP in real terms per hour worked (GDP/L), must increase. In either an imposed or a regulated steady state where resource flows are limited to fixed sustainable levels, the growth of GDP in real terms is restricted by the growth rate of resource productivity (GDP/R) for the resource (R) with the lowest productivity growth rate. If a resource such as energy is essential for production of GDP, then the ability to produce GDP per unit of the resource must increase in order for growth in GDP to be feasible. In other words, the maximum possible growth rate of GDP is equal to min growth rate GDP/R_1 (9.1)

over all I for $I = 1, \ldots, N$, given a total of N different resources.

The limiting resource will consequently be the one with the lowest productivity. Resource productivity for any resource, including the limiting one, can in theory be increased by substitution among different resource inputs and between resources and other inputs, such as labor and capital. The conventional view is that labor and capital can be substituted for the limiting resource input, and resource productivity can be increased, alleviating any constraints on GDP growth. However, beyond some point further substitutions between inputs cannot serve to increase resource productivity (Georgescu-Roegen 1967: 340–341). As both Daly and Georgescu-Roegen have argued, resource flows are ultimately complementary to labor–capital inputs and are thus precluded from playing the substitute role (Daly 1991a: 204–205; Georgescu-Roegen 1984). According to this view, capital and labor are productive by virtue of their capacity to transform material resources through the use of energy into useful commodities and services and, in the final analysis, must be complementary to materials and energy. The point is a simple one: substitutions among inputs are limited in their ability to increase resource productivity. With limits on substitutability and resource input flows fixed at steady-state sustainable levels, improvements in resource productivity will ultimately depend on the introduction of new technologies.

If implemented, a steady-state economy as described in the previous chapter would face serious natural resource constraints. Reducing greenhouse emissions and habitat preservation efforts together would increase the scarcity of both energy resources and developable land. The reduction of greenhouse emissions by 90 percent requires significant energy conservation efforts and expansion of solar energy production. Engineering studies suggest that U.S. energy consumption can be reduced by as much as 50 percent using existing technologies, without significant cost to the U.S. economy (Cline 1992). By international standards energy use in the U.S. is highly inefficient. Energy consumption per capita in the United Kingdom is less than one-half that of the U.S.; U.S. industries are only 60 percent as energy efficient as Japanese industries; and present technology could increase the current 19 mpg automobile fuel efficiency rate in the U.S. to 45 mpg (Pimentel *et al.* 1994). Given a 50 percent reduction in U.S. energy consumption through conservation measures, much of the remaining fossil fuel consumption would have to be replaced by renewable energy sources such as solar.[1] Up to 40 percent of current energy consumption in the U.S. could be replaced by solar energy sources, but doing so would require devoting up to 20 percent of total U.S. land area to solar production. Because non-fossil fuel sources supply approximately 12 percent of current U.S. energy consumption, and because fossil fuel use could continue at low levels under a 90 percent carbon dioxide reduction regime, something less than a 40 percent solar replacement would be required (U.S. Department of Commerce 1993). Still, land requirements for solar energy production would increase significantly. Land requirements for natural habitat

162

preservation and solar together suggest that land would indeed become an extremely scarce resource under a steady-state economic regime. While the productivity of land for nonagricultural uses can be increased in the U.S. by building at higher densities, diminishing returns to increases in land use productivity appear to be inevitable in the long run. The prospects are even poorer for increasing the productivity of land use in already densely populated countries like Japan and the U.K.

If land use productivity growth does not constitute a binding constraint on GDP growth in the future, energy productivity growth probably will. Once a 50 percent reduction in U.S. energy consumption is achieved through conservation measures, diminishing returns to improvements in energy productivity are bound to occur. Moreover, renewable energy resources themselves face supply and environmental constraints (Pimentel *et al.* 1994). As already noted, solar energy production is relatively land intensive and will be constrained by other land use needs. While an environmental steady state does not necessarily consign the economy to an output steady state, it probably means less economic growth than experienced in the past. Such realities are not addressed in the conventional economic models used for estimating the costs of carbon emissions reductions that assume economic growth continuing at historical levels (Cline 1992: 141–194). The costs estimates coming from these models in terms of the proportion of GDP required to achieve emissions limits are not necessarily wrong, just the projection that economic growth can continue at its historical pace once emissions reductions have been achieved and a renewable energy system is in place. A reduced potential economic growth rate will likely have profound effects on the macroeconomy and macroeconomic policy, effects worthy of further investigation and speculation.

Because a capitalist macroeconomy features both short-term and long-term fluctuations in growth rates, a steady-state economy will face critical macroeconomic problems that may require new approaches to macro policy. A short-term rapid expansion in aggregate demand in the context of steady-state energy flows would result in a surge in energy prices. If a steady state were imposed by nature itself as a result of resource scarcity, increases in resource prices would generate higher economic rents to natural resource owners. Because resource owners are generally wealthier than the population at large, the end result would be a redistribution of income in favor of the wealthy, a probable decline in the aggregate propensity to consume, and a resulting reduction in aggregate demand leading to a decline of real GDP.[2] This problem is partly avoided in the early years of the regulated steady state described in the previous chapter, however, where rents from energy price increases would be realized by a large cross-section of the population through ownership of marketable carbon emission permits. In later years of the transition period to a renewable energy system where the volume of carbon emission permits issued is substantially reduced, this would be less the case. Owners of solar energy production capacity would gain significant rents with surges in economic growth and intensified competition for energy resources.

The problem of inflation from energy price increases is, however, unavoidable in either an imposed or a regulated steady state. Rising energy prices would likely initiate a price-cost inflation spiral, one that the monetary authority would undoubtedly try to stop with restrictive monetary policy. This would in turn choke off aggregate demand growth and bring about a decline in real GDP. This seems to be what happened in the early 1980s when the Federal Reserve resisted energy price induced inflation with extremely tight monetary policy. Rising energy prices have invariably preceded years of near zero or negative real GNP growth since World War II and appear to have played a causal role in some post-war recessions (Hamilton 1983; Ott and Tatom 1986; Renshaw 1992).

Not only might short-term expansions in aggregate demand and economic growth be choked off by steady-state energy flows, but long-term expansions could suffer as well. Although the issue is still hotly debated, capitalist economies appear to be driven by long wave growth processes (van Duijn 1983; Freeman *et al.* 1982; Booth 1987; Marshall 1987; Tylecote 1992). In long wave cycles, the underlying growth rate in the economy itself is subject to fluctuations. A long wave lasts from 40 to 60 years and essentially involves a period of rapid economic growth followed by a period of slow growth. During the rapid growth phase of a long wave, the real GDP growth rate is driven to unusually high levels because of bursts in investment spending associated with new products, new forms of economic activity, and related infrastructure investment. During such periods, consumer spending is also growing rapidly not only because of income growth, but because of the introduction of radically new products and the expansion of the market sphere to include new forms of activity formerly restricted to the nonmarket realm (Nell 1988). Such expansions have historically depended on growth in the use of energy and materials. Without the potential for growing use of energy and other resources such as land, the long wave growth phase could be choked off, and a resulting collapse of investment spending could lead to a period of serious economic decline.[3]

As in the case of conventional business cycles, energy prices are apparently a driving element in long waves. Substantial spikes in wholesale energy prices precede detrended long wave troughs in investment spending and pig iron shipments by between nine and 13 years (Watt 1989) for the last three long wave cycles, suggesting that energy scarcity plays a key role in bringing long wave expansions to an end. Such scarcities emerged after periods of growing energy use. Obviously, if there is an absolute lid on energy use, then long wave expansions will be choked off sooner than otherwise.

The concept of the long wave is consistent with a basic premise of this book – new industries are required for long-term economic growth because of retardation in the growth rate of older industries. In a long wave the formation of new industries tends to be concentrated in time, causing the long-term economic growth rate to accelerate. Even if such concentration does not occur, restrictions on energy supplies and other resources could inhibit the ability of new businesses in new industries to form. Such businesses are very sensitive to input costs, as demonstrated by the propensity of new businesses in new industries to avoid locations where existing industries are located and dominate local input markets (Booth 1987; Watkins 1980). In a world of limited energy and developable land supplies, new businesses would have to bid away such resources from other users. Renewable energy and energy conservation would, however, be two sectors that may well attract new businesses based on new technologies under a steady-state energy regime. Still, entrepreneurs would lack the full range of opportunities they would face in a resource-abundant world.

By placing a strait-jacket on growth in the form of limits on energy flows and developable land, a steady state thus creates special problems for capitalist economies driven by both short-term and long-term fluctuations in economic activity. Even if the short- and long-term cyclical problems could somehow be resolved, a structural unemployment problem could also emerge if labor force growth exceeds the growth rate in macroeconomic labor demand, which is approximately equal to the real GDP growth rate minus the growth rate in labor productivity (GDP/hours worked). This problem would be partly alleviated by a substitution of labor for energy resources because of increases in energy prices caused by steady-state policies. Although the substitution of labor for energy is ultimately limited by the inherent complementarity of the two inputs, energy conservation measures, such as installing insulation and energy-conserving recycling (e.g. aluminum cans), are labor intensive. The substitution of labor for energy would reduce labor productivity growth and thus increase growth in the demand for labor.

Whether a slow growth induced unemployment problem emerges depends in the long term on population growth and changes in labor force participation. Obviously, rapid population growth will exacerbate the problem and slow population growth or population stability will mitigate it.

Macroeconomic policy and a steady state

In a steady-state world, conventional fiscal and monetary measures become counter-productive. As demonstrated by recent business cycle history, tight monetary policy to fight resource price induced inflation merely substitutes unemployment for inflation. An alternative that avoids a cost-push inflation cycle without bringing on a recession and unemployment is an incomes policy that restricts the growth of wage and dividend income. Such a policy allows the relative price of energy to rise and stimulate further efficiencies in its use without resulting in incomes chasing prices and prices chasing incomes in an ever upward spiral.

While an incomes policy would help by avoiding excessively restrictive monetary and fiscal policies, the underlying problem of an inherently cyclical and growth-oriented capitalist economy would remain. Surges of growth from normal business cycle upturns as well as long wave economic expansions would still run up against the limits of fixed energy flows and limited supplies of land. The simple multiplier-accelerator business cycle model implies that a ceiling on growth brings forth a slump in induced investment expenditures. If long wave business expansions are driven by the development of new products and technologies that feed booms in investment and consumption spending (van Duijn 1983: 93–111), and if such expansions are highly restricted by fixed energy resource throughput, then slumps in both investment and consumption spending are a possibility in a steady-state world. The growth of consumption spending is at least partly driven by novelty and the transformation of nonmarket into market activities (Nell 1988). Transformational growth involves the taking over of productive activities by corporate enterprises formerly performed in the confines of the family or the traditional craft system (e.g. mass production of canned foods), while novelty involves the satisfaction of basic wants in entirely new and novel ways (e.g. the invention of television as a medium of entertainment). With economic expansion restricted in the aggregate, competition for resources between old and new forms of economic activity will intensify, impinging on the growth of the new. With limits on novelty and transformational growth, both consumption and investment expenditures could easily suffer a chronic slump. The cutting off of both short-term and long-term investment and consumption cycle expansions could lead to a chronic problem of stagnant private sector demand. A likely pattern would be investment- and consumption-driven expansion attempts cut off by fixed resource flows followed by periods of stagnation. An ultimate result could be the discouragement of entrepreneurial activity and its associated investment spending. In order to maintain a fully employed economy in such circumstances, government expenditures may have to be permanently expanded in order to fill in the gap between private sector expenditures and the total needed in order to prevent serious unemployment problems (Nell 1988: 159–183, 228–248).

Whether an energy and land use steady state brings forth a slump in entrepreneurial activity and the creation of new products is a speculative matter. If entrepreneurs are clever enough to seek out products with low energy and land use intensity and focus on energy and land use conservation and new forms of energy production, underinvestment and underconsumption may not emerge as a problem, although multiplier-accelerator investment instability would still result if investment goods themselves required significant energy inputs to produce. Again, entrepreneurs under a steady-state regime would lack the full range of possibilities for innovation they would have in a world of energy and resource abundance.

Even if GDP could be kept on the growth path permitted by resource productivity growth, as already noted slow growth induced unemployment could still result if the growth rate in the labor force exceeds the growth in aggregate labor demand (real GDP growth rate less the labor productivity growth rate). The only way to solve this problem is through some form of work time reduction. A reduction in the length of the workweek would be one means for spreading hours worked over more jobs (Daly 1973: 162). One potentially popular means for accomplishing this objective would be to substitute compensating time off (comp time) for overtime pay, as suggested by Juliet Schor in her widely acclaimed book, *The Overworked American* (1992: 142–146). Schor (1991; 1992: 128–132) presents evidence that most American workers would willingly forgo pay increases in order to obtain more leisure, and advocates an aggregate reduction in work time as an environmental measure.

A second longer-term option for reducing unemployment problems arising from a steady state would be to engage in policies that reduce population growth and thus labor force growth. A stable or shrinking population would clearly reduce the need for job-creating GDP growth as well as reducing pressure on resource use. We need to get beyond the idea that population policy is only for less developed countries.

To accomplish macroeconomic stability and full employment would consequently require macroeconomic policy measures that are not a part of the contemporary policy discourse: an incomes policy, a relatively larger government sector, a reduction in the length of the workweek, and a population policy. In a steady-state world macroeconomic policy would of necessity differ radically from current practice.

The microeconomic feasibility of a macroeconomic steady state

The expansionist nature of capitalist institutions raises doubt about whether they could continue to flourish at the microeconomic level in the context of macroeconomic steady-state limitations on energy and other resource flows. Both entrepreneurial capitalism and the modern expansionist bureaucratic corporation in this setting would face some serious problems.

These problems flow in part from the dynamics of the relationship between the large bureaucratic corporation and the comparatively small entrepreneurial enterprise. The former is run by a managerial class and the latter by individual entrepreneurs. The corporate bureaucracy functions best at solving the problems of large-scale production and marketing, while the more flexible entrepreneurial enterprise is at its best in serving niche markets and devising innovative new products and technologies (Booth 1987: 11–17). The most successful of the entrepreneurial enterprises are either taken over by large corporations, or graduate to that status themselves through growth. The entrepreneurial enterprise and the bureaucratic corporation are thus linked. The former provides the new products and new ideas that feed the growth of the latter. While existing corporate bureaucracies are capable of incremental innovations, it is generally the entrepreneurial enterprise that fosters the creation of entirely new products, technologies, or forms of economic activity. The classic form of the corporate conglomerate growth process is the draining of capital from slow-growth subsidiaries, or "cash cows," to feed the acquisition and expansion of high-growth subsidiaries, the "stars," many of which have their origins as entrepreneurial enterprises (Dugger 1985). The growth of the corporate conglomerate is thus dependent on a growing entrepreneurial sector.

The constraining of the entrepreneurial sector and new forms of economic activity by steady-state resource flows not only impinges on long wave expansions, but also constrains corporate growth by cutting into a key source of expansion, the acquisition of high-growth entrepreneurial businesses. This plus the direct constraint of steady-state resource flows on expansion seriously impinges on the continued rapid growth of large corporate enterprises.

Without growth, a corporation faces serious internal problems with its managerial class. The central motivating force within the managerial hierarchy is the quest by individuals for higher position and expanded income (Dugger 1980; 1989). The primary goal of a manager is elevated status; elevated status comes with positions of greater authority; and authority is related to the scale of the organization. Corporate growth increases the potential for advancement, and corporate stagnation curtails it. With a steady state comes the possibility of corporate stagnation, diminished potential for advancement, and managerial demoralization (Penrose 1968: 54). The net result could be an economy dominated by large corporate bureaucracies staffed by alienated and unmotivated employees. Recent corporate downsizing and compression of the managerial hierarchy make this problem even more significant. With fewer managerial slots, even more growth is needed to provide the middle class with the carrot of economic advancement.

To preserve its vitality, the modern capitalist corporation as an institution relies heavily on relatively rapid macroeconomic growth.[4] Since macro-level restrictions on resource flows limit such growth, the continued health of the corporation in a steady state is an open question. For a steady-state economy to function effectively at both the micro and macro levels, a new form of business organization that relies less heavily on growth may be needed. One such organizational form is the producer cooperative where employees own nonmarketable shares in their workplace that entitle them to a wage payment in return for work performed, a vote in a general assembly of workers that elects a managing board, and a share of surplus earnings paid in proportion to wage income earned (Ellerman 1983). The advantages of such an organization form for environmental policy are addressed in detail in the next chapter.

Conclusion

In Herman Daly's early works on a steady-state economy (1991a), the implementation of a steady state is envisioned as a reform measure not requiring substantial changes in business institutions. Only limited attention was given by Daly to the macroeconomic consequences of a steady state. Once these consequences are more fully understood, a steady-state economy can be seen more readily for what it is and for what it requires. It requires relatively radical changes in both macroeconomic and microeconomic institutions in order to be successful. Modern corporate and entrepreneurial capitalism are each premised on waves of high economic growth, and without these waves neither can function very effectively. In a more recent work, Daly and Cobb (1989) seem to recognize the need for a dramatic restructuring of society not only for its own sake, but also to achieve economic sustainability. While their focus is on the concept of community and the social changes needed to achieve sustainable communities, they do not address in detail the macroeconomic problems associated with a sustainable economy. Specific measures they do propose, however, such as increased employee ownership and reductions in working time, are identical to those suggested here to resolve steady-state macroeconomic problems.

In sum, for a steady-state macroeconomy to function effectively, the requirements at a macroeconomic level are an incomes policy, an expanded government sector, and a reduction in the workweek, and the central need at a microeconomic level may be new organization forms that embody principles of economic democracy, an issue taken up in more detail in the next chapter. While the imposition of a steady state sacrifices economic growth, those things needed to make it work, such as a shorter workweek and increased economic democracy, are appealing in their own right. Moreover, survey research suggests that there is no real connection between increased human happiness and economic growth (Schor 1992: 115). This permits a note of optimism for the eventual adoption of a steady state. On the other hand, against it will be an array of formidable economic interests tied to a high-growth economy. The question of how such interests might be overcome is the subject of the final two chapters.

10

ECONOMIC DEMOCRACY AS AN ENVIRONMENTAL MEASURE

The idea that problems of declining environmental quality and growing natural resource scarcity are attributable to growth of the economic system occurring in the context of a stable ecosystem is gaining growing acceptance (Costanza 1991) and is a basic premise of this book. As the economic system expands, it places increasing demands on the global ecosystem for energy, materials, and ecosystem services. The global ecosystem, however, has a fixed capacity to provide such services (Daly 1991a). As a consequence of economic expansion, the global ecosystem suffers from excessive exploitation, and, as a result, its capacity to provide inputs to the global economy is diminished. This view is consistent with the central thesis of this book, that the forces driving economic growth are also driving environmental change.

As suggested in the last two chapters, a steady-state economy that draws upon global environmental resources at a stable, sustainable level is sufficient for re-solving environmental problems and meeting ethical obligations to future gen-erations as well as the nonhuman natural world.[1] This does not necessarily mean a no-growth economy. Economic growth in the conventional sense could still occur so long as the productivity of environmental resource use increases over time (Chapter 9). However, a steady-state economy would likely grow more slowly than a conventional high-growth capitalist economy.

Given that a steady-state economy is desired to resolve environmental prob-lems, what form of business organization is likely to be most compatible with it? The market-driven capitalist corporation appears to have won the global struggle over the question of organizational superiority. Centrally planned economies and their state-run enterprises are in rapid retreat not only in the former Soviet Union, but in China and elsewhere as well. The central question to be raised in the pages to follow is whether the expansion-minded capitalist corporation is the appropri-ate organizational form in a world of growing environmental resource scarcity, or whether there is some other form of business organization that is not only more efficient but more environmentally benign as well.

A form of business organization that appears to be a promising alternative to the corporation is the producer cooperative. In a producer cooperative, em-ployment brings with it a right to democratic participation in governance of the organization and a right to share in surplus earnings. In the highly successful

Mondragon system of cooperatives in the Basque region of Spain, surplus earnings above wages and retained reserves are deposited in individual employee capital accounts not subject to withdrawal until the employee's retirement (Whyte and Whyte 1988; Thomas and Logan 1982). Like their conventional corporate counterparts, the Mondragon cooperatives compete against other businesses in the European and global economy.

Is a democratically run cooperative that functions in the context of a market economy inherently more environmentally friendly than a hierarchical capitalist corporation? This is the central question to be addressed in this chapter. In the first section, the cooperative and conventional corporation will be compared theoretically. Would a cooperative or a corporation be more growth-oriented and thus more prone to increase its utilization of environmental resources? Which would be more likely to undertake capital investments that will conserve on energy and materials inputs? These are the critical theoretical issues. In the second section, the empirical literature comparing cooperative and conventional business performance will be reviewed for insights into the questions of growth orientation and efficiency of nonlabor input use. The final section will address the question of which form of business organization, the cooperative or the corporation, is more likely to adopt environmental preservation and resource conservation as a goal, and which will be the least resistant to environmental regulation.

Growth and resource conservation in the corporation and the cooperative: theory

The intent of this section is to compare the profit-maximizing corporation and a cooperative that maximizes income per worker in a theoretically rigorous way in order to determine which would be more environmentally friendly. The key conclusions of this comparison are the following:

1   cooperatives will employee fewer workers and produce less output than corporations;
2   corporations are more likely to undertake scale-expanding investments than cooperatives; and
3   cooperatives are more likely to undertake nonlabor (e.g. energy and materials) cost-reducing investments than corporations.

In each case an intuitive argument will be presented prior to the more technical theoretical argument.

Employment and output: cooperative vs. the corporation

The goal of a cooperative where members share in total earnings net of nonlabor costs will be to maximize income per member, assuming that individual members are only interested in income and not other organizational goals. The goal of a corporation is typically to maximize total profits. How will the decision on the number of members to recruit in the case of the cooperative and the number of employees to hire in the case of the corporation differ? The cooperative will recruit more members so long as the income per member either increases or remains the same as membership expands. This will occur if economic efficiencies are available from using more labor that increase output per worker. Beyond some point, however, adding labor will reduce output per worker and added membership will drag down average member income. The addition of members will stop short of declining average member income. At this point, the added net income generated by the last unit of labor added will just be equal to the average member income. If it were less, it would pull average income down, and if it were more it would pull average income up.

The corporation's hiring decision will differ because its goal is to maximize total profits. It will want to expand employment and production so long as the net income increase from employing another worker is greater than or equal to the added wage cost. The going market wage rate will have to be less than the average labor income in a comparable cooperative if returns to capital are earned.[2] The corporation will expand the employment of labor beyond the peak of average labor income to the point where the addition of net income by the last unit of labor hired is just equal to the wage. Beyond the peak the incremental net income from labor will fall, pulling average labor income down. The corporation is interested in the incremental net income relative to the wage it pays. It will go beyond the peak to the point where equality between the incremental net income and the wage occurs. The point is simple: corporations will use more labor and produce more output than comparable cooperatives. Corporations will thus have greater energy/matter throughput rates and pollution emissions than their cooperative counterparts.

Now let's undertake the more rigorous explanation of employment and output differences between cooperatives and corporations. To theoretically compare a typical corporation and a typical cooperative in a rigorous manner, a number of simplifying assumptions are necessary. The cooperative and corporation are assumed to initially have identical capital stocks and to pay out an identical fixed return on capital each year. In the case of the cooperative, the return will be paid for borrowed capital, either to owners of individual capital accounts or to lenders, while for the corporation the return will be paid either to stock holders as dividends, or to lenders. All nonlabor variable inputs are assumed to be used in fixed proportions to output. For the cooperative, the goal is assumed to be the maximization of the net average revenue product (*NARP*) with nonlabor and capital costs netted out. *NARP* is equal to net income per worker. Assuming either diminishing returns to labor or diminishing marginal revenue from output, the *NARP* schedule will rise to a maximum and then decline to zero, as shown in Figure 10.1.[3] *NARP* does not become positive until the fixed annual capital cost is covered by revenues. Irrespective of the wage rate (*W*), the cooperative will choose the level of employment *E* that maximizes income or net revenue per

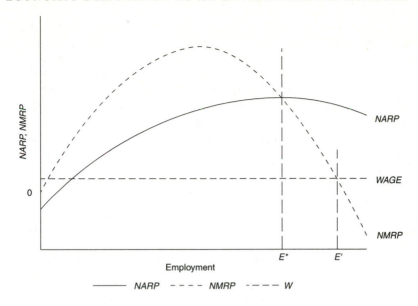

Figure 10.1 Net average revenue product and net marginal revenue product

workers. The wage would simply establish the division between income received immediately and income to be paid into the individual capital accounts.

In what follows, the assumption of a perfectly competitive market is not necessary, although the analysis is consistent with perfect competition in an industry characterized by increasing costs. The underlying production function is assumed to have the usual neoclassical characteristics, apart from the proportionality between nonlabor inputs and output. The proportionality assumption is consistent with Daly's (1991a: 204) view on the complementarity of energy/matter and labor and capital. While the efficiency of energy and materials use can be increased at the margin through new technologies that may use more capital or labor, the extent of such substitutability is ultimately limited. Production will always require an energy/matter input.

The profit-maximizing corporation would behave somewhat differently. The added cost of another worker would be the market-determined wage rate, W. Consequently, the profit-maximizing corporation would expand hiring until the net marginal revenue product (*NMRP*), with the cost of additional nonlabor inputs netted out, is just equal to the wage rate W in Figure 10.1 (at E'). Because *NMRP* intersects *NARP* at the latter's maximum and is thereafter below it, *NMRP* = W at an employment level greater than E^* where average worker income is maximized in the cooperative. Of course, *NMRP* must be declining, not increasing, in order for profits to be at a maximum.

The first conclusion is a simple one and has been recognized previously by a number of authors (Vanek 1970; Ward 1958; Meade 1972). The per worker income-maximizing cooperative will employ fewer workers and produce less than a comparable capitalist profit-maximizing firm. This means that the cooperative will use fewer material and energy inputs and emit less waste into the environment than a comparable capitalist firm, assuming that both face identical production possibilities. Basically, because the cooperative must pay the full *NARP* to additional workers employed rather than just the wage rate *W*, it will be more reluctant to take on additional workers than the corporation.

This is a comparative statics result and is of little real interest in a dynamic world. The more interesting question is whether cooperatives would be inclined to expand their scale of operations and their level of production to the same extent as the capitalist corporation. Would both in similar circumstances always undertake investments that increase the scale of their operations and thus the extent to which they use up material and energy resources and emit wastes into the environment?

Scale-expanding investment: the cooperative vs. the corporation

Consider an investment that would double the size of a given production facility. For a corporation, a doubling of plant capacity and sales with no changes in input or output prices would double profits. A corporation would therefore undertake to double the size of the plant, given that the resulting rate of return is at least equal to the next best investment alternative. The cooperative, however, would have no reason to do this unless the average income per worker increased as a result. In fact, capacity-expanding investments could more than double profits for the corporation while reducing income per worker for the cooperative. Cooperatives are thus less likely to undertake capacity-expanding investments that increase energy/matter throughput and the volume of pollution emissions.

This point can also be made using basic economic theory. In order for a cooperative that maximizes income per worker to undertake an investment project, the peak net average revenue product (*NARP*) would have to increase, taking account of the additional capital cost attributable to the investment in *NARP*.

The story is quite different for the capitalist corporation. For the profit-maximizing corporation, $(NARP - W)E$, or net profit, would have to increase, and this could occur even when the maximum level of *NARP* declines after the investment is undertaken. This is illustrated in Figure 10.2. The loss of profit from the reduction in the level of *NARP* is made up by the increase in employment caused by the outward shift of *NARP*. The loss in profit from the reduction in *NARP*, area *BCDE* in Figure 10.2, is less than the gain in profit from the increase in employment, area *FEGH* (*E'* and *E"* are the respective profit-maximizing employment levels for *NARP1* and *NARP2* and wage *W*). The cooperative would forgo this investment project, whereas the corporation would undertake it. Again, in order for an investment project to be of any benefit to a cooperative, *NARP* would have to shift upwards. Hence, the cooperative is less inclined than the corporation to undertake scale-expanding investment projects. The profit-maximizing corporation will thus be more expansionist than the cooperative and more prone to expand its use of environmental resources.

174

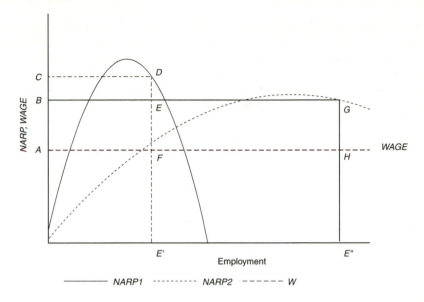

Figure 10.2 Scale-increasing investment: cooperative vs. a corporation

Investments in energy/matter throughput reduction: the cooperative vs. the corporation

The path to higher income per worker-member for cooperatives is to reduce nonlabor input costs. Investments that cut energy and materials needs per unit of output will clearly lift income per worker. If less must be paid out for such inputs, more income will be available to worker-members. For the corporation, scale-expanding investments that cooperatives would reject may well be more profitable than investments reducing the use of nonlabor inputs. Since the scale expansion option is unattractive to cooperatives, they will be more inclined to choose investments that economize on nonlabor inputs. This will mean that cooperatives are likely to be more efficient users of natural resource inputs than corporations.

This point can be made more rigorously using economic theory. Investments that reduce the amount of energy and materials required per unit output will shift the *NARP* schedule upward vertically, increasing net income per worker (*NARP*) in a cooperative. A corporation would respond by expanding employment since such an investment would shift the *NMRP* schedule upwards. Generally speaking, businesses cannot undertake all profitable investment opportunities at once because of limitations on the amount of investment funds available or on the managerial capacity to oversee investment projects. If there is a choice between two alternative investment projects, one causing an upward shift in *NARP* and one causing an outward shift leaving the maximum level of *NARP* unchanged, the corporation will undertake the scale-expanding investment project if it increases profit by a greater magnitude, whereas the cooperative would

175

always undertake the one that shifts *NARP* upwards. In other words, the cooperative will be biased towards investment projects that increase the efficiency
of energy and materials usage in comparison to the corporation. For the cooperative, an investment that increases the productivity of energy and raw materials is more likely to increase net income per worker than an investment that
increases the scale of employment and production. This point is illustrated by
the *NARP* schedules in Figure 10.3. The investment that causes an outward shift
in the *NARP* schedule is more profitable for the corporation, while the cooperative will only undertake the investment that leads to an upward shift in the
NARP schedule.[4]

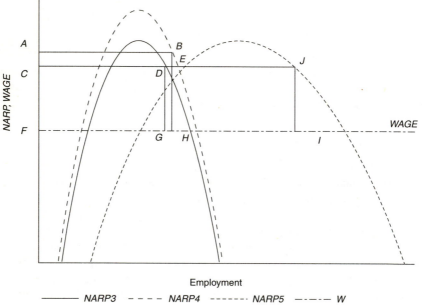

Figure 10.3 Energy/materials productivity-improving investment vs. scale-increasing
investment

Summary

The key points of this discussion are simple. Cooperatives will be strongly driven
to cut nonlabor costs, specifically the cost of energy and materials, and they will
avoid scale increases that fail to increase income per worker. The profit-
maximizing corporation will view scale expansions more favorably than cooperatives and will be less inclined to invest limited capital and managerial resources
in reducing energy and materials costs when scale-expanding investment alternatives are available.

Even in periods of macroeconomic decline cooperatives are more likely to focus on nonlabor cost reductions than corporations. Lacking a contractual commitment to their employees to keep them on the payroll, corporations can cut employment in order to reduce variable labor costs during business downturns. Worker cooperatives are committed to maintaining employment for their members and thus don't have the option of drastic labor cost cuts available to them. Consequently, they are likely to go after nonlabor cost cuts with a vengeance, especially in hard times. While corporations can cut both labor and nonlabor costs, limited capital and bounded managerial capacity are likely to cause them to choose the path of least resistance, which is most likely to be labor cost cuts.

Apart from the question of more efficient nonlabor input use, an economy composed of cooperatives that are individually smaller and less growth-prone than conventional businesses would not necessarily be smaller in the aggregate and use less total energy and material inputs. The result could simply be the same aggregate demand as in a capitalist economy, but smaller and more numerous individual firms. However, in a capitalist economy scale-expanding investments are likely to include investments in advertising, product promotion, and new product development in order to expand the total market. Given that cooperatives are less inclined to such scale expansion, the total market would likely be smaller and aggregate resource use less in a cooperative economy relative to a capitalist one.[5]

Growth and resource conservation in the corporation and cooperative: evidence

Is there evidence that cooperatives in fact focus on nonlabor cost reductions and limit their growth to a greater extent than corporations? Unfortunately, because of the rarity of worker cooperatives, the opportunities for doing comparative studies of cooperatives and corporations are relatively limited. The argument could be made that cooperatives must use inputs less efficiently and must be inferior to the corporate form of business organization simply because so few exist in western capitalist economies. This line of reasoning is flawed, however, because the creation of cooperatives faces a public goods problem not encountered by corporations (Booth 1987: 52–53). The benefit of creating cooperatives will not be fully captured by those individuals who are responsible for their initial organization, but will be shared with all individuals who ultimately become members of the cooperative. The founders of a corporation, on the other hand, by virtue of private ownership, can more fully capture the benefits of its creation. Hence, even if a cooperative is potentially more efficient than a corporation, the corporation is more likely to exist in practice.

Despite this barrier, various forms of cooperative ownership can be found in western capitalist countries, and some comparative studies of cooperatives and conventional businesses have been undertaken. The primary goal of these studies has been to compare the efficiency of production in cooperatives and conventional businesses. The hypothesis implicit in these studies is that cooperatives are more X-efficient than conventional businesses. That is, from given inputs cooperatives are able to produce a greater volume of output, or, to turn the hypothesis on its head, to produce a given volume of output, cooperatives require fewer inputs. The rationale underlying this hypothesis is that workers who share in profits and are able to influence management policy will be more highly motivated and will look for opportunities to use inputs more effectively. In the conventional business, this motivation will be weaker because the benefits of improved input efficiencies will most likely go to the business owners as increased profits, not to the workers (Booth 1987: 41–46; Thomas and Logan 1982: 97–98; Levin 1984). A study of French cooperatives found that value added was positively related to the extent of participation in profits and degree of collective membership and ownership, lending support to the X-efficiency hypothesis (Defourney *et al.* 1985).

The results of several comparative studies of cooperatives and conventional businesses are summarized in Table 10.1. These studies provide insight into whether individual cooperatives are likely to focus on nonlabor cost reductions and to be less growth-prone than their conventional capitalist counterparts, and whether systems of cooperatives are likely to be more or less growth-prone than systems of capitalist businesses. With one exception, the theoretical conclusion of more efficient nonlabor input use in cooperatives is confirmed. While the efficiency of energy and material input use is not explicitly considered in all except one of the studies, these inputs are a part of the broader nonlabor input category. Given that nonlabor inputs in general are used more efficiently in four of the five cooperative groups listed in Table 10.1 relative to their corporate competition, then it is highly likely that energy and material inputs are used more efficiently as well.

Table 10.1 Cooperative input efficiency, size, and growth relative to conventional firms

Cooperatives	Energy/material input efficiency	Nonlabor input efficiency	Individual cooperative size/growth	Cooperative system growth
British	unknown	unknown	less	less
U.S. (plywood)	greater	greater	same	less
French	unknown	greater	greater	greater
Italian	unknown	greater	greater	unknown
Mondragon	unknown	greater	greater	greater

Sources: Stephen (1984); Batstone (1982); Zevi (1982); Berman (1967); Thomas and Logan (1982); Jones and Backus (1977); Oakeshott (1978).

There is a theoretical possibility that superior X-efficiency in a cooperative relative to a corporation would result in production increases sufficient to expand the use of natural resource inputs even if they are utilized more efficiently. In such cases the increase of production would have to be relatively substantial to override the per unit decrease in input use. Moreover, a simple reduction in the amount of natural resource input required per unit of output as a consequence of

X-efficiency would result in an increase in the net price per unit of output. The result would be the perverse supply response so much discussed in the literature on labor-managed firms (Stephen 1982: 5). This means that the peak income per member-worker (*NARP*) would shift inward and less labor would be employed as a result, actually reducing output and the use of natural resource inputs.

A surprising conclusion in Table 10.1 is that individual cooperatives and cooperative systems are in some cases actually more growth-prone than their conventional competitors. This result certainly needs explaining in light of theoretical predictions to the contrary. A full understanding of this issue, however, requires a more detailed description of the studies summarized in Table 10.1.

British cooperatives

A study of British cooperatives and conventional businesses found little difference in output per worker in the footwear industry between cooperative and capitalist firms, and a slightly higher output per worker in capitalist firms relative to cooperatives in other industries (Stephen 1984: 147–148). However, the capital–labor ratio was also found to be higher in capitalist firms in these other industries, making any definite conclusions about X-efficiency impossible.

While the relative efficiency of British cooperatives cannot be determined, it is clear that individual cooperatives tend to be less growth-prone and smaller than their capitalist counterparts. Jones and Backus (1977) found that producer cooperatives in the British footwear industry experienced a reduction of the average number of people employed from 1948 to 1968, while the opposite occurred for capitalist firms in the industry. They also found that the growth of average value added for producer cooperatives was generally less than for comparable capitalist firms and that producer cooperatives were undercapitalized relative to their capitalist counterparts.

Similarly, British cooperatives as a group have experienced decline relative to British industry as a whole. After gaining a foothold in printing, textiles, and clothing in the 1890s, the British worker cooperative movement has slowly declined ever since, although individual cooperatives have been tenacious survivors, outliving many of their capitalist competitors (Oakeshott 1978: 65–67). Between 1881 and 1893 the number of producer cooperatives in England and Wales increased from 13 to 113. After 1893, this group of cooperatives experienced a lengthy period of slow decline to 16 enterprises in 1973 (*ibid.*: 65; Jones 1982; Jones and Backus 1977).

French, Italian, and U.S. cooperatives

Studies of French, Italian, and U.S. cooperatives arrive at more concrete conclusions on the issue of nonlabor input efficiency. A study of the French construction and printing industries in the Paris area found that the value added per unit of labor cost was greater on average for cooperatives than for all firms as a whole in each industry (Batstone 1982: 106–116). These same cooperatives also had a lower level of capital investment per worker and a higher value added per unit of capital, suggesting a stronger propensity to reduce nonlabor costs in cooperatives than in capitalist firms. In a study of the Italian construction industry, cooperatives were found to have a value added per worker 14 percent below that for capitalist enterprises, but the capital–labour ratio in cooperatives was 39 percent less on average than for capitalist firms (Zevi 1982: 245–246), again suggesting a strong propensity towards nonlabor cost reductions in cooperatives.

While worker cooperatives are a rarity in the U.S., they are significantly represented in the plywood industry. Studies have shown that output per worker is 25–40 percent greater in the plywood cooperatives than in the industry as a whole. The plywood cooperatives not only achieve higher output per worker, but apparently extract more plywood per board foot of timber input than their conventional counterparts. The cooperatives also have invested heavily in waste utilization facilities (Berman 1967: 188).

The U.S. plywood cooperatives behave most like the theoretical model described in the previous section. Not only are they efficient users of nonlabor inputs, but they have not exhibited strong tendencies toward growth individually or as a group. In her study of the U.S. plywood cooperatives, Katrina Berman (1967: 67, 99–100) found that the average size of cooperative plants in terms of productive capacity was about the same as for conventional plants and the size distribution of cooperative plants was similar to that for the industry as a whole, with a slightly more heavy concentration of plants in the lower-middle size ranges. Berman suggests that the empire-building motive for growth is likely to be absent in worker-owned companies, noting that worker-owned plywood companies have not expanded beyond a single plant, unlike major corporations. She also argues that taking on more worker-owners is not necessarily in the interest of the existing owners, because doing so won't necessarily increase returns per hour worked. Worker-owned plywood plants have increased their capacity only when it has resulted in improvements of income per hour, taking into account capital costs (*ibid*.: 191–192). After an initial period of rapid formation in the 1940s and 1950s, the share of the total market held by worker-owned firms had shrunk from a peak of 20 percent to 15 percent by 1964 (*ibid*.: 93–94).

In contrast to the British and American cases, French and Italian cooperatives tend to be larger and more growth-prone than their capitalist counterparts (Batstone 1982: 114; Zevi 1982: 244). In his study of Italian construction and manufacturing cooperatives, Zevi (1982: 246) found that cooperatives in both sectors grew more rapidly than their capitalist counterparts from 1976 to 1978. Since value added per employee and profits as a percentage of turnover grew in both manufacturing and construction cooperatives, expansions in firm size did not come at the sacrifice of average employee income. As in the case of the U.S. plywood cooperatives, worker-owners are apparently added only when average worker income does not suffer. The one French cooperative that experienced really dramatic growth is AOIP, a major producer of telephone equipment (Oakeshott

1978: 121–144). From 1950 to 1978 its employment increased from 1,500 to 4,000. Whether this expansion had a positive or negative impact on per worker income is not known.

The French cooperative movement as a whole has a history of slow but steady expansion. From 1901 to 1975, the number of cooperatives grew from 119 to 537, and in 1975 employed around 30,000 workers. The peak in terms of numbers of cooperatives was reached in France in 1947 at 703. More than 50 percent of the cooperatives are very small, employing less than 15 workers. Many are concentrated in the construction industry where capital requirements are not very high (*ibid.*: 123–131). While the cooperative sector is not a large part of the French economy, it has performed well since World War II, increasing its output by more than twice the rate of expansion of French industrial production between 1946 and 1976 (Batstone 1982: 115–116).

The Italian cooperative system is the largest in Europe, made up of some 2,675 cooperatives employing 147,500 workers in 1977. Italy's cooperative movement experienced its most rapid period of expansion from 1896 to 1921, increasing from 68 to 4,302 cooperatives. The movement was suppressed during the Fascist period, and was stagnant in the 1950s and 1960s (Oakeshott 1978: 148). In the 1970s, however, there was steady growth in the number of cooperatives and co-operative employment (Zevi 1982: 240–241). Italian cooperatives, which are heavily concentrated in the construction industry like the French, have focused primarily on saving jobs in older industries through buyouts of businesses that would have otherwise shut down (*ibid.*: 239–251; Oakeshott 1978: 143–164).

Mondragon cooperatives

Perhaps the most prominent example of a highly organized system of coopera-tives is the one found in the Basque region of Spain around the village of Mondragon. Cooperatives in this system are not only efficient users of all nonlabor inputs, but as a group they have experienced substantial growth (Booth 1987: 73). The Mondragon group of cooperatives started in 1956 with a single enter-prise employing 24 workers, and by 1979 had grown to 70 industrial coopera-tives employing 15,672 workers. In addition to the industrial cooperatives, a number of secondary cooperatives have been created, including a bank, a social security cooperative, a technical college, and a research and development cooperative. The products of the industrial cooperatives include refrigerators, ranges, auto-matic washing machines, bicycles, capital equipment, tools, light engineering instruments, and electrical and electronic goods (Thomas 1982: 130–131).

The research department for the Mondragon cooperatives has devised a total factor productivity measure for following productivity trends over time in the cooperatives. For one year in which comparable data were available (1972), total factor productivity was found to be higher for the cooperatives than for the 500 largest companies as well as all other manufacturing businesses in Spanish manufacturing (Thomas and Logan 1982: 107). This occurred even though the amount of fixed capital per worker in the cooperatives was less than for the top 500 Spanish companies (Levin 1984: 19). The ratio of value added per unit of fixed capital was substantially greater for the cooperatives than the top 500, suggesting that the cooperatives were able to squeeze greater productivity out of a unit of capital and keep nonlabor costs to a minimum. In addition, output per worker has generally been higher in the cooperatives, although the gap has been shrinking, apparently as the result of an emphasis on employment creation and growth as a matter of policy on the part of the Mondragon cooperative system (Thomas and Logan 1982: 106–109). Thomas and Logan (*ibid*.: 109–111) found profitability measures to also be generally higher for the cooperatives than private industry.

The average employment in Mondragon cooperatives almost tripled between 1965 and 1978 (*ibid*.: 117). Moreover, over the period 1971 to 1975, Mondragon cooperatives were typically somewhat larger in terms of employment than other industrial companies in the local area, and total factor productivity and profitability (surplus as a percentage of sales) were actually slightly greater for smaller than larger cooperatives within the Mondragon system (*ibid*.: 118–119). This suggests that some Mondragon cooperatives were not only larger than their conventional counterparts, but larger than they should have been to maximize income per worker.

While several countries have umbrella producer cooperative organizations, no cooperative system is so tightly organized as Mondragon, and none has grown so rapidly. Output of the Mondragon cooperatives as a whole has consistently grown more rapidly than the output of comparable sectors in the Spanish economy (*ibid*.: 101; Whyte and Whyte 1988: 201). The key to this growth is the close association of the primary producer cooperatives with a cooperative bank, which provides not only access to capital, which cooperatives have traditionally lacked, but extensive assistance to entrepreneurs who wish to start new cooperatives. An associated research cooperative provides the technical capacity to enter new rapid-growth high-technology industries, while a cooperative technical institute provides training to employees (Thomas and Logan 1982; Whyte and Whyte 1988). Capital availability is increased through the practice of depositing surplus earnings in individual co-op member capital accounts on which a fixed rate of interest is paid. Because members cannot withdraw funds from these accounts until they retire, members in effect are forced to save nonwage earnings, providing a pool of capital to the cooperative system for investment purposes. The Mondragon system is fundamentally structured for growth, unlike any previously existing system of cooperatives. Although an explicit policy of keeping the size of the individual co-ops to less than 350 to 500 members has been adopted (Thomas and Logan 1982: 35, 117), the system as a whole can grow through the creation of new cooperatives and the division of existing cooperatives, both of which are promoted and financed by the cooperative bank.

The surprising result of the empirical studies summarized in Table 10.1, as already noted, is the high growth tendencies of some individual cooperatives and cooperative systems. The absence of growth in the British and American cooperatives is most likely explained by their financial structure and the limited availability of external financial resources and organizational assistance. Most British footwear cooperatives generated their financing for capital investment internally from retained earnings, not allowing worker-owners leaving the cooperative prior to full depreciation of capital assets to fully recapture their investment. As Vanek (1970) and others (Stephen 1982: 10–14) have pointed out, internally financed cooperatives that do not pay the opportunity cost of capital to capital owners are likely to operate on an inefficient scale and are prone to shrinkage and, ultimately, self-destruction. Unlike the British footwear cooperatives, the worker-owner shares in the plywood cooperatives are marketable, permitting workers to recapture internally financed investments at the time of their departure from the cooperative (Berman 1967). However, external sources of finances were limited for the plywood cooperatives and they lacked incentives to create other cooperatives.

The somewhat more expansionist tendencies of the French and Italian cooperatives can be probably be explained by the presence of umbrella organizations providing technical assistance to cooperatives and the financial structure of individual cooperatives. Both Italian and French cooperatives raise some of their capital from member loans at a fixed interest rate, reducing the inclination by cooperatives to underinvest and avoiding the financing problems faced by British cooperatives (Zevi 1982: 241–242; Defourney *et al.* 1985: 201–205). The French and Italian cooperatives also benefit from a favorable legal structure and, in the case of Italy, government assistance. The goal of supporting cooperatives in Italy has been to reduce unemployment.

The Mondragon system of cooperatives appears to be most expansionist of all. The goal of expansion has been to reduce unemployment, even at the expense of forgoing maximum per worker income, and the ability to expand is related to the system's unique financing structure. Levin (1984) argues that in a labor surplus capitalist economy, labor solidarity in cooperatives will manifest itself in sacrifices of income per worker to provide jobs. As a consequence, cooperatives are likely to be larger and more prone to growth than their capitalist counterparts (*ibid*.: 21–23). He also suggests that where employment and income are assured, workers will return to size- and growth-limiting income-maximizing behavior. In order for cooperatives to behave in a growth-limiting mode of the type suggested by the theory in the previous section, employment for all will have to be assured, but this was not the case in the decades following World War II when the French, Italian, and Mondragon cooperatives were experiencing expansion.

The growth-proneness of a system of cooperatives as a whole could thus defeat the tendency to conserve on inputs and limit growth in the individual co-ops, and the net result could actually be more growth in resource use than in a comparable collection of capitalist businesses.

This need not be the case, however. The growth of a capitalist system is not subject to control, while the growth of a Mondragon-style cooperative system is.

By reducing the rate of forced savings through the immediate distribution of some portion of annual surplus earnings to workers, the pressure to grow could be reduced by reducing the pool of available capital. The British and American cases, where capital availability is limited, prove that reduced capital availability reduces growth. The traditional reluctance of cooperative systems to grow could be easily re-established in order to create a steady-state economy. This same measure of regulation is not readily available in a capitalist system of privately held businesses.

The pro-growth structuring of the Mondragon system historically arose from the need for employment opportunities in an area devastated by war and the oppression of the Franco government in Spain. Once adequate employment levels are attained, such a system could be restructured to achieve other goals, such as using energy and material inputs more efficiently and reducing waste emissions. A fully employed economy could be achieved even if economic growth is limited through reductions in the workweek as proposed by Daly (1973) and Schor (1991, 1992). Schor suggests that workweek reductions be accomplished holding real per worker incomes constant by reducing the workweek in proportion to average labor productivity increases.

The practice of democracy and environmental preservation

The central conclusions of the analysis so far are comparatively simple. Cooperatives that maximize income per worker will have a stronger inclination to reduce nonlabor costs than profit-maximizing corporations. This in turn results in greater efficiency of use for natural resource inputs. Moreover, cooperatives in a fully employed economy will be less motivated to expand than their capitalist counterparts, diminishing growth in the use of natural resource inputs and waste emissions. Individual cooperatives will grow to the point where per worker income is maximized, but they won't have any incentive to go beyond that point. The empire-building capitalist firm, on the other hand, will continue efforts to expand markets and add production facilities so long as an increment to profit results, and this can occur even when the peak income per worker is stable or declining. Thus, an economy based on democratically run cooperatives will be inherently more resource-conserving than one based on capitalist corporations.

The final question to be addressed is this: Can the practice of democracy in producer cooperatives itself lead to the conservation of resource inputs and restraint on waste emissions?

Several simple and obvious points can be made, suggesting that economic democracy may lead to a more activist stance on environmental issues by cooperatives than hierarchical corporations. Economists have long recognized that businesses may express motives other than simple profit maximization (Dugger 1980). In a corporation, top management exercises decision-making authority and determines the goals of the business beyond profit maximization. The goals of managers seem to be the accumulation of power and the expansion of their personal income (*ibid.*). This in turn manifests itself in the desire for organizational growth. Improvements in energy efficiency and reductions in waste emissions are not likely to find favor with top management because they divert capital and scarce managerial resources from the goal of growth. Consequently, environmental activism by employees would likely be squelched.

Because management in the Mondragon-style worker cooperative is chosen by members of management councils who are in turn elected by employees, cooperative management policy is more likely to reflect the broader interests and desires of employees than is the case for the hierarchical corporation. In addition to the goal of enhancing member incomes, the Mondragon cooperative system has an explicit goal of employment expansion in the Basque region (Whyte and Whyte 1988: 70). Cooperatives also devote 10 percent of their surplus earnings to social programs. The point is, broader social concerns beyond income or profit maximization do seem to be expressed in Mondragon cooperative management policy.

If environmentalism is a strongly held value in the larger society, then it is more likely to get expressed in a democratically determined cooperative management policy than in a hierarchically determined corporate management policy. In the corporation, the driving motivation is likely to be the enhancement of managerial status. In the cooperative, managers will be constrained by the collective wants of their employees. Of course, if environmentalism is not a strongly held value in the larger society, democratic decision making won't matter as a tool for promoting environmental ends. However, evidence suggests that the concern about environmental issues is widespread (Milbrath 1984). If this is the case, then the democratic cooperative is more likely to be environmentally friendly than the hierarchical corporation. Certainly, employees in democratic cooperatives at the very least are going to push for control of pollutants from their own enterprises that harm the local community in which they live (Tomer 1987).

This analysis of business behavior is consistent with a socio-economic conception of the firm recently suggested by John Tomer (1992). Tomer argues that a firm's environmental behavior is dependent not only on market incentives and the regulatory environment, but on its environmental opportunities and internal organizational capabilities, and on external social forces. Environmental opportunities refers to the potential for the use of "clean technologies" and the sale of environment-friendly products. Internal organizational capabilities refers to a firm's ability to integrate environmental concerns into all aspects of its operations, its capacity for effective decision making in a world characterized by bounded rationality, its degree of social responsibility or ethical concern, its capacity for entrepreneurship, its ability to engage in organizational learning, and its general level of environmental concern and awareness.

Tomer (1992) suggests that firms can be placed on a spectrum in terms of their behavior, ranging from those that simply pursue the maximization of short-run profits and have a strong propensity to resist environmental regulations at one extreme, to those at the other extreme that have highly developed internal organizational capabilities, including a strong sense of environmental responsibility and willingness to integrate environmental goals in all operations. In other words, business behavior is not uniform. Some firms exhibit a greater complexity of behavioral patterns than others. The central hypothesis offered here is that firms structured on the democratically oriented cooperative model will be more likely to exhibit behavior patterns at the complex end of the spectrum. The Mondragon cooperatives, as already noted, exhibit a comparatively broad range of organizational goals that go beyond the simple maximization of income, including economic equity, social solidarity, democracy, and regional development. Entrepreneurship has been effectively institutionalized in the entrepreneurial division of the bank, illustrating a relatively high level of development of internal organizational capabilities. This is also demonstrated in the development of secondary cooperatives, such as a research co-op, that serves the primary cooperatives by fostering technological change. Finally, external social forces and attitudes are manifested in the Mondragon system by cooperative employees through democratic processes. Individuals in a cooperative system have the option of politically advocating for environmental measures without fear of reprisals.

Corporations, as Tomer (1992) argues, have the potential to express a range of motivations in their behavior. Anecdotal evidence suggests that some are environmentally friendly. The extent of our environmental problems, however, provides evidence that most are not. The point being argued here is a simple one. Firms that institutionalize democratic decision making are more likely to be environmentally friendly than those that don't.

Conclusion

The central conclusion of this book leads us to a paradox. Economic growth requires the creation of new industries; new industries create new environmental problems; and new industries become vested political interests opposed to environmental regulations. Politically, then, the steady-state approach to environmental regulation suggested in Chapter 8 and the reforms of macroeconomic policy offered in Chapter 9 are precluded. The discussion of economic democracy in this chapter suggests a way out. Economic enterprises that embody the principles of economic democracy are more likely to be environmentally friendly than the existing corporate form of business organization. Principles of democratic self-management and employee ownership are increasingly being adopted by businesses as a matter of survival in an increasingly competitive world. To the extent that environmental values are widely held, as opinion surveys suggest, businesses may increasingly reflect the values of their employees and become more environmentally friendly over time and less resistant to the concept of an environmental steady state. There is also the possibility that economic democracy will come to be valued by society in its own right and receive a push through political action. Will we continue down the current path of global corporate political and economic dominance and continued growth in the exploitation of nature and its resources and significant environmental destruction and change, or will we choose an alternative path featuring economic democracy and steady-state environmental policies? This is the central topic of the next and final chapter.

11

GROWTH, ENVIRONMENTAL CHANGE, AND STEADY-STATE ECONOMICS

Conclusion

Let us repeat one last time the central themes of this book. First, economic growth is premised on the creation of new forms of economic activity and these new forms are the source of new kinds of environmental change. Second, alongside the growth of new forms of economic activity arise groups with vested political interests opposed to environmental regulation. Third, if there is a moral obligation to preserve the natural environment, then a steady-state economy is a sufficient means for doing so. A significant percentage of the public in the U.S. and the U.K. seem to accept the idea of such a moral obligation.

The unresolved problem in the environmental dynamic suggested here is the question of how the strength of vested interests in high-growth economies is to be overcome in order to move to a steady state. This is not an easy question to answer and any response at this point is highly speculative. Still, it is an issue that must be addressed.

Barriers to change

The primary barrier to national and global steady-state environmental strategies comes from the prosperous countries themselves and their dependence on economic growth. Whether it be a multinational corporation or a local small business, the fundamental striving of the capitalist business enterprise is for growth and the profits it brings. Underpinning this growth is in turn the striving of consumers for higher status associated with the acquisition of what Fred Hirsch (1976: 27–54) calls "positional goods" needed to demonstrate relative material well being. The essential features of positional goods are rarity, high relative cost, and conspicuousness. By virtue of these characteristics, the drive for such goods is a zero-sum game. Individuals attempt to expand their ownership of positional goods through the earning of higher incomes. Incomes as a result increase, a broader cross-section of the population acquires consumer goods whose supply can be expanded, and the prices of positional goods whose supply is fixed are bid up keeping them out of reach of the masses. Average income rises, but average status cannot. Consumption of goods previously thought of as exhibiting status may increase, but their role as positional goods declines because of a decline in rarity and relative cost. For the average consumer, the goal of obtaining more positional goods is defeated.

Survey research has shown that happiness depends not on absolute income levels, but on relative position in the income distribution, as suggested by the theory of positional goods (Scitovsky 1992: 133–145). Even though the average standard of living has increased substantially in the prosperous countries of the world, the proportion of the population claiming to be happy with their lives has remained unchanged. Citizens of these countries seem to be on a merry-go-round in pursuit of the unattainable golden ring of higher relative status for all.

Because steady-state economic policies will result in significantly lower rates of growth in prosperous countries like the U.S., a transformation in attitudes towards consumption is required for broad public acceptance of steady-state economics. The pursuit of positional goods will need to diminish and be replaced by a life centered on intrinsically valuable human activities to which consumption is complementary but subordinate. In such a world, consumption will involve not the hopeless pursuit of positional goods, but the maintenance of a fixed stock of goods needed for human activities essential to a decent human life. The challenge is bringing forth such a transformation in human attitudes in the face of entrenched economic interests that are hooked on high rates of economic growth.

Possible paths to a steady state

One rather obvious possible path to a steady state is its imposition by a Middle East political crisis, one that could cut the global supply of energy overnight, as was the case in the 1970s. In the longer term, a drawing down of finite oil and gas reserves could lead to the same thing. A resulting explosion in energy costs would foster increased energy conservation efforts and a search for renewable substitutes, with salutary environmental effects. One danger is that the substitute turned to first might be coal, an energy source that is globally abundant but heavily laden with pollutants. Coal generates more carbon emissions per unit energy than any other fossil fuel. A second danger is that if the crisis is political, it is reversible, and once resolved we may well return to our old high energy consuming ways as we did after the energy crisis of the 1970s. Finally, the problem with conversion to a steady state by crisis is the unnecessary pain of economic and social disruption avoidable through a planned transition.

A more hopeful trend is increased public concern about environmental problems. This concern is expressed both in public opinion surveys and in the rising membership of environmental groups. Because little is privately gained from membership, the motivation to join environmental groups is probably ethical in its orientation. Ethical commitment is a means by which voluntary organizations overcome the free rider problem that plagues the political organization of large diffuse interests. With increasing political strength, the environmental movement may experience increasing success in winning regulatory battles and be able to incrementally move the global economy toward an environmental steady state. A serious problem here is that the pace of environmental change may well exceed the pace of regulatory progress. By the time global warming takes on crisis proportions, reversing it may be too late.

As suggested by the last chapter, trends towards economic democracy in business organizations could aid and abet the environmental movement. If expanded economic democracy took the form of employee-owned cooperatives, per worker income maximization would result in smaller-scale production organizations that use energy and materials more efficiently. Employee-controlled businesses would think twice about increasing pollution emissions harmful to residents in local communities where employees live. Finally, economic democracy may lead to the expressed desire by employees for the pursuit of nonpecuniary business goals, such as the conserving of environmental resources. Whether current trends in business towards greater employee involvement in organizational decision making go this far remains to be seen. The prospects for employee involvement in management seems to have suffered a setback recently with expanded efforts to downsize businesses by dismissing current employees in large numbers, a practice that seem to increase short-term profits but comes at the expense of employee commitment to business goals by fearful survivors of layoffs, commitment that is essential for effective employee self-management.

A final trend that indirectly supports a more environmentally friendly economy is the desire for more leisure. If a shorter workweek is realized, this could ultimately mean reduced material consumption and a reduction in the negative environmental consequences that go with it. Long workweeks may actually encourage material consumption by increasing the demand for relatively passive consumer activities, such as watching TV, shopping, or playing computer games. With a shorter workweek, a more energetic public may engage in activities that are valuable in their own right as ends in themselves, not just for the comfort and pleasure they bring. With more time, the feasibility of participation in cultural activities and social organizations not requiring massive amounts of consumer goods increases. Instead of going to the mall for recreational shopping or the video store for the latest film, the public may increasingly engage in more active pastimes, such as team sports, volunteer service groups, the arts, amateur theater, book clubs, birdwatching, environmental advocacy groups, and gardening, requiring limited and nonincreasing levels of material consumption.

Whether one of these trends or some combination of them overpower vested economic interests and move the global economy in the direction of an environmental steady state remains to be seen. Only time will tell.

190

NOTES

1 INTRODUCTION: ECONOMIC GROWTH AND ENVIRONMENTAL CHANGE

1 This is Nordhaus's (1991) conclusion for all but very small reductions in greenhouse gas emissions. The method used for arriving at this conclusion involves the usual practice of discounting future cost and benefit flows.

2 ECONOMIC GROWTH AND ENVIRONMENTAL CHANGE: THEORY

1 This pattern has been confirmed by more recent research (van Duijn 1983: 28–29).
2 Liability law is generally ineffective in limiting pollution, for similar reasons. Evidence of damage is often hard to demonstrate, and the damage experienced by any individual is often too small to justify the costs of litigation.

3 THE LINK BETWEEN INDUSTRY CREATION AND ENVIRONMENTAL CHANGE

1 The point here is that certain technological watersheds must be crossed before innovations such as the assembly line are possible. Rosenberg (1972) argues for a more gradualist view of technological change. His view is that the assembly line was made possible by the gradual accumulation of knowledge in the machine tool industry (*ibid.*: 107–113). Even so, a decentralized power source was clearly needed, and that was provided by the electric motor, an innovation that was part of the electricity technological watershed. The truth most likely falls somewhere between. Technological advance is gradual in some spheres and punctuated by sudden changes in others.
2 The Fordist methods of production were incompletely adopted in the early history of the British and European auto industries. Because of a smaller market and resistance by labor, the full-blown machine-paced assembly line methods employed by Henry Ford were only partially applied in the U.K. (Church 1994: 1–42).
3 A major obstacle to expansion of the auto industry prior to 1913 was an insufficient supply of fuel. Only 10 percent of a barrel of oil could be converted to gasoline through distillation. This problem was solved through the development of the cracking process, eventually allowing up to a 42 percent yield of gasoline from a barrel of oil. The cracking process was made possible in part by the availability of steel tanks that could withstand very high pressures (Hogan 1971b: 686; Williamson *et al.* 1963: 131–150).
4 The relative distribution of pollutants by source is similar in the U.K., although domestic sources are more pronounced and the transportation sector plays a somewhat lesser

role. In 1980, power stations were responsible for 61 percent of sulfur dioxide emissions, and industry for much of the rest in the U.K. Nitrous oxide emissions from power stations constituted 46 percent of the total, domestic sources 23 percent, and transportation 28 percent. Volatile organic emissions were about evenly split between transportation (42 percent) and industry (46 percent), while carbon monoxide emissions arose predominantly in the transportation sector (89 percent). The majority of particulate emissions (smoke) come from domestic sources in the U.K. (63 percent). See Park (1987: 35) for the details.

5 Modest regulatory efforts to stabilize emissions at 1990 levels have been undertaken in the U.K. (Maddison and Pearce 1995).

6 The data prior to 1980 are municipal road miles. After 1980, urban is defined as a place with greater than 5,000 population or an urbanized area with population greater than 50,000. As a result, the reported miles were 70,000 less in 1970 than 1980. To adjust the data, a regression with urban road miles as the dependent variable and time as the independent variable was run with a dummy variable equal to 1 for the period 1947–1979. Since the coefficient on the dummy was equal to 66,000, the post-1980 data were adjusted up by this amount in Figure 3.5.

7 The nature of the problems caused by pesticides is addressed in detail in Chapter 5.

8 The point of Fogel's (1964) work on the impact of railroads on the U.S. economy, and to a lesser extent Fishlow's (1965), is that the railroad contributed less to economic growth than commonly thought. Without the railroad, settlement and economic growth would still have occurred, but at a slower pace. Fogel claims that railroads contributed directly and indirectly some 5 percent of GNP in 1890. Williamson (1975) argues that the figure was more like 20 percent, when a general equilibrium perspective is taken. Basically, what Fogel is arguing is that the railroad as a technological innovation could have been skipped without much effect. This approach raises a whole host of questions that Fogel cannot really address. Would large-scale industry have developed so rapidly without the innovations in business organization pioneered by the railroads? Would the steel industry have developed so rapidly without the massive market for steel rails? Would mechanical skills so essential to an industrial economy have developed as quickly without the railroad? How can one even properly evaluate the rapidity of human communication fostered by the railroad? Wouldn't water transportation simply be too slow for the speed of communication needed by a capitalist economy? Would urban street railways and the early application of electricity to them have occurred in the absence of the railroad? Would the arid west have been settled so quickly where canal development is improbable? The full impact of the railroad including a whole host of indirect effects is not easily measurable. The settlement of the Midwest certainly would have been much slower without the railroad, and Chicago would not have been the focal point of the Midwestern economy (Cronon 1991). In any event, the railroad as a technological innovation was not skipped, and it did have a profound impact on the pace and pattern of settlement, as we will see.

9 Fogel suggests that in the absence of railroads, canals along with road improvements could have opened up much of the prairie lands to settlement (1964: 91–110). If this were the case, a substantial investment in transportation improvements would still have been required in order to foster settlement, and it still would have been based on steam technology.

10 Best estimates of the price elasticity of housing are –0.65. When the price of housing declines by 10 percent, the quantity of housing increases by 6.5 percent (Mills and Hamilton 1994: 209). Hence, if land costs on average decline because of an increase in supply caused by reduced transportation costs, then the quantity of housing consumed will increase, together with the amount of construction materials going into housing, such as lumber.

NOTES

4 ECONOMIC GROWTH AND ENVIRONMENTAL CHANGE: NATURAL HABITAT LOSS

1 This information was provided by a personal communication from Nature Conservancy personnel. Prairie fame-flower (*Talinum rugospermum*) is considered to be globally vulnerable (G3) by the Nature Conservancy. (Designations used by the Nature Conservancy include G1 (critically imperiled globally), G2 (imperiled globally), and G3 (vulnerable globally).)

5 ECONOMIC GROWTH AND ENVIRONMENTAL CHANGE: AIR, WATER, AND PESTICIDE POLLUTION

1 More recent studies suggest a somewhat lower rate of significant acidification in Adirondack lakes (Howells 1990: 108).
2 A limiting nutrient is one that is scarce relative to all other nutrients and thus inhibits biological productivity.
3 High productivity will reduce carbon dioxide concentrations, which blue-green algae apparently favor relative to more palatable green algae (Welch 1992: 147–157). Other factors may play a role in blue-green dominance as well.
4 For summaries of research on pesticides, see Brown (1978) and Pimentel *et al.* (1992).

6 ECONOMIC GROWTH AND THE LIMITS OF ENVIRONMENTAL REGULATION

1 The 1977 Amendments to the Clean Water Act created somewhat stronger BAT requirements for toxins, while weakening the requirements for conventional pollutants, replacing the original BAT standards with new "best conventional technology" standards. For conventional pollutants the EPA under the 1977 Amendments was required to consider whether the benefits of water quality improvement exceed the costs (Tietenberg 1994; Goodstein 1995). Also, the deadline for meeting the original BPT regulatory requirements was moved ahead to 1983, and the deadline for meeting toxic BAT requirements was moved ahead to 1984.
2 For examples, see Vogel (1986: 107–145) and Pye-Smith and Rose (1984: 67–72).

7 ETHICS AND THE LIMITS OF ENVIRONMENTAL ECONOMICS

1 Something is said to have value for itself if it unreflectively pursues some programmatic end. Something is said to have value in itself if it consciously and reflectively pursues some end. This requires the capacity for conscious reasoning and determination of purposeful ends. This distinction is discussed in Lee (1996).
2 A holistic objectivist environmental ethic would require that entities like ecosystems or species programmatically pursue some end. Populations of species through evolutionary adaption possess the programmatic end of self-perpetuation and expansion within the limits of environmental and biological constraints. Thus they can be said to have value for themselves. Whether this is the case for ecosystems is a more controversial issue. If ecosystems simply contain opportunistic collections of species, then to argue that they have value for themselves is a problem (Brennan 1988). If, however, ecosystems are tightly co-evolved, then they are something more than a random collection of species and the system itself is following a strategy of self-organization. The same is true if ecosystems follow nonrandom, well specified successional paths where the stage of succession determines the characteristics of the ecosystem. Still, the preservation of ecosystem processes is necessary for the

preservation of populations of species, so the preservation of ecosystems is a necessary condition to preserve individual organisms or species populations, and the specific locus of value is not, as such, of much practical importance for naturally occurring species. To protect populations of individual species requires the protection of ecosystems.

3 This requirement will not hold in all cases. If, for example, the polluter is economically impoverished and is struggling to earn enough to live decently, then compensation would not be required given an ethical standard that gives priority to basic material needs. In Kantian terms, the capacity for our own self-development takes priority over the happiness of others.

4 Such moral dilemmas may in fact be rather common. Consider a farmer who owns land containing a large wetland that improves downstream water quality and prevents flooding, to the benefit of other landowners. This farmer may not be able to earn an income sufficient to live a decent life without converting the wetland to cropland. In such circumstances, the moral claim of the farmer may be greater than the downstream landowners benefiting from the continued existence of the wetland, and the appropriate solution would be to compensate the farmer for preservation of the wetland.

5 Under the criterion of Pareto optimality, an allocation of resources is optimal if there is no other feasible allocation of resources that will make at least some better off without making any others worse off.

6 A contingent valuation study of the spotted owl case finds considerable public support for preserving the spotted owl. The willingness to pay for preservation in this study was found to exceed the benefits of exploitation several-fold. This survey was undertaken from a sample of nonusers of old-growth forests. Why would nonusers value spotted owls and old growth so highly? The only convincing answer is that supporters of preservation are expressing a moral commitment born of an emotional identification with natural beings. If so, their support is noninstrumental. While the study results are reported in a cost-benefit format, they are not at all inconsistent with the notion that the valuation is noninstrumental (Hagen *et al.* 1992). If valuation of the spotted owl is indeed noninstrumental, then to report them in a cost-benefit framework is inappropriate for the reasons discussed above. Simply put, noninstrumental and instrumental values are incommensurable, and cost-benefit analysis is premised on full commensurability in monetary terms.

8 THE STEADY-STATE ALTERNATIVE

1 In a more recent work, Daly (1992) recognizes the need for separately limiting the scale of waste emissions to sustainable levels. In this article he recognizes that tradable emission permits are a means to limit one dimension of the scale of the economy relative to the scale of the global ecosystem.

2 Also, see the discussion in Chapters 4 and 5 above.

3 In addition, nitrous oxide emissions, another precursor to acid rain, are to be reduced by 2.5 million tons per year by the year 2000.

4 In judging whether an environmental protection measure would reduce the living standard below that necessary for a decent human life, whose living standard is of concern? If we adopt a Rawlsian (1971) view of economic justice, then environmental protection measures that protect human and ecosystem health are ethically questionable only if they reduce society's ability to assure that its poorest member receives an adequate standard of living.

5 The central concern of conventional economists in evaluating regulatory schemes is whether or not cost minimization will result. Conventional economists have also been concerned with whether the benefits of regulation exceed the costs. This is not an

issue here because of our rejection of the cost-benefit approach in favor of ethical standards. For a more detailed treatment of the cost minimization issue, see Tietenberg (1994) or Goodstein (1995).

6 This calculation assumes a phase-in period beginning in the year 2001 and an equal percentage reduction in emissions each year to reach a 90 percent reduction by 2025. The total amount of emissions under this reduction plan would be approximately the same over the first 100 years as would occur under a plan of emission reductions of 70 percent in 2000 and a fixed level at 70 percent of the 2000 figure of 7.1 GtC thereafter. This is roughly the amount needed to stop further global warming beyond the amount already in the pipeline. To reduce emissions immediately by 70 percent would probably be impossible. Consequently, a 25-year phase-in with an eventual 90 percent reduction below predicted levels is selected as the preferred option. The data for this calculation are based on Cline (1992: 290–291).

7 Ayres and Walter (1991) suggest the zero net cost reduction of carbon emissions may be as much as 50 percent.

8 These figures assume that the cost per unit of carbon emissions reduction is the same for Europe and the U.S. Because European energy efficiency is already about twice that of the U.S. on a per capita basis and because European carbon emissions in per capita terms are already about half those of the U.S., the incremental cost of carbon reduction is likely to be greater in Europe than in the U.S. The U.S. still has low-cost options for reducing carbon emissions by increasing energy efficiency whereas the Europeans have already exercised many of these. In the interest of equity as well as efficiency, the U.S. requirement for carbon reductions ought to be relatively greater than the European requirement. This means the GDP cost of an across-the-board 90 percent reduction of emissions would be lower than the stated figures for the U.S. and higher for Europe. This could be offset in the name of efficiency and equity by requiring the U.S. to undertake relatively more emissions reductions than the Europeans. To reduce carbon emissions by 90 percent and at the same time equalize per capita emissions in the U.S. and Europe would require a 93 percent reduction by the U.S. and an 85 percent reduction in Europe.

9 Obviously, there is no way of determining with any precision the amount of aid to less developed countries required to gain their support for carbon emissions limits. The 2 percent figure would be substantially above current U.S. contributions to development overseas amounting to approximately 0.2 percent of GDP (Pearce 1993: 31).

10 Permits, for example, could be issued electronically to social security card holders.

11 With crude oil imports substantially reduced, the current U.S. trade deficit could well be converted to a surplus, giving the U.S. leverage in negotiations with its trading partners.

12 The issue of economic development in poor countries takes us beyond the scope of this chapter. The question of whether carbon emissions limitations substantially harm the ability of everyone in low-income countries to live decently is a legitimate question and one not easily answered. As suggested in the text, a properly structured global carbon emission permit system could create economic opportunities for less developed countries. In the end, I suspect the real barriers to a decent living standard in less developed countries are excessive population growth and economic inequality, and any negative impact of carbon emission limits on economic prospects would probably be fairly marginal. For a more detailed treatment of international greenhouse gas control issues, see Cline (1992).

13 Technology forcing was also compatible with the goal of agency capture avoidance discussed in Chapter 6. Because of measurement problems, industry would have an easier time resisting ambient controls than effluent limits.

14 Licht (1994) argues that the Conservation Reserve Program is poorly structured to

provide significant habitat for nongame species. He suggests that if significantly reformed, this program could be used to restore significant tallgrass and mixed-grass prairie habitat.

15 The high-cost watershed is the Menomonee River, which includes industrial areas on the southside of Milwaukee, WI. Cost figures per stream mile for other watersheds surveyed are as follows: Milwaukee River South: $244,000; Upper Fox River: $50,000; Sheboygan River: $3,500. The first is a predominantly urban watershed, while the latter two are more heavily rural (Wisconsin DNR 1991, 1992, 1993, 1994).

16 We will address pesticide threats associated with agricultural runoff in the next section.

17 See Pimentel *et al.* (1991) for an excellent summary of different methods for reducing pesticide use.

18 Such losses amount to over $3 billion a year (Pimentel *et al.* 1992: 757).

19 Permits could be issued to farmers on the basis of historical use patterns, or they could simply be auctioned off to the highest bidder. Such a system would be premised on the ability to assign commensurable risk levels to different kinds of pesticides. Farmers able to reduce pesticides at low cost could reduce more than necessary and sell some of their permits to farmers who can reduce pesticide use only at a very high cost. This would assure that pesticide reduction costs would be minimized. Maximum use limits may still may be required, however, to avoid local pesticide hot spots.

20 Raphael (1981) suggests this approach to forestry management, only he argues that forestland ought to be leased to forest stewardship cooperatives whose earnings would be determined by audits of forest characteristics.

21 Because of the absence of substantial amounts of public land in the U.K., the problem of preserving semi-natural habitat features and biodiversity is somewhat different. The basic problem is getting private landowners to manage critical habitat in such a fashion as to preserve semi-natural features. Incentive programs currently exist to accomplish this, but they tend to be underfunded and in some cases poorly managed (Winter 1996: 225–256). One possible source of funding could be through the sale of some portion of carbon emission permits reserved from public distribution.

22 While I applaud efforts to reduce population growth and bring forth population stability, or even decline, I have no great insight on how to do it. Herman Daly's (1991a) birth permit idea has merit in the eyes of some economists, but many people, including my students, seem to think it infringes on reproductive freedom. I have no great insight either into how a decent standard of living can be achieved in the poor nations of world. My only point here is that a steady-state economy can be achieved by prosperous nations without excessive sacrifices while at the same time assistance can be provided to poor countries in such a way as to encourage the sustainable use of ecosystems, such as the preservation of forests for the sequestering of carbon and the maintenance of biodiversity.

9 THE MACROECONOMICS OF A STEADY STATE

1 Given the current relatively high land use density in northern European countries like the U.K., and the limited number of sunny days, replacing fossil fuel energy with renewables seems like a pipe dream. However, solar energy could be used to produce hydrogen in desert areas of the African subcontinent and the hydrogen could be shipped by pipeline or tanker to Europe. In a solar energy world, deserts would become tremendously productive assets.

2 For a complete analysis of this and other mechanisms by which energy prices can lead to reductions in aggregate output, see Helliwell (1981).

3 Because of the energy price rises in the mid-1970s, capital investment and productivity growth suffered (Hudson and Jorgenson 1978; Jorgenson 1981).

4 For an argument that growth is the driving motivation of the managerial corporation, see Penrose (1968).

10 ECONOMIC DEMOCRACY AS AN ENVIRONMENTAL MEASURE

1 Some would go so far as to argue that a "declining-state" economy is needed, where the use of energy and materials is actually reduced over time. This is ultimately necessary for matter, given the impossibility of 100 percent recycling.

2 Because cooperative members own their stock of capital goods, a portion of their membership income constitutes a return to capital and the remainder the return to labor.

3 In other words, in what follows a perfectly competitive market is not assumed, although the analysis is consistent with perfect competition in an industry characterized by increasing costs.

4 Area *DJIG*, the increase in profit from the scale-expanding investment that shifts *NARP* outwards (*NARP3* to *NARP5*), is greater than area *ABEC+DEHG*, the increase in profit from the energy/materials-saving investment that shifts *NARP* upwards (*NARP3* to *NARP4*). For the case where the output price is constant, a reduction of per unit input costs used in fixed proportions to output will result in a reduction of employment for the cooperative. This is another situation in which the so-called perverse supply response holds, one that may actually be desirable where reduced resource use is needed to achieve a sustainable steady state. A reduction in nonlabor input costs is equivalent to the perverse supply response caused by a price increase. See Stephen (1982: 4–5) for a simple proof of the perverse supply response.

5 My thanks to John Tomer for bringing this issue to my attention. Obviously, a mixed cooperative/capitalist economy would not serve to reduce aggregate demand and the scale of economic activity because capitalist firms would simply step into the breach.

BIBLIOGRAPHY

Abrahamson, D. E. (1989) "Global warming: the issue, impacts, responses," in D. E. Abrahamson (ed.) *The Challenge of Global Warming*, Washington D. C.: Island Press.

Ackerman, B. A. and Hassler, W. T. (1981) *Clean Coal/Dirty Air*, New Haven, Conn.: Yale University Press.

Adler, R. W., Landman, J. C. and Cameron, D. M. (1993) *The Clean Water Act 20 Years Later*, Washington D. C.: Island Press.

Ahlgren, C. E. and Ahlgren, I. F. (1983) "The human impact on northern forest ecosystems," in S. L. Flader (ed.) *The Great Lakes Forest: An Environmental and Social History*, Minneapolis, Minn.: University of Minnesota Press.

Allin, C. W. (1982) *The Politics of Wilderness Preservation*, Westport, Conn.: Greenwood Press.

Alverson, W. S., Waller, D. M. and Solheim S. L. (1988) "Forests to deer: edge effects in northern Wisconsin," *Conservation Biology* 2: 348–358.

Arp, H. A. (1993) "Technical regulation and politics: the interplay between economic interests and environmental policy goals in EC car emission legislation," in J. D. Liefferink, P. D. Lowe and A. P. J. Mol (eds) *European Integration and Environmental Policy*, London: Belhaven Press.

Ashby, E. and Anderson, M. (1981) *The Politics of Clean Air*, Oxford: Clarendon Press.

Axelrod, D. I. (1985) "Rise of the grassland biome, central North America," *Botanical Review* 51: 163–201.

Ayres, R. U. and Walter, J. (1991) "The greenhouse effect: damages, costs and abatement," *Environmental and Resource Economics* 1: 237–270.

Balling, R. C., Jr. (1992) *The Heated Debate: Greenhouse Predictions versus Climate Reality*, San Francisco, Calif.: Pacific Research Institute for Public Policy.

Bartlett, R. V. (1984) "The budgetary process and environmental policy," in N. J. Vig and M. E. Kraft (eds) *Environmental Policy in the 1980s: Reagan's New Agenda*, Washington D. C.: Congressional Quarterly Inc.

Batstone, E. (1982) "Country studies: France," in F. H. Stephen (ed.) *The Performance of Labor-Managed Firms*, New York: St Martin's Press.

Behm, D. (1994) "Scientists warn of chemical devastation," *Milwaukee Journal,* 20 April: A10.

Berger, J. (1991) "Greater Yellowstone's native ungulates: myths and realities," *Conservation Biology* 5: 353–363.

Berman, K. (1967) *Worker-Owned Plywood Companies: An Economic Analysis*, Pullman, Wash.: Washington State University Press.

Blowers, A. (1984) *Something in the Air: Corporate Power and the Environment,* London: Harper & Row.

Boehmer-Christiansen, S. and Skea, J. (1991) *Acid Politics: Environmental and Energy Policies in Britain and Germany*, London: Belhaven Press.

Bogue, A. G. (1963) *From Prairie to Corn Belt: Farming on the Illinois and Iowa Prairies in the Nineteenth Century*, Chicago, Ill.: University of Chicago Press.

Booth, D. E. (1987) *Regional Long Waves, Uneven Growth, and the Cooperative Alternative*, New York: Praeger.

—— (1989) "Hydroelectric dams and the decline of chinook salmon in the Columbia River," *Marine Resource Economics* 6: 195–211.

—— (1990) "Review essay: In defense of the land ethic and respect for nature," *Review of Social Economy* 48: 84–96.

—— (1994) *Valuing Nature: The Decline and Preservation of Old-Growth Forests*, Lanham, Md.: Rowman & Littlefield.

Bosso, C. J. (1987) *Pesticides and Politics: The Life Cycle of a Public Issue*, Pittsburgh, Pa.: University of Pittsburgh Press.

—— (1988) "Transforming adversaries into collaborators: interest groups and the regulation of chemical pesticides," *Policy Sciences* 21: 3–22.

Boulding, K. E. (1966) "The economics of the coming Spaceship Earth," in H. Jarrett (ed.) *Environmental Quality in a Growing Economy*, Baltimore, Md.: Johns Hopkins University Press.

Bourdo, E. A., Jr. (1983) "The Forest the Settlers Saw," in S. L. Flader (ed.) *The Great Lakes Forest: An Environmental and Social History*, Minneapolis, Minn.: University of Minnesota Press.

Brennan, A. (1988) *Thinking about Nature*, London: Routledge.

Brimblecombe, P. (1987) *The Big Smoke: A History of Air Pollution in London since Medieval Times*, London: Methuen.

Brittingham, M. C. and Temple, S. A. (1983) "Have cowbirds caused forest songbirds to decline?" *Bioscience* 33: 31–35.

Bromley, D. W. (1978) "Property and liability rules," *Journal of Economic Issues* 12: 43–60.

Brookshire, D. S., Eubanks, L. S. and Sorg, C. F. (1986) "Existence values and normative economics: implications for valuing water resources," *Water Resources Research* 22: 1509–1518.

Brown, A. W. A. (1978) *Ecology of Pesticides*, New York: John Wiley & Sons.

Brown, E. R. (1985) *Management of Wildlife and Fish Habitats in Forests of Western Oregon and Washington*, Portland, Oreg.: USDA Forest Service, Pacific Northwest Region.

Brown, L. (1985) *Grasslands*, New York: Alfred A. Knopf.

Burns, A. F. (1934) *Production Trends in the United States since 1870*, New York: National Bureau of Economic Research.

Button, K. (1995) "UK environmental policy and transport," in T. S. Gray (ed.) *UK Environmental Policy in the 1990s*, London: Macmillan.

Byatt, I. C. R. (1979) *The British Electrical Industry: 1875–1914*, Oxford: Clarendon Press.

Callicott, J. B. (1985) "Intrinsic value, quantum theory, and environmental ethics," *Environmental Ethics* 7: 257–273.

—— (1989) *In Defense of the Land Ethic: Essays in Environmental Philosophy*, Albany: State University of New York Press.

—— (1990) "The case against moral pluralism," *Environmental Ethics* 12: 99–124.

Canham, C. D. and Loucks, O. L. (1984) "Catastrophic windthrow in the presettlement forests of Wisconsin," *Ecology* 65: 803–809.

Carson, R. (1962) *Silent Spring*, Boston, Mass.: Houghton Mifflin.

Christensen, P. (1991) "Driving forces, increasing returns and ecological sustainability," in R. Costanza (ed.) *Ecological Economics: The Science and Management of Sustainability*, New York: Columbia University Press.

Church, R. (1994) *The Rise and Decline of the British Motor Industry*, London: Macmillan.

Clapp, B. W. (1994) *An Environmental History of Britain since the Industrial Revolution*, Harlow: Longman.

Cleveland, C. J. (1991) "Natural resource scarcity and economic growth revisited: economic and biophysical perspective," in R. Costanza (ed.) *Ecological Economics: The Science and Management of Sustainability*, New York: Columbia University Press.

Cline, W. R. (1992) *The Economics of Global Warming*, Washington D. C.: Institute for International Economics.

Coase, R. (1960) "The problem of social cost," *Journal of Law and Economics* 3: 1–44.

Coffin, B. and Pfannmuller, L. (eds) (1988) *Minnesota's Endangered Flora and Fauna*, Minneapolis, Minn.: University of Minnesota Press.

Conway, G. R. and Pretty, J. N. (1991) *Unwelcome Harvest: Agriculture and Pollution*, London: Earthscan.

Cooper, C. C. (1958) "The role of railroads in the settlement of Iowa: a study in historical geography," unpublished M. A. thesis, University of Nebraska.

Costanza, R. (ed.) (1991) *Ecological Economics: The Science and Management of Sustainability*, New York: Columbia University Press.

Cronon, W. (1991) *Nature's Metropolis: Chicago and the Great West*, New York: W. W. Norton.

Culhane, P. J. (1981) *Public Lands Politics – Interest Group Influence on the Forest Service and the Bureau of Land Management*, Baltimore, Md.: Johns Hopkins University Press.

Curtis, J. T. (1959) *The Vegetation of Wisconsin: An Ordination of Plant Communities*, Madison, Wis.: University of Wisconsin Press.

Daily, G. C., Ehrlich, P. R., Mooney, H. A. and Ehrlich, A. H. (1991) "Greenhouse economics: learn before you leap," *Ecological Economics* 4: 1–10.

Daly, H. E. (1973) "The steady-state economy: toward a political economy of biophysical equilibrium and moral growth," in H. E. Daly (ed.) *Toward a Steady-State Economy*, San Francisco, Calif.: W. H. Freeman & Company.

—— (1985) "The circular flow of exchange value and the linear throughput of matter-energy: a case of misplaced concreteness," *Review of Social Economy* 43: 279–285.

—— (1990) "Toward some operational principles of sustainable development," *Ecological Economics* 2: 1–6.

—— (1991a) *Steady State Economics*, 2nd edn, Washington D. C.: Island Press.

—— (1991b) "Towards an environmental macroeconomics," *Land Economics* 67: 255–259.

—— (1992) "Allocation, distribution, and scale: toward an economics that is efficient, just, and sustainable," *Ecological Economics* 6: 185–193.

Daly, H. E., and Cobb, J. B., Jr. (1989) *For the Common Good: Redirecting the Economy toward Community, the Environment, and a Sustainable Future*, Boston, Mass.: Beacon Press.

Davies, J. E. and Doon, R. (1987) "Human health effects of pesticides," in G. J. Marco, R. M. Hollingworth and W. Durham (eds) *Silent Spring Revisited*, Washington, D. C.: American Chemical Society.

Davis, L. N. (1984) *The Corporate Alchemists: Profit Takers and Problem Makers in the Chemical Industry*, New York: William Morrow & Company.

Defourney, J., Estrin, S., and Jones, D. C. (1985) "The effects of workers' participation on enterprise performance: empirical evidence from French cooperatives," *International Journal of Industrial Organization* 3: 197–217.

Downs, A. (1972) "Up and down with ecology – the 'issue-attention cycle'," *The Public Interest* 28: 38–50.

Dugger, W. M. (1980) "Corporate bureaucracy: the incidence of the bureaucratic process," *Journal of Economic Issues* 14: 399–409.

—— (1985) "The continued evolution of corporate power," *Review of Social Economy* 43: 1–13.

—— (1989) "Emulation: an institutional theory of value formation," *Review of Social Economy* 47: 134–154.

Duijn, J. J. van (1983) *The Long Wave in Economic Life*, London: George Allen & Unwin.

Dunlap, R. E. (1991) "Trends in public opinion toward environmental issues: 1965–1990," *Society and Natural Resources* 4: 285–312.

Edwards, S. F. (1986) "Ethical preferences and the assessment of existence values: does the neoclassical model fit?" *Northeastern Journal of Agricultural and Resource Economics* 15: 145–150.

—— (1987) "In defense of environmental economics," *Environmental Ethics* 9: 82–85.

Ehrlich, P. R. (1989) "The limits to substitution: meta-resource depletion and a new economic-ecological paradigm," *Ecological Economics* 1: 9–16.

Ehrlich, P. R., Ehrlich, A. H., and Holdren, J. P. (1977) *Ecoscience: Population, Resources, Environment*, San Francisco, Calif.: W. H. Freeman.

Ellerman, D. P. (1983) "A model structure for cooperatives: worker co-ops and housing co-ops," *Review of Social Economy* 41: 52–67.

—— (1988) "The Kantian person/thing principle in political economy," *Journal of Economic Issues* 22: 1109–1122.

Etzioni, A. (1986) "The case for a multiple-utility conception," *Economics and Philosophy* 2: 159–183.

Fishlow, A. (1965) *American Railroads and the Transformation of the Ante-Bellum Economy*, Cambridge, Mass.: Harvard University Press.

Fogel, R. W. (1964) *Railroads and American Economic Growth: Essays in Econometric History*, Baltimore, Md.: The Johns Hopkins Press.

Foreman, D. and Wolke, H. (1992) *The Big Outside: A Descriptive Inventory of the Big Wilderness Areas of the United States*, New York: Harmony Books.

Fox, W. (1990) *Transpersonal Ecology: Developing New Foundations for Environmentalism*, Boston and London: Shambhala Publications.

Franklin, J. F., Cromach, K., Denison, W., McKee, A., Maser, C., Sedell, F., Swanson, F. and Juday, G. (1981) *Ecological Characteristics of Old-Growth Douglas-Fir Forests*, Portland, Oreg: USDA Forest Service, GTR, PNW-8.

Franklin, J. F., Shugart, H. H. and Harmon, M. E. (1987) "Tree death as an ecological process: the causes, consequences, and variability of tree mortality," *BioScience* 37: 550–556.

Freeman, A. M. III (1990) "Water pollution policy," in P. Portney (ed.) *Public Policies for Environmental Protection*, Washington D. C.: Resources for the Future.

Freeman, C., Clark, J. and Soete, L. (1982) *Unemployment and Technical Innovation: A Study of Long Waves and Economic Development*, Westport, Conn.: Greenwood Press.

Gallman, R. E. (1960) "Commodity output, 1839–1899," in National Bureau of Economic Research. *Trends in the American Economy in the Nineteenth Century*, Princeton, N. J.: Princeton University Press.

Gates, D. M., Clarke, C. H. D. and Harris, J. T. (1983) "Wildlife in a changing environment," in S. L. Flader (ed.) *The Great Lakes Forest: An Environmental and Social History*, Minneapolis, Minn.: University of Minnesota Press.

Gates, P. W. (1960) *The Farmer's Age*, White Plains, N. Y.: M. E. Sharpe.

Georgescu-Roegen, N. (1967) *Analytical Economics: Issues and Problems*, Cambridge, Mass.: Harvard University Press.

—— (1971) *The Entropy Law and the Economic Process*, Cambridge, Mass.: Harvard University Press.

—— (1973) "The entropy law and the economic problem," in H. E. Daly (ed.) *Toward a Steady-State Economy*, San Francisco, Calif.: W. H. Freeman.

—— (1977) "Inequality, limits and growth from a bioeconomic viewpoint," *Review of Social Economy* 35: 361–375.

—— (1984) "Feasible recipes versus viable technologies," *Atlantic Economic Journal* 12: 21–31.

Gillis, A. M. (1991) "Why can't we balance the globe's carbon budget?" *BioScience* 41: 442–447.

Glick, D., Carr, M. and Harting, B. (1991) "An environmental profile of the greater Yellowstone ecosystem," Bozeman, Minn.: The Greater Yellowstone Coalition.

Goodpaster, K. E. (1978) "On being morally considerable," *Journal of Philosophy* 75: 168–176.

Goodstein, E. S. (1995) *Economics and the Environment*, Englewood Cliffs, N. J.: Prentice-Hall.

Gould, R. (1985) *Going Sour: Science and Politics of Acid Rain*, Boston, Mass.: Birkhauser.

Graber, R. R. and Graber, J. W. (1963) "A comparative study of bird populations in Illinois, 1906–1909 and 1956–1958," *Illinois Natural History Survey Bulletin* 28: 383–519.

Green, B. (1985) *Countryside Conservation: The Protection and Management of Amenity Ecosystems*, London: George Allen & Unwin.

Grossman, G. M. and Krueger, A. B. 1993. "Environmental impacts of a North American Free Trade Agreement," in P. M. Garber (ed.) *The Mexico–US Free Trade Agreement*, Cambridge, Mass.: MIT Press.

Guthrie, J. A. (1972) *An Economic Analysis of the Pulp and Paper Industry*, Pullman, Wash.: Washington State University Press.

Hagen, D. A., Vincent, J. W. and Welle, P. G. (1992) "Benefits of preserving old-growth forests and the spotted owl," *Contemporary Policy Issues* 10: 13–26.

Hamburg, J. F. (1981) *The Influence of Railroads upon the Processes and Patterns of Settlement in South Dakota*, New York: Arno Press.

Hamilton, J. D. (1983) "Oil and the macroeconomy since World War II," *Journal of Political Economy* 91: 228–248.

Hargrove, E. C. (1980) "Anglo-American land use attitudes," *Environmental Ethics* 2: 121–148.

Harmon, M. E. and Franklin, J. F. (1989) "Tree seedlings on logs in *Picea–Tsuga* forests of Oregon and Washington," *Ecology* 70: 45–59.

Harris, L. D. (1988) "Edge effects and conservation of biotic diversity," *Conservation Biology* 2: 330–332.

Harrison, D., Jr. (1975) *Who Pays for Clean Air: The Cost and Benefit Distribution of Federal Automobile Emission Controls*, Cambridge, Mass.: Ballinger Publishing.

Helliwell, J. F. (1981) "The stagflationary effects of higher energy prices in an open economy," *Canadian Public Policy* 7: 155–164.

Hirsch, F. (1976) *Social Limits to Growth*, Cambridge, Mass.: Harvard University Press.

Hogan, W. T. (1971a) *Economic History of the Iron and Steel Industry in the United States, Volume I*, Lexington, Mass.: Lexington Books.

—— (1971b) *Economic History of the Iron and Steel Industry in the United States, Volume II*, Lexington, Mass.: Lexington Books.

Holden, K., Peel, D. A. and Thompson, J. L. (1987) *The Economics of Wage Controls*, New York: St Martin's Press.

Holderness, B. A. (1985) *British Agriculture since 1945*, Manchester: Manchester University Press.

Holtby, L. B. (1988) "Effects of logging on stream temperatures in Carnation Creek, British Columbia, and associated impacts on the coho salmon (*Oncorhynchus kisutch*)," *Canadian Journal of Fisheries and Aquatic Science* 45: 502–515.

Howells, G. (1990) *Acid Rain and Acid Waters*, Chichester, West Sussex: Ellis Horwood.

Hudson, E. A. and Jorgenson, D. W. (1978) "Energy prices and the U. S. economy, 1972–1976," *Natural Resources Journal* 18: 877–897.

Hunter, S. and Waterman, R. W. (1992) "Determining an agency's regulatory style: how does the EPA Water Office enforce the law?" *Western Political Quarterly* 45: 403–417.

Hynes, H. P. (1989) *The Recurring Silent Spring*, New York: Pergamon Press.

Ingram, H. M. and Mann, D. E. (1984) "Preserving the Clean Water Act: the appearance of environmental victory," in N. J. Vig and M. E. Kraft (eds) *Environmental Policy in the 1990s*, Washington D. C.: Congressional Quarterly Inc.

Ingram, H. M. and Mann, D. E. (1989) "Interest groups and environmental policy," in J. P. Lester (ed.) *Environmental Politics and Policy: Theories and Evidence*, Durham, N. C.: Duke University Press.

Jackson, K. T. (1985) *Crabgrass Frontier: The Suburbanization of the United States*, New York: Oxford University Press.

Johnson, R. N. (1985) "U. S. Forest Service policy and its budget," in R. T. Deacon and M. B. Johnson (eds) *Forestlands: Public and Private*, San Francisco, Calif.: Pacific Institute for Public Policy Research.

Jones, D. C. (1982) "British producer cooperatives, 1948–1968: productivity and organizational structure," in D. C. Jones and J. Svejnar (eds) *Participatory and Self-Managed Firms*, Lexington, Mass.: Lexington Books.

Jones, D. C. and Backus, D. K. (1977) "British producer cooperatives in the footwear industry: an empirical evaluation of the theory of financing," *Economic Journal* 87: 488–510.

Jorgenson, D. W. (1981) "Energy prices and productivity growth," *Scandinavian Journal of Economics* 83: 165–179.

Kapp, K. W. (1970) "Environmental disruption and social costs: a challenge to economics," *Kyklos* 23, 4: 833–847.

Kelman, S. (1981) "Cost-benefit analysis: an ethical critique," *Regulation* 5: 33–40.

Kinnersley, D. (1988) *Troubled Water: Rivers, Politics and Pollution*, London: Hilary Shipman.

—— (1994) *Coming Clean: The Politics of Water and the Environment*, London: Penguin.

Kleinknecht, A. (1984) "Observations on the Schumpeterian swarming of innovations," in C. Freeman (ed.) *Long Waves in the World Economy*, London: Frances Pinter.

Knopf, F. L. (1996) "Prairie legacies – birds," in F. B. Samson and F. L. Knopf (eds) *Prairie Conservation: Preserving North America's Most Endangered Ecosystem*, Washington, D. C.: Island Press.

Knopman, D. S. and Smith, R. A. (1993) "20 Years of the Clean Water Act," *Environment* 35: 17–41.

Kornbluh, H., Crowfoot, J. and Cohen-Rosenthal, E. (1985) "Worker participation in energy and natural resources conservation," *International Labour Review* 1, 24: 737–754.

Kraft, M. E. (1994) "Environmental gridlock: searching for consensus in Congress," in N. J. Vig and M. E. Kraft (eds) *Environmental Policy in the 1990s*, Washington, D. C.: Congressional Quarterly Inc.

Lacey, A. (1992) *Bioresources: Some U. K. Perspectives*, London: Institute of Biology.

Lee, K. (1996) "The source and locus of intrinsic value," *Environmental Ethics* 18: 297–309.

Lettenmaier, D. P., Hooper, E. R., Wagoner, C. and Faris, K. B. (1991) "Trends in stream quality in the continental United States, 1978–1987," *Water Resources Research* 27: 327–339.

Levin, H. M. (1984) "Employment and productivity of producer cooperatives," in R. Jackall and H. M. Levin (eds) *Worker Cooperatives in America*, Berkeley, Calif.: University of California Press.

Licht, D. S. (1994) "The Great Plains: America's best chance for ecosystem restoration, part 1," *Wild Earth* 4, 2: 47–53.

Liddell, B. E. A. (trans.) (1970) *Kant on the Foundation of Morality: A Modern Version of the Grundlegung*, Bloomington and London: Indiana University Press.

Ling, P. J. (1990) *America and the Automobile: Technology, Reform, and Social Change*, Manchester: Manchester University Press.

MacArthur, R. H. and Wilson, E. O. (1967) *The Theory of Island Biogeography*, Princeton, N. J.: Princeton University Press.

McCormick, J. (1991) *British Politics and the Environment*, London: Earthscan.

MacDonald, G. (1982) *The Long-Term Impacts of Increasing Atmospheric Carbon Dioxide Levels*, Cambridge, Mass.: Ballinger Publishing.

—— (1989) "Scientific basis for the greenhouse effect," in D. E. Abrahamson (ed.) *The Challenge of Global Warming*, Washington, D. C.: Island Press.

McGrath, J. J. and Barnes, C. D. (eds) (1982) *Air Pollution – Physiological Effects*, New York: Academic Press.

Maddison, D. and Pearce, D. (1995) "The UK and global warming policy," in T. S. Gray (ed.) *UK Environmental Policy in the 1990s*, London: Macmillan.

Madson, J. (1982) *Where the Sky Began: Land of the Tallgrass Prairie*, Boston, Mass.: Houghton Mifflin.

Maloney, W. A. and Richardson, J. (1994) "Water policy making in England and Wales: policy communities under pressure?" *Environmental Politics* 4: 110–138.

Mannan, R. W., Meslow, E. C. and Wight, H. M. (1980) "Use of snags by birds in Douglas-fir forests, western Oregon," *Journal of Wildlife Management* 44: 787–797.

Manning, R. (1995) *Grassland: The History, Biology, Politics, and Promise of the American Prairie*, New York: Viking.

Marshall, M. (1987) *Long Waves of Regional Development*, New York: St Martin's Press.

Maser, C. and Trappe, J. M. (eds) (1984) *The Seen and Unseen World of the Fallen Tree*, Portland, Oreg.: USDA Forest Service, Pacific Northwest Forest and Range and Experiment Station, GTR PNW-164.

Maser, C., Trappe, J. M. and Nussbaum, R. A. (1978) "Fungal–small mammal interrelationships with emphasis on Oregon coniferous forests," *Ecology* 59: 799–809.

Maser, C., Maser, Z., Witt, J. W. and Hunt, G. (1986) "The northern flying squirrel: a mycophagist in southwestern Oregon," *Canadian Journal of Zoology* 64: 2086–2089.

Mattson, D. J. and Reid, M. M. (1991) "Conservation of the Yellowstone grizzly bear," *Conservation Biology* 5: 364–372.

Mead, W. J., Muraoka, D. D., Schniepp, M. and Watson, R. B. (1990) "The economic consequences of preserving old growth timber for spotted owls in Oregon and Washington," Community and Organization Research Institute, University of California, Santa Barbara.

Meade, J. E. (1972) "The theory of labor-managed firms and of profit sharing," *Economic Journal* 82: 402–428.

Melnick, R. S. (1983) *Regulation and the Courts: The Case of the Clean Air Act*, Washington D. C.: The Brookings Institution.

Melosi, M. V. (1985) *Coping with Abundance: Energy and Environment in Industrial America*, Philadelphia, Penn.: Temple University Press.

Mengel, R. M. (1970) "The North American central plains as an isolating agent in bird speciation," in W. Dort, Jr. and J. K. Jones, Jr. (eds) *Pleistocene and Recent Environments of the Central Great Plains*, Lawrence, Kans.: University Press of Kansas.

Meybeck, M., Chapman, D. V. and Helmer, R. (eds) (1989) *Global Freshwater Quality: A First Assessment*, Oxford: Blackwell.

Milbrath, L. (1984) *Environmentalists: Vanguard for a New Society*, Albany, N. Y.: State University of New York Press.

Mills, E. S. and Hamilton, B. W. (1994) *Urban Economics*, 5th edn, New York: Harper-Collins.

Mitchell, B. R. (1984) *Economic Development of the British Coal Industry: 1800–1914*, Cambridge: Cambridge University Press.

Mitchell, R. C. and Carson, R. T. (1989) *Using Surveys to Value Public Goods: The Contingent Valuation Method*, Washington D. C.: Resources for the Future.

Mitchell, R. C., Mertig, A. G. and Dunlap, R. E. (1991) "Twenty years of environmental mobilization: trends among national environment organizations," *Society and Natural Resources* 4: 219–234.

Murphy, M. L. and Hall, J. D. (1981) "Varied effects of clear-cut logging on predators and their habitat in small streams of the Cascade Mountains, Oregon," *Canadian Journal of Fisheries and Aquatic Science* 38: 137–145.

Muth, R. F. (1969) *Cities and Housing: The Spatial Pattern of Urban Residential Land Use*, Chicago, Ill.: University of Chicago Press.

Nash, R. (1982) *Wilderness and the American Mind*, 3rd edn, New Haven, Conn.: Yale University Press.

National Academy of Sciences, National Academy of Engineering, Institute of Medicine (1992) *Policy Implications of Greenhouse Warming: Mitigation, Adaption, and the Science Base*, Washington D. C.: National Academy Press.

Nature Conservancy (1996) *Priorities for Conservation: 1996 Annual Report Card for U.S. Plant and Animal Species*, Arlington, Va.: Nature Conservancy.

NCC (1984) *Nature Conservation in Great Britain*, Shrewsbury: Nature Conservancy Council.

Nell, E. (1988) *Prosperity and Public Spending: Transformational Growth and the Role of Government Spending*, Boston, Mass.: Unwin Hyman.

Nelson, R. H. (1985) "Mythology instead of analysis: the story of public forest management," in R. T. Deacon and M. B. Johnson (eds) *Forestlands: Public and Private*, San Francisco, Calif.: Pacific Institute for Public Policy Research.

Nordhaus, W. D. (1991) "To slow or not to slow: the economics of the greenhouse effect," *Economic Journal* 101: 920–937.

—— (1992) "An optimal transition path for controlling greenhouse gases," *Science* 258: 1315–1319.

North, D. C. (1974) *Growth and Welfare in the American Past: A New Economic History*, 2nd edn, Englewood Cliffs, N. J.: Prentice-Hall.

Norton, B. G. (1987) *Why Preserve Natural Variety?*, Princeton, N. J.: Princeton University Press.

—— (1989) "Intergenerational equity and environmental decisions: a model using Rawls' veil of ignorance," *Ecological Economics* 1: 137–159.

—— (1991) *Toward Unity among Environmentalists*. New York: Oxford University Press.

—— (1992) "Policy implications of Gaian theory," *Ecological Economics* 6: 103–118.

Norton-Taylor, R. (1982) *Whose Land Is It Anyway? Agriculture, Planning, and Land Use in the British Countryside*, Wellingborough: Turnstone Press.

Noss, R. F. and Cooperrider, A. Y. (1994) *Saving Nature's Legacy: Protecting and Restoring Biodiversity*, Washington D. C.: Island Press.

Nownes, A. J. (1991) "Interest groups and the regulation of pesticides: Congress, coalitions, and closure," *Policy Sciences* 24: 1–18.

Oakeshott, R. (1978) *The Case for Workers' Co-ops*, London: Routledge & Kegan Paul.

OECD (1991) *The State of the Environment*, Paris: Organisation for Economic Cooperation and Development.

—— (1995) *OECD Environmental Data*, Paris: Organisation for Economic Cooperation and Development.

Oelschlaeger, M. (1991) *The Idea of Wilderness: From Prehistory to the Age of Ecology*, New Haven, Conn.: Yale University Press.

Olson, M., Jr. (1971) *The Logic of Collective Action: Public Goods and the Theory of Groups*, New York: Schocken Books.

O'Neill, R. V., DeAngelis, D. L., Waide, J. B. and Allen, T. F. H. (1986) *A Hierarchical Concept of Ecosystems*, Princeton, N. J.: Princeton University Press.

O'Toole, R. (1988) *Reforming the Forest Service*, Washington D. C.: Island Press.

—— (1993) "Last stand: selling out the national forests," *Multinational Monitor* 14: 25–29.

Ott, M. and Tatom, J. A. (1986) "Are energy prices cyclical?" *Energy Economics* 8: 227–236.

Park, C. C. (1987) *Acid Rain: Rhetoric and Reality*, London: Methuen.

Passer, H. C. (1953) *The Electrical Manufacturers, 1875–1900: A Study in Competition, Entrepreneurship, Technical Change, and Economic Growth*, Cambridge, Mass.: Harvard University Press.

Patrick, R. (1992) *Surface Water Quality: Have the Laws Been Successful?*, Princeton, N. J.: Princeton University Press.

Pearce, D. (1993) *Blueprint 3: Measuring Sustainable Development*, London: Earthscan.

Penrose, E. T. (1968) *The Theory of the Growth of the Firm*, Oxford: Basil Blackwell.

Peters, R. L. (1989) "Effects of global warming on biodiversity," in D. E. Abrahamson (ed.) *The Challenge of Global Warming*, Washington, D. C.: Island Press.

Peters, R. L. and Lovejoy, T. E. (eds) (1992) *Global Warming and Biological Diversity*, New Haven, Conn.: Yale University Press.

Petts, G. E. (1984) *Impounded Rivers: Perspectives for Ecological Management*, New York: John Wiley & Sons.

Pike, L. H., Radial, R. A. and Denison, W. C. (1977) "A 400-year-old Douglas fir tree and its epiphytes: biomass, surface area, and their distributions," *Canadian Journal of Forest Research* 7: 680–699.

Pimentel, D. and Perkins, J. H. (1979) *Pest Control: Cultural and Environmental Aspects*, Boulder, Colo.: Westview Press.

Pimentel, D., McLaughlin, L., Zepp, A., Lakitan, B., Kraus, T., Kleinman, P., Vancini, F., Roach, J. W., Graap, E., Keeton, W. S. and Selig, G. (1991) "Environmental and economic effects of reducing pesticide use," *Bioscience* 41: 402–409.

Pimentel, D., Acquay, H., Biltonen, M., Rice, P., Silva, M., Nelson, J., Lipner, V., Giordano, S., Horowitz, A. and D'Amore, M. (1992) "Environmental and economic costs of pesticide use," *BioScience* 42: 750–760.

Pimentel, D., Herdendorf, M., Eisenfeld, S., Olander, L., Carroquino, J., Corson, C., McDade, J., Chung, Y., Cannon, W., Roberts, J., Bluman, L. and Gregg, J. (1994) "Achieving a secure energy future: environmental and economic issues," *Ecological Economics* 9: 201–220.

Plumwood, V. (1991) "Ethics and instrumentalism: a response to Janna Thompson," *Environmental Ethics* 13: 139–149.

Poor, H. V. and Poor, H. W. (1868–1900) *Poor's Manual of Railroads*, New York: H. V. and H. W. Poor.

Pye-Smith, C. and Rose, C. (1984) *Crisis and Conservation: Conflict in the British Countryside*, Harmondsworth: Penguin.

Rae, J. B. (1984) *The American Automobile Industry*, Boston, Mass.: Twayne Publishers.

Raphael, R. (1981) *Tree Talk: The People and Politics of Timber*, Washington D. C.: Island Press.

Rasker, R. (1993) "Rural development, conservation, and public policy in the greater Yellowstone ecosystem," *Society and Natural Resources* 6: 109–126.

Rasker, R. and Glick, D. (1994) "Footloose entrepreneurs: pioneers of the new West?" *Illahee* 10: 34–43.

Rasker, R., Tirrell, N. and Klopfer, D. (1991) "The wealth of nature: new economic realities in the Yellowstone region," Washington D. C.: The Wilderness Society.

Rawls, J. (1971) *A Theory of Justice*, Cambridge, Mass.: Belknap Press.

Regan, T. (1981) "The nature and possibility of an environmental ethic," *Environmental Ethics* 3: 19–34.

Reisner, M. (1987) *Cadillac Desert: The American West and Its Disappearing Water*, New York: Penguin Books.

Renshaw, E. (1992) "Identifying no growth years in the U. S. economy using increases in crude oil prices," *Energy Economics* 14: 132–135.

Richardson, K. (1977) *The British Motor Industry: 1896–1939*, London: Macmillan.

Risser, P. G., Birney, E. C., Blocker, H. D., May, S. W., Parton, W. J. and Wiens, J. A. (1981) *The True Prairie Ecosystem*, Stroudsburg, Penn.: Hutchinson Ross Publishing Company.

Rolston, H. III (1981) "Values in nature," *Environmental Ethics* 3: 113–128.

—— (1988) *Environmental Ethics: Duties to and Values in the Natural World*, Philadelphia, Penn.: Temple University Press.

Romme, W. H. and Turner, M. G. (1991) "Implications of global climate change for biogeographic patterns in the greater Yellowstone ecosystem," *Conservation Biology* 5: 373–386.

Rosenbaum, W. A. (1989) "The bureaucracy and environmental policy," in J. P. Lester (ed.) *Environmental Politics and Policy: Theories and Evidence*, Durham, N. C.: Duke University Press.

—— (1991) *Environmental Politics and Policy*, 2nd edn, Washington D. C.: Congressional Quarterly Inc.

Rosenberg, N. (1972) *Technology and American Growth*, New York: Harper & Row.

Ross, H. H. (1970) "The ecological history of the Great Plains: evidence from grassland insects," in W. Dort, Jr. and J. K. Jones, Jr. (eds) *Pleistocene and Recent Environments of the Central Great Plains*, Lawrence, Kans.: University Press of Kansas.

Roth, D. M. (1984) *The Wilderness Movement and the National Forests: 1964–1980*, Washington D. C.: USDA Forest Service.

Royal Commission on Environmental Pollution (1995) *Transport and the Environment*, Oxford: Oxford University Press.

Sagoff, M. (1988) *The Economy of the Earth: Philosophy, Law, and the Environment*, Cambridge: Cambridge University Press.

Saunders, D. A., Hobbs, R. J. and Margules, C. R. (1991) "Biological consequences of ecosystem fragmentation: a review," *Conservation Biology* 5: 18–32.

Schneider, K. (1994) "Progress, not victory, on Great Lakes pollution," *New York Times* 7 May: 1, 7.

Schor, J. B. (1991) "Global equity and environmental crisis: an argument for reducing working hours in the North," *World Development* 19: 73–84.

—— (1992) *The Overworked American: The Unexpected Decline of Leisure*, New York: Basic Books.

Schorger, A. W. (1942) "Extinct and endangered mammals and birds of the upper Great Lakes region," *Transactions of the Wisconsin Academy of Sciences, Arts and Letters* 34: 23–44.

Schumpeter, J. A. (1939) *Business Cycles*, New York: McGraw-Hill.

—— (1950) *Capitalism, Socialism, and Democracy*, New York: Harper & Row.

Schurr, S. H. and Netschert, B. C. (1960) *Energy in the American Economy, 1850–1975: An Economic Study of Its History and Prospects*, Baltimore, Md.: Johns Hopkins Press.

Schurr, S. H., Burwell, C. C., Devine, W. D. and Sonenblum, S. (1990) *Electricity in the American Economy*, Westport, Conn.: Greenwood Press.

Schwartz, R. E. and Hackett, D. P. (1984) "Citizen suits against private industry under the Clean Water Act," *Natural Resources Lawyer* 27: 327–368.

Scitovsky, T. (1992) *The Joyless Economy: The Psychology of Human Satisfaction*, revised edition, New York: Oxford University Press.

Scrivener, J. C. and Brownlee, M. J. (1989) "Effects of forest harvesting on spawning gravel and incubation survival of chum (*Oncorhynchus keta*) and coho salmon (*O. kisutch*) in Carnation Creek, British Columbia," *Journal of Fisheries and Aquatic Science* 46: 681–696.

Sen, A. K. (1977) "Rational fools: a critique of the behavioral foundations of economic theory," *Philosophy and Public Affairs* 6: 317–344.

Sher, V. M. and Stahl, A. (1990) "Spotted owls, ancient forests, courts and congress: an overview of citizens' efforts to protect old-growth forests and the species that live in them," *Northwest Environmental Journal* 6: 362–383.

Skea, J. (1995) "Acid rain: a business as usual scenario," in T. S. Gray (ed.) *UK Environmental Policy in the 1990s*, London: Macmillan.

Smith, W. B. (1986) "Wisconsin's fourth forest inventory: area," *Resource Bulletin* NC-97, USDA Forest Service.

Smith, W. H. (1990) *Air Pollution and Forests: Interaction between Air Contaminants and Forest Ecosystems*, 2nd edn, New York: Springer-Verlag.

Snyder, S. A. (1994) "Homes in wildlife habitat: learning to share the land," *Greater Yellowstone Report* 11: 10–11.

Solins, P., Grier, C. C., McCorison, F. M., Cromack, K., Jr. and Fogel, R. (1980) "The internal element cycles of an old-growth Douglas-fir ecosystem in western Oregon," *Ecological Monographs* 50: 261–285.

Soule, M. E. (1985) "What is conservation biology?" *Bioscience* 35: 727–734.

Spencer, J. C., Jr. (1983) "Michigan's fourth forest inventory: area," *Resource Bulletin* NC-68, USDA Forest Service.

Spies, T. A. and Franklin, J. F. (1988a) "Old growth and forest dynamics in the Douglas-fir region of western Oregon and Washington," *Natural Areas Journal* 8: 190–201.

—— (1988b) "Coarse woody debris in Douglas-fir forests of western Oregon and Washington," *Ecology* 69: 1689–1702.

Steinauer, E. M. and Collins, S. L. (1996) "Prairie ecology – the tallgrass prairie," in F. B. Samson and F. L. Knopf (eds) *Prairie Conservation: Preserving North America's Most Endangered Ecosystem*, Washington D. C.: Island Press.

Stephen, F. H. (1982) "The economic theory of the labor-managed firm," in F. H. Stephen (ed.) *The Performance of Labor-Managed Firms*, New York: St Martin's Press.

—— (1984) *The Economic Analysis of Producers' Cooperatives*, New York: St Martin's Press.

Stern, A. C., Boubel, R. W., Turner, D. B. and Fox, D. L. (1984) *Fundamentals of Air Pollution*, 2nd edn, New York: Academic Press.

Stevens, W. K. (1996) "Too much of a good thing makes benign nitrogen a triple threat," *New York Times* 10 December: B5, B8.

Swaney, J. A. and Evers, M. A. (1989) "The social cost concepts of K. William Kapp and Karl Polanyi," *Journal of Economic Issues* 23: 7–33.

Taylor, P. (1981) "The ethics of respect for nature," *Environmental Ethics* 3: 197–218.

—— (1986) *Respect for Nature*, Princeton, N. J.: Princeton University Press.

Thedinga, J. F., Murphy, M. L., Heifietz, J., Koski, K. V. and Johnson, S. W. (1989) "Effects of logging on size and age composition of juvenile coho salmon (*Oncorhynchus kisutch*) and density of presmolts in southeast Alaska streams," *Canadian Journal of Fisheries and Aquatic Science* 46: 1383–1391.

Thomas, H. (1982) "The performance of the Mondragon cooperatives in Spain," in D. Jones and J. Svejnar (eds) *Participatory and Self-Managed Firms*, Lexington, Mass.: Lexington Books.

Thomas, H. and Logan, C. (1982) *Mondragon: An Economic Analysis*, London: Allen & Unwin.

Thomas, J. W., Forsman, E. D., Lint, J. B., Meslow, E. C., Noon, B. R. and Verner, H.

(1990) "A conservation strategy for the northern spotted owl," Interagency Scientific Committee to Address the Conservation of the Northern Spotted Owl, Portland, Oreg.

Tietenberg, T. (1994) *Environmental Economics and Policy*, New York: HarperCollins.

Titus, J. G. (1989) "The causes and effects of sea level rise," in D. E. Abrahamson (ed.) *The Challenge of Global Warming*, Washington, D. C.: Island Press.

Tomer, J. F. (1987) *Organizational Capital: The Path to Higher Productivity and Well-Being*, New York: Praeger.

—— (1992) "The human firm in the natural environment: a socio-economic analysis of its behavior," *Ecological Economics* 6: 119–138.

Transeau, E. N. (1935) "The prairie peninsula," *Ecology* 16: 423–437.

Twight, B. W. (1983) *Organizational Values and Political Power: The Forest Service versus the Olympic National Park*, University Park, Penn.: Pennsylvania State University Press.

Tylecote, A. (1992) *The Long Wave in the World Economy: The Present Crisis in Historical Perspective*, London: Routledge.

U. S. Census Office (1854) *The Seventh Census of the United States, 1850, Vol. 1*, Washington D. C.: U. S. Government Printing Office.

—— (1864) *Agriculture of the United States in 1860, the Eighth Census*, Washington D. C.: U. S. Government Printing Office.

—— (1872) *Ninth Census, Volume III. The Statistics of the Wealth and Industry of the United States*, Washington D. C.: U. S. Government Printing Office.

—— (1883) *Report of the Productions of Agriculture, Tenth Census*, Washington D. C.: U. S. Government Printing Office.

—— (1895) *Report on the Statistics of Agriculture in the United States, Eleventh Census*, Washington D. C.: U. S. Government Printing Office.

—— (1902) *Twelfth Census of the United States, Census Reports Volume V, Agriculture, Part I*, Washington D. C.: U. S. Government Printing Office.

—— (1922) *Fourteenth Census of the United States, Agriculture, Volume VI, Part I*, Washington D. C.: U. S. Government Printing Office.

U. S. Council of Economic Advisors (1995) *Economic Report of the President*, Washington D. C.: U. S. Government Printing Office.

U. S. Department of Commerce, Bureau of the Census (1975) *Historical Statistics of the United States: Colonial Times to 1970*, Washington D. C.: U. S. Government Printing Office.

—— (1948–1993) *Statistical Abstract of the United States*, Washington D. C.: U. S. Government Printing Office.

U. S. Department of Commerce, Bureau of Economic Analysis (1995) "Regional economic information system," Regional Economic Measurement Division, Washington D. C.

U. S. Department of the Interior, Bureau of Reclamation (1991) *Summary Statistics: Water, Land, and Related Data*, Denver, Colo.

U. S. Environmental Protection Agency (1991) "National air pollutant emission estimates, 1940–1990," Office of Air Quality Planning and Standards, Research Triangle Park, N. C.

U. S. Federal Highway Commission (1947–1965) *Highway Statistics*, Washington D. C.: U. S. Government Printing Office.

U. S. International Trade Commission (1974–1988) *Synthetic Organic Chemicals: United State Production and Sales*, Washington D. C.: U. S. Government Printing Office.

U. S. Tariff Commission (1959–1973) *Synthetic Organic Chemicals: United State Production and Sales*, Washington D. C.: U. S. Government Printing Office.

Vanek, J. (1970) *The General Theory of Labor-Managed Market Economies*, Ithaca, N. Y.: Cornell University Press.

Vig, N. J. (1994) "Presidential leadership and the environment: from Reagan and Bush to

Clinton," in N. J. Vig and M. E. Kraft (eds) *Environmental Policy in the 1990s*, Washington D. C.: Congressional Quarterly Inc.

Vogel, D. (1986) *National Styles of Regulation: Environmental Policy in Great Britain and the United States*, Ithaca, N. Y.: Cornell University Press.

Wall, B. R. (1972) *Log Production in Washington and Oregon: An Historical Perspective*, Portland, Oreg.: USDA Forest Service, Resource Bulletin, PNW-42.

Ward, B. (1958) "The firm in Illyria: market syndicalism," *American Economic Review* 48: 566–589.

Waring, R. H. and Franklin, J. F. (1979) "Evergreen coniferous forests of the Pacific Northwest," *Science* 204: 1380–1385.

Warner, R. E. (1994) "Agricultural land use and grassland habitat in Illinois: future shock for midwestern birds?" *Conservation Biology* 8: 147–156.

Warner, S. B., Jr. (1974) *Streetcar Suburbs: The Process of Growth in Boston, 1870–1900*, Cambridge, Mass.: Atheneum.

Watkins, A. J. (1980) *The Practice of Urban Economics*, Beverly Hills, Calif.: Sage.

Watt, K. E. F. (1989) "Evidence for the role of energy resources in producing long waves in the United States economy," *Ecological Economics* 1: 181–195.

Weaver, J. E. (1954) *North American Prairie*, Lincoln, Nebr.: Johnsen Publishing Company.

Welch, E. B. (1992) *Ecological Effects of Wastewater: Applied Limnology and Pollutant Effects*. London: Chapman & Hall.

Wells, P. V. (1970) "Vegetational history of the Great Plains: a post-glacial record of coniferous woodland in southeastern Wyoming," in W. Dort, Jr. and J. K. Jones, Jr. (eds) *Pleistocene and Recent Environments of the Central Great Plains*, Lawrence, Kans.: University Press of Kansas.

Wenner, L. M. (1989) "The courts and environmental policy," in J. P. Lester (ed.) *Environmental Politics and Policy: Theories and Evidence*, Durham, N. C.: Duke University Press.

Whitney, G. G. (1987) "An ecological history of the Great Lakes forest of Michigan," *Journal of Ecology* 75: 667–684.

Whyte, W. F. and Whyte, K. K. (1988) *Making Mondragon: The Growth and Dynamics of the Worker Cooperative Complex*, Ithaca, N. Y.: ILR Press.

Williams, M. (1989) *Americans and Their Forests: A Historical Geography*, Cambridge: Cambridge University Press.

Williamson, H. F., Andreano, R. L., Daum, A. R. and Klose, G. C. (1963) *The American Petroleum Industry: The Age of Energy, 1899–1959*, Evanston, Ill.: Northwestern University Press.

Williamson, J. G. (1975) "The railroads and midwestern development, 1870–90: a general equilibrium history," in D. C. Klingaman and R. K. Veddar (eds) *Essays in Nineteenth Century Economic History: The Old Northwest*, Athens, Ohio: Ohio University Press.

Wilson, E. O. (ed.) (1988) *Biodiversity*, Washington D. C.: National Academy Press.

—— (1992) *The Diversity of Life*, Cambridge, Mass.: Belknap Press.

Wilson, S. D. and Belcher, J. W. (1989) "Plant and bird communities of native prairie and introduced Eurasian vegetation in Manitoba, Canada," *Conservation Biology* 3: 39–44.

Winter, M. (1996) *Rural Politics: Policies for Agriculture, Forestry, and the Environment*. London: Routledge.

Wisconsin DNR (1991) "A nonpoint source control plan for the Milwaukee River South Priority Watershed Project: project summary," Madison, Wis.: Wisconsin Department of Natural Resources.

—— (1992) "A nonpoint source control plan for the Menomonee River Priority Watershed Project: project summary," Madison, Wis.: Wisconsin Department of Natural Resources.

—— (1993) "A nonpoint source control plan for the Sheboygan River Priority Watershed Project: project summary," Madison, Wis.: Wisconsin Department of Natural Resources.

—— (1994) "A nonpoint source control plan for the Upper Fox River Priority Watershed Project," Winconsin Department of Natural Resources, Madison, Wisc.

Wisconsin Legislative Fiscal Bureau (1995) "Nonpoint source water pollution and soil conservation programs," Information Paper 63, Madison, Wisc.

Wittfogel, K. (1957) *Oriental Despotism: A Comparative Study of Total Power*, New Haven, Conn.: Yale University Press.

Wood, C. (1989) *Planning Pollution Prevention: A Comparison of Siting Controls over Air Pollution Sources in Great Britain and the USA*, Oxford: Heinemann Newnes.

Woodwell, G. M. (1989) "Biotic causes and effects of the disruption of the global carbon cycle," in D. E. Abrahamson (ed.) *The Challenge of Global Warming*, Washington D. C.: Island Press.

Wolke, H. (1991) *Wilderness on the Rocks*, Tucson, Ariz.: Ned Ludd Books.

Woolf, A. G. (1984) "Electricity, productivity, and labor saving: American manufacturing, 1900–1929," *Explorations in Economic History* 21: 176–191.

World Resources Institute (1995) *World Resources: A Guide to the Global Environment: 1995–96*, Oxford: Oxford University Press.

—— (1996) *World Resources: A Guide to the Global Environment: 1996–97*, Oxford: Oxford University Press.

Worster, D. (1985) *Rivers of Empire: Water, Aridity, and the Growth of the American West*, New York: Pantheon Books.

Wright, H. E., Jr. (1970) "Vegetational history of the Central Plains," in W. Dort, Jr. and J. K. Jones, Jr. (eds) *Pleistocene and Recent Environments of the Central Great Plains*, Lawrence, Kans.: University Press of Kansas.

Wright, R. G., MacCracken, J. G. and Hall, J. (1994) "An ecological evaluation of proposed new conservation areas in Idaho: evaluating proposed Idaho national parks," *Conservation Biology* 8: 207–216.

Yahner, R. H. (1988) "Changes in wildlife communities near edges," *Conservation Biology* 2: 333–339.

Young, S. C. (1995) "Running up the down escalator: developments in British wildlife policies after Mrs Thatcher's 1988 speeches," in T. S. Gray (ed.) *UK Environmental Policy in the 1990*, London: Macmillan.

Zevi, A. (1982) "The performance of Italian producer cooperatives," in D. Jones and J. Svejnar (eds) *Participatory and Self-Managed Firms*, Lexington, Mass.: Lexington Books.

INDEX

acid rain 10, 22, 83–6, 139–40; in the Adirondack Mountains 84; and aluminum 84, 86; and aquatic ecosystems 84–5; in the Black Forest of Germany 84, 86, 117; and bird population losses 85; buffering of by calcium carbonate 84; in Canada 84; control of in the U.S. 144–5; deposition of 21, 83–5; and epiphytic lichens 86; and fish population losses 85; and forest ecosystems 85–6; and heavy metals 84; in Norway 84, 116; and politics in Europe 116–18; and politics in Germany 117–18; and politics in the U.K. 115–18; in Scandinavian countries 83, 117–18; and species losses 85; and sulfur dioxide emissions from the U.K. 116; in Sweden 116; and tree damage 86; in the U.K. 86; in the U.S. 83–6

Adirondack Mountains: acid deposition in 84

agency capture problem 104

Agricultural Act of 1986 123

agricultural policy: and countryside preservation 123; and pesticides 110; in the U.K. 37; and water pollution regulation in the U.K. 120

agricultural settlement 55, 99

agriculture 9, 22, 53, 80; early development of in the U.K. 46–7; and global warming 89–90; modernization of in the U.K. 37, 47–8, 80, 121; and natural habitat destruction 39–43; and nonpoint water pollution 34–5;

northern Great Lakes growing season too short for 46; northern Great Lakes soil too poor for 46; and pesticides problems 96–8, 110; and prairie settlement 39–44; and productivity increases from CO_2 enrichment 89; and semi-natural habitat in the U.K. 120–4; use of chemicals in 34, 52; use of pesticides in 21–2; and water pollution 33–5, 95; and water pollution in the U.K. 37; and yield losses 89

air pollution 1–2, 5, 9, 81–6, 99, 150; and asthma 82; from carbon monoxide 25–31, 81–3; and cardiovascular disease 82; and forests 85–6; from fossil fuels 23–31, 82; from hydrocarbons 81; from hydrochloric acid 116; from nitrous oxides 25–31, 81–2; and ozone 81–2, 86; from particulates 2, 25–31, 82; and photochemical smog 83; and primary pollutants 81–2; and pulmonary functioning 82; and secondary pollutants 81–2; from smoke 20, 29, 53; sources 25–6, 29; from sulfur oxides 25–31, 81–2, 85–6; and the tall-chimney policy 83; and tree damage 86; from volatile organic compounds 28–30, 81; U.S. 25–8; U.K. 29–30, 82–4

air pollution emission limits: U.S. 104–6

air pollution regulation 26–8, 82–3, 104–6; and the Alkali Inspectorate 116; and the auto industry 106; and the auto industry in Germany 118; and the auto industry in the U.K. 118; and the

212

British environmental lobby 116–17; and coal-fired electric utilities 105–6; and coal in the U.K. 115–16; and Congress 105–6; and coal mines 105; and the domestic fire in the U.K. 115–16; early history of in the U.K. 116; and Federal District Courts 106; and new performance standards 105; and politics in Europe 116–18; and politics in Germany 117–18; and politics in the U.K. 115–18; and presidential administrations 105–6; 116–18; and prevention of significant deterioration (PSD) 104–5; resistance to 104–6, and the Scandinavian countries 116–18; and scrubbers 105; and the Reagan administration 106; and State Implementation Plans (SIPs) 106

air quality 53, 82–4

air quality standards 26, 28, 82, 86; U.S. 104–6

alder (*Alnus glutinosa*) 73

aldrin 38

Alkali Act (1874) 82, 115

Alkali Inspectorate 83; and air pollution regulation 116

Alkali Works Regulation Bill (1863) 115

aluminum: and acid rain 84, 86

American crocodile 91

American Petroleum Institute 104

Arctic National Wildlife Refuge 129

Arctic Ocean: global warming and primary productivity reduction 91; marine food chains in the and global warming 91–3

arsenic 38

ash (*Fraxinus excelsior*) 73

aspen (*Populus tremula*) 46, 64–5, 73; adaptation to fire by 64–5; and deer population eruption 66

assembly line 24

asters (*Aster spp.*) 58

Atlantic brant geese: poisoning of by pesticides 96

atrizine 38

Audubon Society 102

automobile: history of 24–5; and petroleum 24–5; and road construction 24; and suburbanization 24

Backus, D. K. 179

Baird's sparrow (*Ammodramus bairdii*) 61

bald eagle 10, 69

balloon frame 45

balsam fir (*Abies balsamea*) 64

Basque region 171, 181

basswood (*Tilia americana*) 64

bear 78; brown 47; grizzly 78–80, 91–2, 157

beaver 47

beech: air pollution damage to 86; *Fagus grandifolia* 64; *Fagus sylvatica* 73; and global warming 91

benefits: intangible 10

Berman, K. 180

best available technology (BAT) 107–8

best conventional technology (BCT) 107–8

best practicable means 36, 82, 115

best practicable technology (BPT) 107

big bluestem (*Andropogon gerardi*) 57, 63

bighorn sheep 79

biochemical oxygen demand (BOD) 34, 93–5, 150

biodiversity 1, 155–8; decline of 9–11, 59–63; and pesticides 98; and road density 157

biological reserves 156–9; and incompatible uses 156; and roadless area protection 156–7

biotic communities 9; altered composition of prairie avian 62; moral concern for 126

birch (*Betula spp.*) 73; white 64; yellow and global warming 91

bison 10, 58–9, 80

blackeyed Susan (*Rudbeckia hirta*) 58

black-footed ferret (*Mustela nigripes*) 58

Black Forest 84, 86

boar 47

Bosso, C. J. 103, 109, 111

bounded rationality 147, 185

budget maximization: and Congress 112;

by the U.S. Forest Service 112–13
Bureau of Land Management *see* U.S.
   Bureau of Land Management
Burns, A. F. 13
Bush, G. 114, 124

calcium carbonate 84
California 138
California sea lion: and global warming
   91, 93
Callicott, J. B. 141
Canada 78
Canada wild rye (*Elymus canadensis*) 57
Canada yew (*taxus canadensis*) 66
capital accumulation 11–12
capitalism 11
carbamates 38
carbofuron: and bird kills 96
carbon dioxide (CO_2) emissions 3, 10,
   29–31, 86–8, 143, 145–50, 162–3;
   accumulation of in the atmosphere 53,
   86–8, 145; and agricultural
   productivity 89; and coal consumption
   189; limits on 118, 143, 145–50, 159,
   162–3; limits and costs 146–50, 163;
   regulation of 114; U.K. contribution to
   30–1; U.S. contribution to 30–1; *see
   also* global warming
carbon monoxide (CO) emissions 26–8,
   81–3
carbon sinks 30
caribou (*Rangifer caribou caribou*) 65
Carson, R. 39, 95–6, 98, 103, 109–10
catalytic converters 29
cedar: western red 68; white (*Thuja
   occidentialist*) 63; loss of seedlings to
   deer 66
Central Electricity Generating Board: and
   opposition to emission controls 117
CFCs (chlorofluorocarbons) 87, 145–6
Chernobyl 103
Chicago 40, 45
China 170
chlordane 38
chloride 35
chlorinate hydrocarbons 38, 96, 98–9
chlorine 30
cholera 118

circular flow 7–8
Clean Air Act of 1956 (U.K.) 83, 116
Clean Air Act of 1970 (U.S.) 26–8, 82,
   104–7
Clean Air Act of 1990 (U.S.) 114, 144
Clean Water Act Amendments of 1987
   (U.S.) 151
Clean Water Act of 1972 (U.S.) 32–4,
   107–9, 150–1, 153; cost of 153
Cline, W. R. 89, 147–8
climate change *see* global warming
climate simulation models 87
Clyde River 33
coal 22; history of use in the U.K. 23–30;
   history of use in the U.S. 23–30;
   pollution from 16; use in home heating
   16
Coase, R. 17, 132
Cobb, J. B. 168
Colorado 56
Columbia River 78
commitment *see* moral commitment
compensation for environmental damage
   132; and economic efficiency 132;
   impossibility of and moral
   considerability 135–8; and substitution
   between instrumental values 132–3
complementarity of inputs 162, 165, 168
conservation biology 60–1, 155–7
Conservation Reserve Program (USDA)
   151–2, 158
consumers: biotic 9
consumption spending 164–6
contingent evaluation studies 137–8
Control of Pollution Act of 1974 (U.K.)
   36, 119
conventional environmental economics
   1–2
Cooper, C. C. 40
cooperatives 6; as an alternative to the
   corporation 168–87; British 178–9,
   183–4; capital accounts in 171; and
   differences from corporations 168–87;
   and economic efficiency 177–84; and
   economic growth 178–85; employee-
   owned producer 168–87, 190; and
   employment 171–4; and energy/matter
   throughput 175–6, 190; French

178–81, 183–4; and investment 174–7, 179–84; Italian 178–81, 183–4; and maximization of income per worker 171–7; Mondragon 181–6; and nonlabor input costs 175–6, 178–84; and pollution emissions 185, 190; and the public goods problem 177; and unemployment 183; U.S. 178–81, 183–4; and X-efficiency 178–9

copper 34–5

coppicing 73

corporations: and acquisition of subsidiaries 167; and bureaucracy 167–8; and cash cows 167; and cooperatives as an alternative form of business organization 170–87; and energy/matter throughput 175–6, 185; and entrepreneurs 167–8; and environmental activism 185; the goals of 184–6; and investment 174–7; and macroeconomic growth 168; and nonlabor input costs 175–6; and profit maximization 171–7, 185, 188; and socio-economics 185; and steady-state growth constraints 168

cost-benefit analysis 3: and environmental ethics 125–41; the limits of 125–41

cost internalization failure problem 2

costs: of biological reserves 157–8; externalization of 2, 17–18, 102, 132; climate stabilization 146–50, 163; internalization of 2; nonpoint pollution control 152–3, 159; of nonrenewable resource extraction 159; of pesticide use 154; pollution control 140; of reduced pesticide use 154, 159; resistance to internalization of 3–4; of sea level increase from global warming 89; of species preservation 140; of a steady-state economy 142–60

cougar (Felis concolor couguar) 66, 78

Country Landowners' Association 123

countryside: U.K. 10, 46–8, 55, 72–5; preservation of and agricultural policy 123; and the environmental lobby in the U.K. 122–4; and habitat loss in the U.K. 72–5; and habitat preservation efforts 120–4; and land use planning

121–2; politics of the 115, 120–4; pre-settlement flora and fauna 73

cowbirds (Molthrus ater): nest parasitism by 66

crayfish 49, 85

creative destruction 12, 18–19; and competition 12; and economic growth 11–13; and industry life-cycles 11–13, 18–19

cryptosporidium 153

Cuyahoga River: conflagration of 107

Daly, H. E. 4, 7–8, 142–3, 160–2, 168, 173

dams 22; as barriers to fish migration 77–8; effect of on biodiversity 77–8; and flood control 76–8; and floodplain loss 77–8; and inundation of fish spawning habitat 77–8; and irrigation 76–8; and riparian habitat change 50, 55, 76–8; and salmon losses from nitrogen poisoning 78; and salmon losses in reservoirs 78; and salmon losses in turbines 78; and salmon mortality 78; and water temperature changes 77–8

DDT 39, 95–9, 102, 110; atmospheric deposition of 98; regulation of 39, 53, 95–8, 110

decent human life 140–1, 148–9, 159

deep ecologists 141

deer 65; key 91; population eruption of 66

Deere, J. 42

Department of Environment 123

diazinon 38; and bird kills 96

dieldrin 38

Dickens, C. 115

dissolved solids 35, 150

dog's mercury (Mercurialist perennis) 72–3

Douglas fir 67–70

Downs, A. 102–3, 114

Earth Day 103

Earth Summit 118

economic democracy: and the conservation of resource inputs 184–6;

and cooperatives 168–87; as an environmental measure 168–87, 190; and waste emissions 184–6

economic development: and threats to the Yellowstone ecosystem 78

economic efficiency: and cooperatives vs. corporations 177–84

economic growth 2, 6, 7, 11–19; benefits of 3; and cooperatives 178–84; and cost externalization 2, 17–18; and disruption of ecosystem services 10–11; and energy prices 164; engines of 12; and environmental change 7, 11–17, 19, 20–100, 124–5, 141, 186, 188; and environmental decline 3, 5, 11–19, 20–100, 124–5, 141; and the global ecosystem 8, 170; and new consumer goods 11–12; and new industries 2, 5, 11–13, 20–54, 124–5, 186, 188; and new technologies 11–13, 50–1; and novelty 166; retardation of 13; social costs of 3; and steady-state throughput limits 162–7, 170; transformational 166; and vested interests 2, 101, 124–5; zero 4

economic inequality 149

economic models: bottom-up and cost estimates for carbon limits 147–8; top-down and cost estimates for carbon limits 147–8

economic system: impact of on ecosystems 9, 13–17; growth of 11; regional 45

economy: capitalist 17; the global 4, 142

ecosystems 5–6; abiotic components of 8; acidification of aquatic 140; anthropogenic 9–10; biotic components of 8–9; global 4, 8, 142; conversion of natural to anthropogenic 10–11; decline of natural 16, 148; and economic growth 8, 170; ethics and preservation of representative types of 140, 156; evolution of 128; and global warming 90–3; harm to 10–11, 16–18, 90–3; health of 4, 18, 90–3, 142, 144, 160; human-created 9; human identification with 128; landscape approach to preservation of 140;

marine 91–3; moral concern for 126, 128–9, 140; moral standing of 141; natural 9–10; and pesticides 97–8; preservation of the functioning of 156, 158; preservation of natural 143, 158; the role of fire in 156; scientific study of 10; services of 9–11, 139; stability of productivity of 11; see also health

Eerie Canal 40

electricity: and air pollution 28; history of use 23–4

elk 51, 78–80

Ellerman, D. P. 130

elm (Ulmus spp.) 73

emissions permits: carbon 149–50, 163; marketable 144, 153

employee self-management 190

Endangered Species Act 113

endrin 38

energy: and economic growth 161–70; flow of 7–8

energy conservation 147–8; and bounded rationality 147

energy consumption: coal 25, 189; fossil fuel 25; gas 25, 189; petroleum 25, 189; by sector 28; steady-state 143; sustainable 99, 162; in the U.K. 162; in the U.S. 25, 162

energy crisis 189; and the issue-attention cycle 103, 106

energy prices: role in business cycles 163–4; role in long waves 164

entrepreneurs 12, 166–9, 182, 186

entropy 4, 7–8, 159

environment: benign use of the 131, 137; damage to the 132; destructive use of the 131–2; material use of the 131; morally relevant damage to the 140; nonmaterial use of the 131; scale of the economy and the global 161

environmentalism 185

environmental change: as a cumulative process 16–17, 20–1; and economic growth 1, 7, 10, 13–17, 20–100, 124–5, 141, 159, 186, 188; irreversible 21; reversible 21; and technology 1, 7; and wealth accumulation 1

Environmental Defense Fund 102

environmental economics: and
environmental ethics 125–41
environmental economists 125
environmental ethic: holistic 128, 140;
instrumentalist 129; objectivist 127–9;
and the protection of human, species,
and ecosystem health 153; subjectivist
holistic 128–9
environmental ethics 3–4, 5–6, 11, 102,
125–41; and the free rider problem 102
environmental groups 189; ethical
orientation of 102; U.S. membership in
102
environmental problems 16–17, 20–100,
102
Environmental Protection Agency (EPA)
see U.S. Environmental Protection
Agency
environmental quality 53
environmental regulation 1, 5, 53, 101–
24, 189–90; and agency capture 104;
politics of 101–24; resistance to 1–2;
101–24; in the U.K. 114–124; in the
U.S. 101–14
Environmentally Sensitive Areas (ESAs)
123
ethical concern 125–41, 185, 189
ethics: and environmental change 3; and
environmental harm 18; and the
evaluation of ecosystems 5, 124–41;
and human values 1; and priority
principles 140–1; and rules of conduct
140–1; see also environmental ethics;
moral considerability; moral costs
ethical standards 140–2; for sulfur
emissions 144
evolutionary potential 61–3
evolutionary processes 128, 156, 158
European Community/Union 1; and air
pollution directives 29, 117–18; and
climate stabilization costs 148;
Common Agricultural Policy of the
121; and conservation of wild birds
directive 123; and economic inequality
149; and environmental regulation 115,
117–18; steady-state policies for the
150; and water pollution directives 120
Everglades mink 91

exotic species 157–8

farmland (U.S.) 33–4, 39–43
fecal coliform 35
Federal District Courts: and air pollution
regulation 106
Federal Insecticide, Fungicide, and
Rodenticide Act (FIFRA) 110–11, 114
Federal Reserve Bank 164
fertilizers 16, 32, 37; and nonpoint water
pollution 34; use of in the U.K. 47
fisher (Martes pennanti pennanti) 66
fisheries: and global warming 91–3;
management of 159; and water
pollution 94
Flint Hills 59, 63
Florida: global warming and 92
Florida panther 91
flying squirrel 70
forest birds: and the decline of songbirds
66; endangerment of 66–7; threats to
66–7
forest mammals: extinction of northern
Great Lakes 65–6; population
reductions of northern Great Lakes 65–
6
forest plants: and deer population
eruption 66
Forestry Commission 47
forests 10; boreal 64; and carbon storage
10, 139; characteristics of old-growth
68; damage to from global warming
90–2; decline of the diversity of in the
U.K. 48; effect of deer population on
northern Great Lakes 65–7, 80; effects
of fire protection on 65; and
endangered species 72; exploitation of
in the U.K. 46–8, 72–3; fir 56; and fire
frequency changes from global
warming 92; fragmentation of northern
Great lakes 66; hydrologic budget in
old-growth 69; large trees and downed
logs in the ecology of 69–71; logging
of and water pollution 93; logging of
old-growth 43, 67; multilayer canopy
in old-growth 67–8; nitrogen cycle in
70; northern Great Lakes 44–6, 55, 63–
7; northern Great Lakes and pulpwood

harvesting 65; old-growth 9–10, 22, 53, 55, 69–72, 80, 99, 131, 138–40; Pacific Northwest 10, 22, 43, 48–9, 53, 55, 69–72, 80; phosphorus cycle in 70; plantation in the U.K. 48; post-harvest fires in 64–5; post-settlement northern Great Lakes 65–7; primary production in 68; role of fire in northern Great Lakes 64; role of wind in northern Great Lakes 64; and salmonid productivity 70–1; snags in ecology of 69; spruce 56; stream ecology in 70–1; suburbanization and the decline of old-growth 48–9, 99; succession of 67

fossil fuels 3, 99; and air pollution 23–30; consumption 25–30, 51; and global warming 146–8, 150

France: and acid rain 117; cooperatives in 178–81, 183–4

Franklin, J. 67

free rider problem 101–2, 132, 189; and environmental ethics 102

Friends of the Earth 117, 120, 122

freshwater clams 85

future generations 139, 148

gain seeking 17–18

GDP (Gross Domestic Product) 146–8, 150, 153, 154, 158–9, 161–9

genetic engineering 139

genetic variation 60–2

Georgescu-Roegen, N. 8, 162

Germany 115; and acid rain 117–18; sulfur dioxide emissions from the former East 83

glacial till 58

glaciation 61

global warming 1, 3, 9, 17, 21–2, 86–93, 99, 145–50; adaptation of ecosystems to 90–1; and agricultural damage 88–90; and agricultural productivity increases 89; and air conditioning costs 90; and California sea lions 91, 93; and carbon dioxide emissions 3, 10, 29–31, 86–8, 143, 145–50, 162–3; causes of 29–30, 86–8; and clouds 87; and coastal wetland losses 91–3; and commercial forest damage 90; costs of

limiting 146–50; and deep ocean mixing 87; and ecosystem changes 90–3; estimates of 87, 145–8; and feedback effects 87–8; and fire frequency increases 91–2; and fish productivity 91; and forest damage 88; and greenhouse gases 86–8; and hardwood tree species 91; and marine ecosystem damage 91–3; and marine mammal habitat decline 91, 93; and migration patterns 90; and moral obligations 153; ocean upwelling patterns 91, 93; and ozone pollution 89; policies to limit 145–50; and precipitation 87; and sea ice declines 91, 93; and sea level increase damages 88–9, 91–3; and sea level increases 88–9; and species losses 91; steady-state policies for 145–50; and sulfate emissions 88; and tree death 87–8; and tundra vegetation decline 91–2; and vegetation zone shifts 91–2

goldenrods (Solidago spp.) 58

government expenditures 166

Grand Coulee Dam 78

grassland biome 56

grasslands 9, 37, 56, 80; loss of in the U.K. 74–5, 121; U.K. 72, 74–5; loss of species in 74–5

Great Britain see United Kingdom

Great Lakes 40, 44, 8, 91; PCB and DDT concentrations in the 98

Great Plains 56, 89, 158

Green Party 115, 117–18

greenhouse warming see global warming

habitat: and biodiversity 53, 155–6; destruction (loss) of 21, 55–80; diversity of in the U.K. 47, 72–5; fragmentation of 22, 49–50, 59–63; 66–7; modification of in the U.K. 47, 72–5; modification of riparian 49–50; preservation of natural 143, 155–9, 162–3; semi-natural in the U.K. 46–8, 72–5, 120–4

Hamburg J. F. 40

hazel (Corylus avellana) 73

happiness 6, 130–3, 139, 189

health: air pollution and human 82; of
    ecosystems 4, 18, 142, 144, 160; of
    humans 4, 16–18, 39, 142, 144, 160; of
    humans and global warming 90; of
    humans and the Kantian imperative
    134–5; of humans and nonpoint water
    pollution 153; morally relevant harm to
    human 140; pesticides and human 96,
    98; pesticides and nonhuman species
    96–8; of species 4, 18, 142, 144, 160;
    see also ecosystems, species
heath 72, 74–5, 80; loss of in the U.K.
    74–5; loss of species in; plowing up of
    47, 121
heavy metals 34–5; and water pollution
    93
hedgerows 47, 121
hemlock (*Tsuga canadensis*) 44, 63–4;
    loss of seedlings to deer 66; and global
    warming 91; western 68
Henslow's sparrow (*Ammodramus
    henslowii*) 61
heptachlor 38
Her Majesty's Pollution Inspectorate 83;
    see also Alkali Inspectorate
Hetch Hetchy Valley 133
Hirsh, F. 188
hornbeam (*Carpinus betulus*) 73
House of Commons 117, 123
human ethics 126; and environmental
    economics 130–5; individualistic 140
human individuals: as ends in themselves
    134
hydrochloric acid: regulation of by the
    Alkali Inspectorate 116
hydroelectric plants 43, 50, 80
hydrogen cyanide 38
hydrogen sulfide: and water pollution 94

Idaho 157
Illinois 40–1, 55
income distribution 149–50, 163
incomes policy 165
Indian cucumber root (*Medeola
    virginiana*) 66
Indiana 40
Indians: use of fire 56
industrial forestry 48, 52

industries: birth dates of 20–2, 50–4;
    creation of 2, 5, 20–1, 51–4, 124–5,
    159, 164–5, 186, 188; cumulative
    creation of 20–1, 51–4; as engines of
    growth 13; and environmental change
    7, 124–5, 159; high growth 7; new 2, 5,
    12, 51–4, 99, 124–5, 164–5, 186, 188;
    old 12–13
industry: biotechnology 100; coal 54;
    construction 180; electrical goods
    22, 24, 54; electricity generation
    22–4, 54, 116–18; 144; fertilizer 22;
    highway construction 22, 24, 54;
    information processing 100; lumber
    22, 54, 48–9; microelectronics 22,
    50–1, 54, 80,100; motor vehicle 22,
    23–4, 54, 104, 106, 118; organic
    chemicals 22, 24, 51, 54, 109–10;
    pesticides 22, 37–9; petroleum 22, 24–5,
    54; plywood 180; printing 180; pulp and
    paper 22, 46, 54, 80; railroad 22, 39–42,
    54, 80; steel 23; telecommunications 22,
    100, 180–1; textiles 179
industry life-cycle 12–17, 99, 100–2; and
    environmental change 13–19; and
    environmental damage 12–19; and the
    long wave 164–5
inflation: cost-push 163–6; and energy
    prices 163–4
information age 100
innovation 7; in markets 12; in methods
    of organization 12; in products 12; in
    technologies 12
interest groups: and air pollution 104–6;
    and environmental regulation 101–24;
    and the national forests 111–13; and
    pesticides 109–11; and water pollution
    107–109; *see also* political interest
    groups, vested interests
intrinsic value 127–8
investment spending 164–7
Iowa 40–1; 43, 55
irrigation 22, 50
island biogeography 59–63
Isle Royale 65
issue-attention cycle 102–4, 109, 113–15,
    116–17, 124
Italy: cooperatives in 178–81, 183–4

Jones, D. C. 179
Junegrass (*Koeleria cristata*) 57
Jurassic Park 100

Kansas 40–1, 43, 56, 59, 63
Kant, E. 130
Kantian ethic 130–5, 139
Kentucky bluegrass 63
kingfisher 85
Kirtland's warbler (*Dendroica kirlandii*)
  67; and global warming 91
Kuznets curve hypothesis 21

labor force participation 165
labor productivity 161, 166
Lake Michigan 13, 45
Lake Superior 65
land: limited supplies of 162–6
land development 16
land use planning 35, 121–2
land use productivity 163
large number problem 101–2
lead 34–5
leadplant (*Amorpha canescens*) 58
Lee, K. 127
Levin, H. M. 183
lichens (*Lobaria sp.*) 69; and acid rain
  86
limes (*Tilia spp.*) 73
little bluestem (*Andropogon scoparius*)
  57
log production: Oregon and Washington
  49
Logan, C. 182
logging technology 45
London: killer smog of 1952 116; smog
  28, 82–3, 115
long waves 164–6; and natural resource
  scarcity 164–6; role of energy prices in
  164–6
loon 85
Los Angeles: smog 29, 82
lumber 45, 48–9; milling technology 45

macroeconomics 2, 6, 143; and the
  environment 7, 161; and the steady-
  state economy 160–9

macroeconomic policy: and fiscal
  measures 165–7; and government
  expenditures 165–7; and an incomes
  policy 165, 169; and monetary
  measures 165–7; and population
  growth reductions 167; and steady-state
  economics 165–9; and workweek
  restrictions 166–7, 169
macroeconomy: fluctuations in the 163–
  5; scale of and the global environment
  161
Madson, J. 42
Maine 104
malathion 38
Manning, R. 80
marbled murrelet 72
marine ecosystems: and global warming
  91–3
market saturation 13
marten (*Martes americana americana*) 66
matter: flow of 7–8; and entropy 8; and
  economic circular flow 8
Mead's milkweed (*Asclepias meadii*) 61
merganser 85
Mersey River 33
methane 30, 87, 145–6
Michigan 63, 65
microeconomics 2, 12; and a steady-state
  economy 167–8
Middle East political crisis 189
Midwest 56
Milwaukee, WI 153
Ministry of Agriculture, Fisheries and
  Food 120–1, 123
Minnesota 43, 55, 63
Mississippi River 33, 39–40, 44; and
  water pollution 33, 95
Missouri 43, 55
Mondragon cooperatives 171, 178, 181–6
monocultures 9
moose 65
moral behavior: holistic 128
moral commitment 133, 135–6
moral concern 126; widening circle of
  141
moral considerability 5, 11, 18, 102, 127,
  129–30; of nature 135–8; *see also*
  ethics, environmental ethics

moral costs 3; *see also* ethics
moral dilemmas 135–6, 140
moral ends 135–41; and instrumental values 136–7
moral harm 142
moral obligations: and the health of ecosystems, humans, and species 160; and global warming 153; and nonpoint water pollution 153
moral selves 131: development of 133
moss (*Sphagnum spp.*) 75
motor vehicles: and air pollution 28–9; in the U.K. and U.S. 36; and water pollution 31–2
mountain lion *see* cougar
Muir, J. 133
mule deer 51, 78
multiplier-accelerator model 165–6
Muskie, E. 104, 107
mussels 50
mycorrhizal fungi 70

National Coal Association 104
National Farmers' Union 121
National Forest Management Act 113
national forests: administration of 104, 111–14; and below-cost timber sales 112–13; as biological reserves 156–8; and budget maximization 112; and Congress 112–13; and fees for recreation use 158; land area in 156; and the spotted owl 113, 157; and sustained yield timber management 112–13; timber harvest restrictions in Pacific Northwest 157; and timber sale subsidies 157–8; vegetation types in 157; U.S. Forest Service policy toward 111–14, 157–8
National Nature Reserves 121
National Parks (U.K.) 121–2
national parks (U.S.) 10; and incompatible land use on borders 156; and native species 156
National Rivers Authority (NRA) 119–20
National Society for Clean Air 116; *see also* Smoke Abatement Society
National Stream Quality Accounting Network (NASQAN) 35

National Wildlife Federation 102
natural areas 10; destruction of 22; fragmentation of 22; semi- in the U.K. 22, 46–8; *see also* natural habitat
natural habitat: decline of 5, 9, 39–51, 55–80; fragmentation of 39–51, 49–50; land requirements for 162–3; preservation of 143, 155–9; protection measures for 158; protection of on the national forests 112–14, 143, 156–8; *see also* natural areas
natural resources: constraints on from steady-state policies 162–5; dependence on 51
Natural Resources Defense Council 104
Nature Conservancy 50, 51, 61
Nature Conservancy Council 121
Nebraska 43
neoclassical economics 4–5, 12
Neolithic 46
net average revenue product (NARP) 172–6
net marginal revenue product (NMRP) 173–5
New England 44
new source performance standards 105
New York: acid rain in 84
New Yorker 110
nitrates 33–5, 37, 95
nitrogen: cycle of in forests 70; and water pollution 93–5, 150–1
nitrous oxides 15, 25–30, 81–5, 145–6
Nordhaus, W. D. 89
Norton, B. G. 127, 133
North Dakota 40–3, 55
northern Great Lakes 22; forests 55, 63–67; poor soil in 46; post-harvest fires in 64–5; pulpwood industry 46; short growing season in 46; transformation of forests 44–6
Norway: acid deposition in 84
nuclear power 25

oak (*Quercus spp.*) 44, 63, 73; air pollution damage to 86; California black and air pollution 86
Office of Water Services (OFWAT) 120
Oklahoma 42, 55

orchid 73; blunt-leaved orchid
(*Habenaria obtusata*) 66; purple
fringed (*Habenaria psycodes*) 66;
showy lady's-slipper (*Cypripedium
reginae*) 66; tall northern bog orchid
(*Habenaria hyperborea*) 66; yellow
lady's slipper orchid (*Cypripedium
calceolus*) 66
Oregon 49, 138; wilderness in 113
organic phosphates 38, 96, 98
O'Toole, R. 112–13, 158
The Overworked American 166
oxygen deficit 35; *see also* biochemical
oxygen demand
ozone 1; and air pollution 81–2, 86, 139;
pollution from and global warming 90;
and pollution in the Black Forest of
Germany 86; and smog 14–15;
stratospheric 53, 159; and tree damage
86; tropospheric 30, 145–6
ozone layer: destruction of 22

Pacific silver fir 70
Pacific yew 10, 72
parathion 38
Pareto criterion 135, 137
Parliament 36, 118
particulates *see* air pollution
pasqueflower (*Anemone patens*) 57; blue
74
PCBs (polychlorinated byphenols) 13, 98
peregrine falcons: and pesticides 97
Peshtigo fire 64
pesticides 16, 32, 37–9, 95–9; and animal
poisonings 97–8, 154; concentration in
wildlife food chains 38, 96–7;
contamination 21–2; costs of to society
154; and damage to bird populations
96–8, 154; and damage to fish
populations 96, 154; and damage to
human health 96, 154; and damage to
nontarget insects 97–8, 154; and the
decline of floristic diversity in the U.K.
98; and egg shell thinning 97; inorganic
38; and nonpoint water pollution 34,
39; organochlorine 38, 96;
organophosphate 38, 96; and peregrine
falcons 97; poisonings from 96;

production in the U.S. 38; toxicity of
38, 53; use on corn and cotton 38
pesticides regulation 104, 109–11, 114,
143, 154–5, 159; and agricultural
policy 110; and Congress 109, 114; and
costs of reduced use 154–5, 159; and
the issue-attention cycle 109; and
marketable use permits 154–5; and
measures to reduce use 154–5, 159;
and the Reagan administration 111;
resistance to 109–11; and
subgovernments 109–10
phosphorus 33–5, 37; cycle of in forests
70; and water pollution 93–5, 150–1
photosynthesis 30
pileated woodpecker 69
Pinchot, G. 111
pine: adaptation to fire by jack 65; air
pollution damage to 86; air pollution
damage to ponderosa 86; harvest of
white 64–5; jack 44, 63 (*Pinus
banksiana*); jack and global warming
91–2; red (*Pinus resinosa*) 44, 63;
white (*Pinus strobus*) 44, 64
political interest groups 2; and
environmental regulation 101–24; *see
also* interest groups, vested interests
pollution 8; compensation for damage
from 18; control of and ethics 140;
cumulative emissions of 13–17;
emissions of 13–17; externalizing the
cost of 2, 17–18; and property rights
17–18; social costs of 18
population growth 160, 165, 167
positional goods 188–9
poverty: and income 140
prairie: aridity of the 56; biological
reserves in the 158; disappearance of
tallgrass 22, 39–44, 55–63, 99;
farmland in the 43; mixed-grass 56;
northern Great Lakes forests and
tallgrass 44; rainfall in the 56;
settlement of the 39–42, 59–63; short
grass 55; soils in the 42, 58–9; tallgrass
and national forests 158
prairie birds 58; decline of populations 62
prairie bush clover (*Lespedeza
leptostachya*) 61

prairie cat's-foot (*Antennaria neglecta*) 57
prairie chicken (*Tympanuchus cupido americanus* Reich) 61
prairie ecosystem 55–63; creation of 61; and global warming 91–2; grasses in the 56–7; pre-Columbian 61, 63; role of fire in 56, 62
prairie endemics 61–2
prairie farms: and drainage problems 42; and breaking plows 42; and lumber 42, 44–5
prairie forbs 57–8; adaptation to fire 58
prairie fringed orchid (*Platanthera leucophaea*) 61
prairie grasses 56–8; adaptations of prairie 57; diversity of 57; as dominant primary producer 58; evolution of in prairies 57
prairie habitat 16, 39–43; fragmentation of 59–63; and global warming 63; remnants along railways 63; remnants of 42–3, 59–63
prairie mammals 58–9
prairie moonwort (*Botrychium capestre*) 61
prairie violet (*Viola pedatifida*) 57
prevention of significant deterioration (PSD) 104–5
pricing: failure of the system 2; and social costs 2; as a solution to environmental problems 2
privatization 117
production 7
productivity: biological 9; environmental resource 5; labor 5; stability of ecosystem
pronghorn 58
property rights 17–18, 177
public goods problem 177
Public Health Act of 1875 (U.K.) 116
public opinion polls: and environmental issues 103, 114, 186, 188–9
pulpwood 46

rabbits 128
railroads: and logging 45; and prairie settlement 39–43; role in U.S.

economic development 40
rain forests 9; tropical 129
rain shadow 56
RARE I, II 113
Reagan administration 103; cuts in environmental regulation 106, 111, 114
recreation: outdoor 10
recycling 159
Regional Water Authorities (RWAs) 119–20
regulatory capture 104
renewable energy 147, 150
resource productivity 161–2
resources: extraction costs for nonrenewable 159; nonrenewable 9, 159; steady-state consumption of 159; taxes on nonrenewable 159
riparian habitat 22, 55, 80; and dams 76–8; loss of in the U.K. 75; loss of in the Yellowstone ecosystem
River Boards 36, 119–20
river otter 75
River Pollution Prevention Act of 1867 (U.K.) 36
Rivers Act of 1951 (U.K.) 119
Rivers and Pollution Prevention Act of 1876 (U.K.) 119
road density: and biodiversity 157; and roadkills 157
roadless areas 113; as core habitat preserves 157; protection of 156–7
Rocky Mountains 55; Northern 157
Rolston, H. III 127
Royal Society for the Protection of Birds 122–3

safe minimum standards 140–1
salmon 71; chinook 78; coho 71; productivity of and forests 71–2; and water pollution 93
salmonids: and acid rain 84
San Bernardino 86
sandhill crane (*Grus canadensis tabida* Peters) 61
savannah 56
Schor, J. B. 166
Schumpeter, J. A. 2, 11–12
Schumpeterian growth 5, 21–2, 114–15

sea level: increase from global warming 88–9

semi-natural habitat preservation: and agricultural policy 123; and the environmental lobby in the U.K. 122–4; and the politics of the U.K. countryside 120–4

services sector 50–1

Severn River 33

Sevin 38

sewage treatment 36

shooting star (*Dodecatheon meadia*) 57

sideoats grama (*Bouteloua curtipendula*) 57

Sierra Club 102, 113; law suit against the EPA by the 104

Silent Spring 95, 98, 103, 109–10

silicon: in grasses 57

silvex 38

Sites of Special Scientific Interest (SSSIs) 121, 124

slough grass (*Spartina pectinata*) 57

smog 29; 1952 London killer 116

smoke: control of in the U.K. 29, 82–3, 115–16

Smoke Abatement Society 116; *see also* National Society for Clean Air

Smoke Nuisance Abatement Act of 1853 (U.K.) 82, 115

Snake River 78

snails 85

Snowdonia National Park 122

SO$_2$ *see* sulfur dioxide

social costs and benefits 3, 18

sodium carbonate: production of 116

soil erosion 10; and nonpoint water pollution 34

solar energy 143, 147, 162–3; land requirements for 162

solid wastes 53

songbirds: endangerment of 66–7; predators on 66–7

South Dakota 40–3

Soviet Union 170

Spain 171, 181–4

species 5; diversity of 139; endangered 49, 61–3, 138–40, 156; evolution of human 128; exotic 62, 78; extinction of 49, 61–3, 148; and global warming 91; harm to 17–18; harm to from acid rain 84–6; harm to from ozone 86; health of 4, 18, 142, 144, 160; human identification with other 128; moral standing of 141; national parks and native 156; protection of 4, 158; small populations of 61; threatened 79–80; threats to from demographic accidents 61; threats to from inbreeding 61; wilderness areas and native 156; *see also* health

spotted owl 49, 72; habitat of 113; and noninstrumental value 138, 140

spruce 44; air pollution damage to 86; black (*Picea mariana*) 63; Sitka 70; white (*Picea glauca*) 64

State Implementation Plans (SIPs) 106

status 6, 188

steady-state economy 1, 4, 6, 142–70, 186–90; and macroeconomics 160–9

steam technology 22; and air pollution 23

streams: ecology of 70–1; order of 71; pools and riffles in 71; productivity of 70–1; species in 70–1

subgovernments 103, 109–10, 116, 124

subsidies: of timber sales 157–8

substitution: limits of between inputs 162, 165, 173; between instrumental values and compensation 132–3

suburban development 22; and forests 48–9; and freeways 32; and nonpoint water pollution 30–4; in the U.K. 35–6

Sudbury, Ontario: and air pollution damage to forests 85

sugar maple (*Acer saccharum*) 63; and global warming 91

sulfate 35, 88

sulfur dioxide: emissions of 21, 25–30, 81–6, 105, 139; emissions limits in the U.S. 144; scrubbers for emissions of 105

sundew (*Drosera spp.*) 75

sunflowers (*Helianthus spp.*) 58

suspended solids 35; and water pollution 93–5, 150–1

sustainability: weak 4; strong 4

sustainable economies 4

swift fox (*Vulpes velox*) 58
switch grass (*Panicum virgatum*) 57
synthetic organic herbicides 38

tamarack (*Larix larician*) 44, 63
taxol 10
Taylor, P. 140
technological change 99; and the
   environment 7, 20–54
technology: clean 185; high 50–1
technology forcing 107
Thames River 36; pollution in 33, 36, 95,
   118–19
Thatcher, M. 124; government of Prime
   Minister 117
Thomas, H. 182
thermodynamics: laws 8
thirty (30) percent club 117
throughput: matter and energy 142–3,
   165; sustainable 142–3
Times Beach 103
Tomer, J. F. 185–6
total suspended solids (TSS) 34–5
Town and Country Planning Act of 1947
   121
toxic pollution 1, 5, 9, 21–2, 39, 159
transactions costs 18, 102
Transeau, E. 56
transformative values 129, 133
trillium: large-flowered (*Trillium
   grandiflorum*) 66
trout: cutthroat 71
truffles 70
Twight, B.W. 111

unemployment 165–7, 183
United Kingdom (U.K.): and air pollution
   23–4, 28–30, 81–4; and air pollution
   regulation 114–18; and carbon
   emissions limits 118; cooperatives in
   the 178–9, 183–4; and countryside
   issues 120–24; and environmental
   protection 1; and the issue-attention
   cycle 124; and pesticides 38, 98; and
   semi-natural habitat 46–8, 72–5,
   120–4; steady-state policy for the
   159; and water pollution 35–7, 93; and
   water pollution regulation 118–20

United States (U.S.): and air pollution
   23–8, 81–6; and air pollution
   regulation 104–6, 114; and climate
   stabilization costs 148–9; cooperatives
   in the 178–80, 183–4; and economic
   inequality 149; and the environmental
   movement resurgence 114; and
   environmental protection 1; and
   pesticides 37–9, 98; and pesticides
   regulation 109–11, 114, 154–5; and
   national forest policy 111–14, 156–8;
   and natural habitat 39–46, 48–51,
   55–71, 76–80; and natural habitat
   protection 111–14, 155–8; steady-state
   policies for the 150, 159; and sulfur
   dioxide emission limits 144; and water
   pollution 30–5, 93; and water pollution
   regulation 107–9, 151–3
U.S. Army Corp of Engineers 50
U.S. Bureau of Land Management 158
U.S. Bureau of Reclamation 50
U.S. Congress 104–9
U.S. Department of Agriculture 109, 110
U.S. Environmental Protection Agency
   (EPA) 1, 21; and pollution regulation
   104–10; and marketable emissions
   permits 144
U.S. Fish and Wildlife Service 113
U.S. Forest Service 49; behavior of
   111–13; and budget maximization
   112–13; and sustained yield policy
   112–13
utilitarian 129
utilitarian ethics 3, 5: and compensation
   for environmental damage 131; non-
   129
utility 11

value: extended version of instrumental
   127, 129; instrumental 126–7, 129–36;
   noninstrumental 126–9, 135–41;
   objectivist view of noninstrumental
   127–9; subjectivist view of
   noninstrumental 127–9
Vanek, J. 183
vested interests 2, 5, 99–125, 160, 186,
   188, 190; and political organization
   101–4; in the U.K. 115–24; *see also*

interest groups, political interest groups
volatile organic compounds 14, 25–30
voles: California red-backed 70

Washington 49, 138; wilderness in 113
wastes: hazardous 159; solid 159
water fowl: decline of migratory 62
water-oriented transportation: and prairie
    settlement 39–43
water pollution 1, 5, 9–10, 93–5, 99; and
    agriculture 33–5, 93; and agriculture in
    the U.K. 37; and algae blooms 94; and
    biochemical oxygen demand (BOD)
    93–5, 150; and endangered species 49;
    and eutrophic lakes 94–5; and fish 94;
    indicators of nonpoint 33; and logging
    93; in the Mississippi River 33, 95; and
    nitrates 33; and nitrogen 93–5, 150–1;
    nonpoint 16, 21–2, 30–7, 93–5, 150–3;
    in OECD countries 95; and
    oligotrophic lakes 94; and pesticides
    93, 95, 151; and phosphorus 33, 93–5,
    150–1; point sources of 32–3; rural
    nonpoint 33–5; secondary treatment of
    32; sources of urban nonpoint 32; and
    suspended solids 93–5; 150–1; and
    swimmer's itch 95; in the Thames
    River 33, 35–7, 95; in the U.K. 33, 35–
    7; and urban highways 32–3; urban
    nonpoint 30–4; from urban runoff 32–
    3, 93–5, 150; in the Yellowstone
    ecosystem 79
Water Pollution Control Act of 1965
    (U.S.) 107, 151
water pollution regulation 32–3, 36, 104,
    107–9, 150–3; and agricultural policy
    in the U.K. 120; and best available
    technology (BAT) 107–8; and best
    conventional technology (BCT) 107–8;
    and best practicable technology (BPT)
    10; and the Code of Good Agricultural
    Practices 120; and Congress 108; and
    the Conservation Reserve Program
    151; and cryptosporidium 153; and
    ecosystem health 153; and emission
    permits 107–9; and the health of
    species 153; and human health 153;
    and moral obligations 153; and Nitrate

Sensitive Areas 120, 152; and nonpoint
    control costs 152–3; and nonpoint
    control measures on farms 152; and
    nonpoint sources 109, 143, 150–3; and
    the Office of Water Services (OFWAT)
    120; and politics in the U.K. 118–20;
    and politics in the U.S. 107–9; and
    priority watersheds in Wisconsin 152;
    resistance to 108–9, 120; and
    secondary treatment 107; and
    stormwater control measures 152; and
    technology-based standards 151; and
    threatened species 152; in the U.K.
    118–20
water quality 32–7, 53; and dams 76;
    monitoring of 32–3; steady-state 153
water supplies 53
wealth: accumulation of 7
western prairie white-fringed orchid
    (*Platantherea praeclara*) 61
wetlands 10–11, 51, 80; and biodiversity
    11; draining of in the U.K. 47, 75, 121;
    ecology of 75; and flooding 11, 75;
    global warming and loss of coastal
    91–3; loss of in the U.K.; loss of
    species in 75; protection of 158; and
    water quality 11, 75, 152
white pine blister rust 65
whitebeam (*Sorbus aria*) 73
wilderness 46; preservation movement
    49, 111–13
wilderness areas: and Congress 113; as
    core habitat preserves 157; land area
    reserved in 156; and native species
    156; in the U.S. 10, 113
Wilderness Society 102, 113
wildlife 39
Wildlife and Countryside Act of 1981 123
willingness-to-accept 136–8
willingness-to-be-compensated 136–7
willingness-to-pay 136–7
willow (*Salix spp.*) 73
Wisconsin 40, 43, 63, 65; priority
    watersheds in 152–3
Wisconsin glaciation 42
wolf 47, 78, 128; timber (*Canis lycaon*)
    66
wolverine (*Gulo luscus*) 66

woodlands 80; conversion of to conifer plantations 73; ecological identification of primary in the U.K. 72; exploitation of 73–4; habitat loss in 73–4; loss of 73–4; loss of species in 73–4

workweek: reduction of 166–7, 169, 190

World War I 48

World War II 37, 47

X-efficiency 178–9

yellow archangel (*Galeobdolon luteum*) 72–3

Yellowstone 22

Yellowstone ecosystem 50–1, 78–80, 157; area population of 43; and economic growth in 50–1, 78–9; and global warming 91–2; habitat loss in 78–9; and high technology 50–1, 78–9; natural habitat deterioration 50–1, 55, 78–9; and threats from economic development 78–9; and threats to species 78–9

Yellowstone National Park 50, 78–9, 100, 157

yew (*Taxus baccata*) 73; air pollution damage to 86

zinc 34–5